The Bond Street Burlesque

The
BOND STREET
BURLESQUE

An Historical Novel of Murder

RAYMOND PAUL

W. W. Norton & Company
New York : London

Published simultaneously in Canada by Penguin Books Canada Ltd., 2801
John Street, Markham, Ontario L3R 1B4.
Printed in the United States of America.

The text of this book is composed in Baskerville, with display type set in
Colwell Handletter. Composition and manufacturing by The Haddon
Craftsmen, Inc. Book design by Lilly Langotsky.

First Edition

Library of Congress Cataloging-in-Publication Data

Paul, Raymond.
The Bond Street burlesque.
I. Title.
PS3566.A8266B6   1987   813'.54   86–18149

ISBN 0-393-02402-4

W. W. Norton & Company, Inc., 500 Fifth Avenue, New York, N. Y. 10110
W. W. Norton & Company Ltd., 37 Great Russell Street, London WC1B 3NU

1 2 3 4 5 6 7 8 9 0

FOR ABBY THOMAS
my partner in crime

Men have died from time to time, and worms have eaten them, but not for love.

—AS YOU LIKE IT

No other Odysseus will ever come,
For he and I are one, the same.

—THE ODYSSEY

The events portrayed in the pages which follow are drawn from and based on documented fact.

—THE AUTHOR

Contents

The Bond Street Burlesque

Prologue

It is approximately 11:45 P.M.—the dying hour of a dank, foreboding Friday. The heavy fog which has rolled in during the afternoon from the East River still blankets Manhattan Island, and nowhere does it lie thicker than on Bond Street, the heart of New York's medical district. Bond Street is lined with neat, three-story homes unseparated by passable alleys, crowned by narrow chimney stacks and gabled windows, their shutters locked against the winter dampness and the rising winds. These houses are fronted by scrubbed marble stoops and attended by skeletal trees which struggle up from the cement walk. Nearly leafless even in summer, in winter they seem to have given up their fight for life and to stand as a row of mummified corpses, lifting twisted branches pathetically toward the angry sky.

At length the figure of a man appears from the eastern end of Bond Street and is briefly visible in shadowy detail as he passes through the eerie shafts of gaslight thrown out from one of the avenue's lamps. He is thickset, fully bearded, middle-aged, though perhaps not as old as his stooped shoulders and heavy step would suggest. He is costumed well against the weather in a greatcoat and shawl with a stovetop hat pulled down over his ears and rubber boots on his feet—the dress of a man tender of his health, a circumspect man. Yet he seems in no hurry to escape the clammy drizzle for the warmth and cheer of his fireside. His walk is reluctant, almost ponderous, until at last he reaches the steps of number 31. Here he pauses as if uncertain of his course and peers westward in the direction of the bright lights and bustling crowds that, even at this dark hour, illuminate and popu-late Broadway. A few blocks' brisk stroll would bring him to that cheerful thoroughfare where he might have his choice of hotels and the comfort of a late supper, a hot toddy, and a warm bed. Such an adventure would, however, not be cheaply bought, and the gentleman is as careful of his money as of his health. He turns back to the darkened house and stares at its white door and great brass knocker with loathing and a dread bordering on terror. A convulsive shake of his shoulders seems to conquer his fear and he slowly mounts the stoop, his hand prowling through the jumble of keys in his coat pocket for the one that will open the latch.

His name is Dr. Harvey Burdell. In less than eight minutes he will be dead. Now, as he climbs the staircase to his rooms on the second floor, another man, alerted by the creaking footfalls of his victim, shrinks back into the gloom of a closet containing a small laboratory that connects the dentist's front bed chamber with the inner room which serves as his office. The door to this closet opens into the office from right to left. This door the intruder now pulls nearly shut, hearing, as he does so, the jingling of the doctor's keys outside the office door.

By the dim gaslight in the hall Burdell has selected the appro-priate key from the many he carries, most hanging from a ring; a few, and this is one, separated from the rest and carried loosely. With it he enters the blackness of the office—then turns back immediately and relocks the room, leaving the key inside the door. He crosses directly to the desk opposite and ignites the gas lamp above it. By its glow Burdell's broad back is abruptly visible to the man within the closet. Not three feet separate him from his prey. He withdraws a dagger from his pocket. His whole body tenses, perhaps thrills with both excitement and horror at the bloody work to be done. But the moment has come too quickly. He has waited an instant too long. His victim moves out of view, away from his grasp.

Burdell removes coat, hat, and shawl, laying them on the sofa that stands beside the hall door. He tugs off his rubber boots, crosses to the hearth, and lights the fire he himself had laid that afternoon. With a key from his ring he opens a small safe and takes out several papers and a bank ledger. These he spreads on the desk and, tossing the key ring beside them, he sits and bends forward over the book.

In one corner a grandfather's clock ticks ponderously, measuring out the final seconds of Harvey Burdell's life. Its minute hand inches toward midnight. For a time this ticking and the crackling of the fire are the only sounds to be heard.

Then the closet door flies open and the beast springs. He seizes his victim's neckerchief from behind, jerking his head back, and drives the blade down into his chest until the point reaches the apex of the heart. Instinctively, Burdell turns to his left, away from the blow, and staggers toward the hall door, grasping the knob and turning it furiously. But his key remains in the lock. As the dentist whirls to defend himself the dagger slices deeply into his face and then again into his throat, severing the great vessels of the neck. He throws up his arms against the blows. Three times the knife cuts his arms before thrusting under the left armpit into the chest. Burdell slumps to the floor, sprawled on his left side less than six inches from the door, while his murderer, like a blood-maddened shark, tears at his entrails until at last his weapon pierces upward into the auricle of the heart.

On his knees beside the corpse, Harvey Burdell's killer, his savage fury spent, heaves for breath and gapes stupidly at his victim as if the vicious crime he has just committed were the work of a stranger's hand. The sudden chiming of the grandfather's clock shocks him out of his stupor and he quickly pockets the dagger. There are eight other people in the house. Sounds of the violent struggle may have been heard. Escape is now his paramount concern. Once in the hall, he makes his way hesitantly down the dark staircase and back along the ground floor corridor past the closed doors of the front and rear parlors to the back stairs that lead to the basement. The basement hall leads him to an outside door, the tradesmen's entrance, opening on Bond Street below the level of the sidewalk. He gropes on the door's right side near the hinge before finding the knob on the left. Then, yanking the door back, he flees from the scene of horror into the soul-chilling drizzle of the night.

Book I

PORTRAIT
OF THE ATTORNEY
AS A YOUNG MAN

1

The Coach

"I have always found travel by coach so much more congenial and amiable than the bustle and boisterousness of the railway cars," observed Mrs. Serafin Fairgood, letting her hand fall carelessly upon my thigh. "Don't you agree, Squire Brendon?"

"My very sentiment, madam," said I.

"It is not merely the abominable racket and the omnipresence of soot that is so repulsive," the lady continued. "A journey by rail is always so hectic and conditions so cramped—there is such jogging of elbows and trampling of feet—and one is always in terror of missing one's train or losing one's luggage or being robbed. It is enough to put one quite out of sorts. Indeed, the passengers on the cars are unfailingly sullen, not to say surely, my dear Squire, whereas—" And here a violent and unexpected lurch of the carriage threw her against me so that we pressed extremely close together. "Whereas a sojourn by coach is so convivial that the briefest encounter may promote the deepest intimacy, even between strangers. Is it not true, sir?"

"Quite true, madam," I replied, still rocked by the motion of the stage and putting forth my hand, as the lady did hers, to grasp whatever might steady us. "In my experience many a friendship struck up on a trip such as ours has led to a very pleasant intercourse."

"How happily at one we are," cried Mrs. Serafin Fairgood, smiling. "Indeed, Squire Brendon, you touch me in a most responsive place."

"What nonsense you talk, Serafin!" said one of the two gentlemen seated opposite the lady and myself (a stout, flushed fellow of fifty) removing his top hat and swabbing his bald head with an enormous bandanna. "Why on earth you should wish to be jostled and rattled about in this contraption when we might ride the railway in perfect comfort and arrive in New York two hours before times is past my comprehension."

"My husband," Mrs. Fairgood explained to me, "is an exception to our rule of affability. Were we drifting down the Nile in the royal barge he would still insist on being cranky. But," turning to our other companion, "let us leave it to you, Mr. Quinncannon, to settle the dispute."

The gentleman thus addressed was tall and slim with shrewd brown eyes, a long sloping nose, and a dark, close-cropped moustache that lined his upper lip. His face was tanned and a tinge of gray at his temples gave him a distinguished air, but along with his polished manners and aristocratic bearing there lurked an almost sinister quality. He was the sort of man who commands attention and inspires speculation. I thought him a professional gambler, or perhaps a confidence man. Though I had seen no sign of a weapon I felt a certainty that he was armed.

Mr. Quinncannon lowered his newspaper and smiled. "In company as charming as yours, dear lady," he replied in a soft brogue, "the more leisurely and cordial mode of travel is always to be preferred."

Smooth as Irish silk. I watched her blush at his compliment and decided I was annoyed.

"Possibly," the Irishman went on, "your husband favors the cars because the presence of so many more passengers provides a greater market for his curatives."

The fat man brightened. "Ah, then you recognized me, sir."

"I have been reading your advertisements in the papers, Doctor. You are, I assume, the patentee of 'Dr. Fairgood's Unfortunate's Friend' concocted, I see, 'for invigorating the debilitated and completely eradicating all the distressing consequences arising from complicated diseases in their various aspects.' "

"The victims of misplaced confidence may call on me with the certainty of being radically cured," Dr. Fairgood announced. "Only one dollar for a hundred pills," he added, producing a jar from his satchel. "My word on it, sir, it is a veritable panacea!"

"Yet, I *have* heard some praise the virtues of 'Dr. Cobbett's Matchless Sanative,' " Quinncannon said, watching Fairgood out of the corner of his eye.

"Cobbett is a quack and a fraud, sir! Laudanum and epsom salts—*there* is his magic recipe! Oh, trust me, Mr. Quinncannon. I can provide you with a preparation *even more effective* than 'Dr. Fairgood's Unfortunate's Friend.' It is—," lowering his voice to a whisper, *"new, improved* 'Dr. Fairgood's Unfortunate Friend'! Believe me, sir, it is guaranteed to arrest the ravages of all bodily malfunctions and shortly exterminate all poisonous viruses." The little man's eyes darted from the Irishman's face to mine. "Perhaps you might be interested, Squire?" When I shook my head he added quickly, "Ah, possibly there is a lady in your life, eh? A handsome young fellow like you must have a lady in his life, unless I'm much mistaken."

"Not just at present, Doctor," and I watched Mrs. Fairgood smile as I added, "but I am not without hope."

"Splendid!" the doctor cried, extracting another bottle. "Then I may interest you in 'Dr. Fairgood's Golden Pills" for female derangements. I treat illnesses of a certain class, sir, without change of diet or interruption of business, as one may say, and I cure all maladies no matter how obstinate or terrific."

"Now, Doctor," I said, "I believe you are pulling my leg."

"As a matter of fact, Mr. Brendon, he's not," Quinncannon said. "His notice is here in the newspaper. It seems the ladies can obtain his potions by sending one dollar to a post office box in New York. He also provides consultations by mail. 'All communications strictly confidential.' " The Irishman caught my eye over his paper. "The doctor specializes in 'diseases of imprudence.' "

"I regret to inform you, Doctor," I said coldly, "that no young ladies of my acquaintance suffer from diseases of imprudence."

"Ah, but Squire," Fairgood returned, ever optimistic, "surely you have a mother."

2

Mr. Hasty

By the merest coincidence I had engaged to stay at the same hotel as Dr. and Mrs. Fairgood, the Metropole on Broadway. Our stage arrived at about five o'clock that warm April afternoon and, as we stepped down, we were immediately inundated by a swarm of tattered street urchins clamoring to take charge of our luggage, guide us through the city, shine our boots, or in general to accommodate us in whatever we might wish.

One youth in particular, a grimy ragamuffin of perhaps fourteen or fifteen, seemed to make me his especial target. So eager was this fledgling entrepreneur that he bumped up against me several times while assuring me that there was no labor too great nor favor too small but he could accomplish it. "For, sir," he cried earnestly, "these others are only spindle-shanked boys or drooling, half-witted louts, but a fine gentleman like yourself, sir, requires the services of a professional on-too-rage, sir, which happens to be my calling."

With this he snatched off his cap, a torrent of rusty curls cascading over his forehead, and after thrusting his hand deep into a pocket of his multicolored coat of patches he extended a filthy, dog-eared card on which was printed: ZACHARIAH LAMENTATIONS HASTY.

I looked up from the card and found the boy gaping in dismay at something, or someone, behind me. Turning, I saw Mr. Quinn-cannon standing at my elbow and, at the same moment, the youth again jostled me and I reached down instinctively, seizing his wrist and yanking his hand out of my own coat pocket. His fingers were wrapped around my wallet.

"So, you little thief!" I exclaimed. "Caught in the act, are you?" The youngster struggled helplessly in my grasp while I searched the street for a constable. He was pleading his case, not to me but to the Irishman.

"Honest, Mr. Quinncannon, I didn't know he was a friend of yours, sir! I'd never pinch nothing from any citizen was a friend of yours, sir!"

Quinncannon put a hand on my shoulder. "Why not let the lad go, Mr. Brendon. He wasn't stealing your wallet."

"And what, sir, would you say he *was* doing?"

"Putting it back," the Irishman said simply.

"Your pardon, sir," I replied. "It occurs to me that the boy could not return an item unless he had first removed it. The case is open and shut."

"Matters are not always as they appear, my friend," said Quinncannon with a wry smile. "Now if you were to search this lad and find something else of value belonging to you—say, a pocket watch. . . ."

The youth went a ghastly white. He gaped up at me in terror and plunged his free hand into his pocket, rummaging furiously through its contents, and then turned a look of wide-eyed wonder at the Irishman while I reached into my vest pocket and extracted my watch.

A gasp of relief and astonishment escaped the boy.

"Ah, I see you have your timepiece," said Quinncannon. "I wonder, Mr. Brendon, if you would be good enough to return mine."

I did not relish being made to look the fool. "I am not aware that I have your watch, sir," I said with some heat.

"I believe it is in the right pocket of your coat along with my wallet and my diamond stick pin."

I knew before I made the search that his valuables were now on my person. Pricking my finger on his damn stick pin did not improve my humor. When I handed them over Quinncannon smiled. "You see, Mr. Brendon, it is sometimes possible to return something without first removing it."

"The boy is a thief," I insisted. "He committed a crime and he should be punished. That is the law, sir."

"The law, sir, would pitch him into the workhouse for an indefinite stay during which he would labor beside older, hardened criminals, learning their tricks and becoming sufficiently embittered to ply them when he was again cast out on the streets. Or, Mr. Brendon, worse yet, the law would condemn him to one of those hideous 'orphanages' incorporated by this state to receive 'friendless waifs,' where some cold-blooded, canting, ordained hypocrite would starve and beat him until his spirit was broken."

Quinncannon glanced up the street. "Here is a constable coming, Mr. Brendon. If you wish to press charges against the lad this is your opportunity. The matter is entirely in your hands."

It was, of course, emotional blackmail. We had gathered rather a large crowd of spectators whose sympathies for the most part favored the boy. The Fairgoods were divided, the doctor for "jugging the little cutpurse" while his wife urged me to mercy. For all that, I was inclined to have the boy arrested, if only to avenge myself on the Irishman. In the end it was the attitude of the boy himself that decided me. Had he cringed or whimpered I would have abandoned him to the law without a second thought, but he straightened his spine and faced, or rather confronted, me squarely, his bright eyes glowing with defiance. I found myself admiring that defiance and I released my grip on his wrist.

The policeman passed by without stopping. He touched his stick to his helmet and nodded. "Afternoon, Mr. Quinncannon."

"Good afternoon, Charlie," the Irishman said.

"Why do I have the feeling," I said under my breath, "that it was immaterial whether I brought charges or not?"

"You've done a fine, decent thing, Mr. Brendon. Relax and enjoy it."

I shook my head. "It goes against my conscience, sir."

He raised one eyebrow. "And have you one of those? I'm sorry to hear it."

I was trying to determine whether he was patronizing me. "I am an attorney, Mr. Quinncannon, and therefore an officer of the court. The purpose of the law is to protect honest citizens from those who would prey upon them, no matter how young or vulnerable the criminals may seem. I can hardly condone what you have done here."

"What have I done, Squire?"

"You have tampered with evidence, sir. You have manipulated facts and circumstances. You have resorted to sleight of hand trickery to make guilt appear as innocence."

Again there was that wry, exasperating smile. "Well, well, it's a disreputable business, no doubt, Squire Brendon, but it's a living."

The crowd had drifted away, the Fairgoods had gone into the hotel, the gang of urchins had assaulted a newly arrived coach, and Quinncannon and I stood alone on the sidewalk. Surprisingly, the young pickpocket, whom I had expected to take to his heels, still loitered nearby as if awaiting orders.

"Since we've managed to save this mongrel pup from the bridewell," I said, "what do you propose we do with him?"

"Give him honest employment. He has a profession."

I gave the Irishman a long look, then shrugged and signaled to the little beggar. I still held his dog-eared card. "What do I call you? Zachariah or Lamentations . . . or, perhaps you prefer Z.L.?"

"Mr. Hasty suits me," he replied without a hint of impertinence. I smiled in spite of myself.

"Very well, Mr. Hasty, I find after all that I have need of an on-too-rage. Take my luggage into the hotel and wait for me at the desk."

The boy grinned broadly. "Yes, *sir*, Squire!" He went for the bags, then stopped and approached me again shyly. He extended his hand. "Can I have it back?"

I had no idea what he wanted.

"My card, Squire," he said. "It's the only one I got, you see."

I nodded and returned it to him—then watched him struggle manfully under the weight of two valises and a trunk. When I turned around Quinncannon had vanished. I checked my pockets but nothing was missing. Then I strolled into the Metropole.

The boy was standing at the desk, scratching vigorously in areas where well-bred young men do not even itch, and blissfully unaware of the scowl on the face of the hotel clerk who motioned me aside. "This—this *child* claims to be with you, sir," he hissed.

I felt constrained to admit as much. "I merely allowed him to fetch in my baggage."

"The Metropole employs persons for that purpose. *Really,* sir, it is bad enough that these ragamuffins are permitted to swarm about like gnats outside the hotel, bedeviling our guests in spite of all our efforts to scatter them, but when a guest actively *encourages* the little beggars by bringing one of them into the *lobby—!* Why, it is not only insupportable, it's . . . it's . . . *unsanitary!*"

Unfortunately Mr. Hasty chose that very moment to snort thunderously and, hitching up his sleeve, to wipe it slowly across his upper lip. I found myself apologizing—mind you, actually begging the pardon of that most servile of all functionaries, the hotel clerk! It was damned infuriating.

The boy was tugging on my coat. "I can tote your bags up to your room for you, Squire. No extra charge. Anything else I can do for you? On the house." He looked up at me, still smiling.

I tore my coat from his grasp. "Stop pawing me, you little guttersnipe," I growled. He backed rapidly away. I flung a coin at his feet, and he snatched it up. "Now get out of here and keep clear of me, boy, or I'll have the law on you," I barked. He bolted for the door.

I wheeled on the clerk. "Are you satisfied now?" I snapped.

The man seemed to shrink before me. "You understand, sir, I was only trying to do my job. . . ."

I allowed him to address the rest of his obsequences to my back and then ordered the luggage taken to my room and stalked into the taproom for a double Scotch.

3

The Locked-Room Murder

It was as if a nightmare had, in a flash, become real. And yet my dream had been most pleasant, what I could remember of it. The lady and I lay beside each other on our backs in a lush meadow with a warm sun above us. My head was resting on her arm, and I rolled over toward her and threw my arm over her, and my fingers felt something—I was going to say moist but it was something wet—wet and sticky. Then the pounding began.

I opened my eyes. I was still in my hotel room, still in my bed, but I no longer shared it with the lady beside whom I had drifted into soothing slumber and pastoral dreams. My new bedfellow was the lady's husband, the tedious, balding little peddler of patent medicines. He lay on his bulging belly, his jowled face toward me, his eyes like droplets of laundry bluing and nearly popping out of his head as though he were astonished to find me occupying half of the mattress. I was somewhat surprised myself. A dagger had been thrust, up to the hilt, into his back between the shoulder blades. The gummy wetness on my hand was his blood.

The pounding grew more insistent.

I fought to shrug off my sluggishness. My limbs were heavy and my head ached. I managed to stand. The room seemed close, stifling—the air stagnant. I staggered back against the only window and tried to raise the sash but it would not budge. Painted shut—perhaps nailed down. The pounding was coming from the single door, from the passageway beyond the door. I wondered vaguely why whoever was so anxious to enter did not simply turn the knob.

Now I could hear voices—the low, angry bulldog growls of a man, and, rising above them, the frightened screams of a woman. I stumbled toward the door, using the bedpost, then a chair, to steady myself, and as I reached it I realized the cause of my visitors' frustration. The slide bolt just above the knob was drawn shut. The room key protruded from the keyhole at an angle such that I knew the deadbolt was also in place.

I was locked and bolted inside a room with the corpse of a man whose wife I had seduced only hours before—a man who, from the position of his death wound, could not conceivably have destroyed himself. It was impossible that anyone had murdered that fatuous little cuckold and escaped from that chamber. It came to me just as the bolts gave way and the door crashed in and the constable lurched into the murder room: *I had not killed Dr. Walter E. Fairgood, and no one else could have.*

I rose to greet the captain of police as he entered the hotel taproom where I was being detained, but the constable detailed to guard me seized my shoulder and yanked me back into the chair. I recall my regret that a gentleman like myself, a graduate of the University of Virginia, and a newly admitted member of the New York bar, should be manhandled by a common peeler merely because of a slightly awkward misunderstanding. They order these things better, I thought, in Virginia.

My watchdog, the same who had forced my bedroom door, conferred briefly with his superior, handing him my wallet and papers, through which the captain shuffled, once glancing up at me sharply, then down again at the documents, whistling and shaking his head. At last he waved the patrolman away and the latter withdrew, protesting, however, his commander's imprudence in remaining unprotected in the company of "a cold-blooded killer." The burly captain, who at six-foot-two towered four inches over me, and at 220 pounds outweighed me by more than 60 pounds, eyed my slender frame and coughed a laugh. "He's a dangerous character, Fincher, and no mistake, but, my word on it, I'll not turn my back on him."

He was a grizzly of a man with a great red beard and a high forehead crowning a ruddy face the features of which seemed chiseled in granite. He wore the blue uniform well, the lamp light glimmering off the brass buttons and copper shield—all spit and polish and official business, the model of the perfect policeman. He said, "Name!"

"Tobias Brendon, sir."

"Your address?"

"I've just arrived in New York last evening, sir. I have no permanent quarters yet. I suppose you could put down this hotel, or perhaps," I added with a smile, "it would be more appropriate to say the Tombs."

He did not return my smile. "What is your age, youngster?" Then, as I told him, he echoed, "Twenty-two. Have you any idea of the lady's age?"

Charity prompted me to underestimate the figure by five years. "I should guess Mrs. Fairgood to be, perhaps, thirty."

"Forty-four," he said grimly, but whether his tone was meant to imply that she was robbing the cradle or I was robbing the grave was not altogether clear. He scribbled a few jottings before looking up and licking his pencil. "Now, Mr. Tobias Brendon, in your own words, what happened in this hotel tonight?"

For the second time I told my story.

My interview with Captain George Walling lasted more than an hour. It was nearly four o'clock in the morning when he closed the notebook and pushed his bulk up from his chair. I watched him rise until he loomed above me, his brow dark, his eyes angry.

My account of the evening's events, which had seemed to me so logical and credible when I first recited them to the constable, had increasingly taken on a doubtful, even an absurd sound in the retelling. That Walling did not believe me was obvious—yet every word I'd spoken was the truth. At least I thought it was the truth. It was, of course, impossible to explain the circumstances of the death wound and the locked room unless I was the killer —yet I had no motive. I clung to that, and to the certainty that I was incapable of the crime, though the fact was I had no memory of any occurrence between falling asleep beside the lady and waking beside her dead husband. I stared up at Walling and for the first time the desperation of my situation burst full upon me.

"There are a few things, youngster, you had better understand. The case against you is watertight and the charge will be first-degree murder. By rights you should have been arrested and booked three hours ago."

He thumbed through my papers. "I find you are carrying letters to Mr. Ogden Hoffman of this city. Just what is your relationship to Mr. Hoffman, Mr. Brendon?"

"I've not actually met him, Captain Walling, though we've corresponded. The letters are from his friends in Washington City, asking him to help me obtain a position with his law firm here in New York."

"I see." He passed his hand over his eyes. "I'm taking a damn stupid risk. The mayor and the district attorney will melt down my shield for a paperweight if I'm wrong. But, if I turn you over to Coroner Connery and Mr. Hall—you being connected with Mr. Hoffman—that whole Tammany mob will pick your bones clean, son." He began to pace. "I've never seen *anything* like this. Motive, weapon, opportunity. You were locked inside the goddamn room, for Christ's sake! You *must* have done it! Only . . . only. . . ."

I held my breath and waited.

"*Only* for the sake of my friendship with Hoffman—"

"Sir?"

"I've decided to give your attorney one hour to prove your innocence."

"But," I said, "I have no—"

"In this town," Walling cut in, "when a man is charged with a hanging offense he has two choices. If he's innocent he hires Henry Clinton to defend him. If he's guilty he screams for Lon Quinncannon." He waited a moment before adding, "I've already sent for Quinncannon."

4

Legerdemain

"There is a fond belief in this country," said Lon Quinncannon from the doorway of the Metropole taproom, "that bad little boys grow up to be good men. A close examination of your recent exploits, Mr. Brendon, may cause some rethinking of the theory."

He took the Windsor chair opposite my own and placed his hat and walking stick on the table between us.

His reference to my mischievous childhood made me curious. He obviously knew more of my history than could be gathered from our conversation in the coach.

At his gesture a pretty little barmaid no older than seventeen entered with a tray containing a bottle of Irish whiskey and two tumblers. She set them down, keeping her eyes on me and smiling sweetly, and so she remained after she had poured the liquor until I looked up and our eyes met. She was quite charming in a milk-fed, milkmaid fashion, and under almost any other circumstances I would have taken a keen interest in her affairs.

It may be difficult for many of my male readers to believe, but when a man, particularly a young man, finds himself to be unfailingly attractive to women he soon realizes he is under the severest of maledictions. This affliction, you must understand, is no fault of his own. He can no more help his smooth, brown skin, finely chiseled features, and dark, curly hair than he can alter his erect carriage or the jaunty spring in his step. Sad to relate, these physical handicaps are inevitably joined to a nature so guileless and sentimental that he can hardly resist the dozens of temptations that chance throws into his path almost daily. The upshot is that such an unfortunate young man is perpetually plunged into the most maddening, not to say dangerous, of situations.

Here sat I, I reflected, under the shadow of the gallows because of one romantic entanglement, yet already on the edge of being seduced into another.

"May I be of further service to you, sir?" she inquired sweetly.

The question was directed only to me. I believe she had forgotten that Quinncannon was there. I was having some trouble remembering it myself.

"Not just at present, Miss," I said with some reluctance.

"Should you think of any way in which I may accommodate you, sir," said she, withdrawing a small, delicately wrought purse that she had up to then concealed beneath her apron, "I would be most honored," opening her purse as wide as it would allow.

"I shall wrack," I responded, thrusting my largest coin into her purse, "my brain."

When she was gone Quinncannon leaned back in his chair, downing his drink and observing me under an elevated eyebrow.

"It's really a curse," I said.

"Your story of this evening's events," he said, "would make a cat smile."

"I know."

"Tell it again."

"From the outset Mrs. Fairgood played the coquette, sir, under her husband's very nose. I could not believe the man could be so blind."

"Nor could I."

"We had arranged to dine together. The doctor was late to the table. She had some powders to put in his coffee. He had a second cup. I inquired whether that might not keep him awake. He said, on the contrary, coffee invariably had a soothing effect on him.

They went to their room immediately after supper. I remained in the taproom for half an hour."

"Your rooms were adjacent?"

"Directly opposite, at the far end of the hall. She came to me about ten-thirty. She said her husband would not awake before morning. She brought a bottle of champagne."

"You drank it before, during, or after?"

"Yes."

"When you fell asleep was she still in your room?"

"We were in each other's arms."

"The window and door were locked from inside?"

"The window is sealed in some manner. I locked the door myself. I turned the key and drew the slide bolt."

"Does the key trigger a spring lock or a dead bolt?"

"A dead bolt."

"Is the slide bolt above or below the keyhole?"

"Just above the knob, three or four inches higher than the keyhole."

"And you remember nothing after falling asleep in Widow Fairgood's loving embrace until you revived, covered with her husband's blood and locked inside your room with his corpse?"

I nodded solemnly while he poured us each another whiskey. "Well, Toby, it certainly looks as though you killed the old quack."

I gulped hard at my drink while Quinncannon rapped sharply on the table with his cane. It was evidently some sort of signal. I felt a terror rising in me. "Is there no way you can help me, sir? There *must* be another explanation. Possibly the chimney?"

"It couldn't be negotiated by a cockroach with a thyroid condition."

"Might there not be a trap door or a secret passage in the wall?"

His expression conveyed that he would not dignify that suggestion with a response.

"I read," I said, "a story like this once about two murders in a locked room in Paris. The window appeared to be nailed shut but it wasn't really. The killer was an Ourang-Outang as I recall."

He was filling his pipe. "I doubt we could sell even a New York policeman on a homicidal monkey."

I gave up in despair. "Then it's hopeless and you're right. I must have killed him. I can't remember, but I *must* be guilty."

"Toby," he said quietly. "I did not say you murdered Fairgood. I said it looked as though you did."

The door at the rear of the taproom opened suddenly and Mrs. Serafin Fairgood entered, still in nightdress and in disarray, escorted by the stolid Captain Walling. Her eyes were ringed in black and puffed as if she had been crying. Corsetless, her bovine figure sagged. Her face in the flickering candlelight suggested an attempt to apply cosmetics without a mirror. Staring at her now, I could not imagine why I had ever thought her desirable.

The Irishman smiled. "Come in, Sally, and join the party." There was an edge to his voice. The brogue grew thicker with every word. "Do ye think you can control your grief long enough to tell us what transpired here tonight?"

She stiffened and pointed to me. "That young man murdered my husband. Surely there can be no question of that." She turned on Walling. "Really, Captain, must I endure this?"

The officer offered her a chair. "Just answer Mr. Quinncannon's questions, Mrs. Fairgood. After that you'll be allowed to rest."

"Very well!" She threw an angry glare at the Irishman. "Perhaps I can anticipate your cross-examination, sir. You, yourself, were a witness to Squire Brendon's shameless advances yesterday in the coach. After our arrival he became even bolder and I," withdrawing a handkerchief from her bodice, "I, to my shame, at last submitted to his passionate pleas though I should never have done so had the boy not become so distracted that he actually threatened to do rash violence to himself. I am but a poor, frail woman," dabbing at her eyes and addressing the policeman, "and I have a woman's tender heart. I could not bear the thought of one so young and so handsome cut down in first bloom by his own hand when one word, one gesture of affection from me might prevent such a tragedy. A beautiful, mature woman is not unaware of the emotions she may inspire, however inadvertently, in the breast of an inexperienced but ardent stripling, but," flashing fierce eyes at me, "in *this* faithless, murderous puppy I was horribly deceived. No sooner had he had his way with me than he sprang from the bed, his rapturous frenzy agitated with drink, and swore that if he could not possess me no man would. He staggered to the room where my poor husband slept and dragged him from his couch. I tried," choking out a sob, "oh! I tried to prevent him but he flung me away and bolted his door against me and I, overcome by fear, sank down in a faint from which I did not recover for almost an hour. At last I was able to summon a policeman but when he broke through the door he found my husband weltering in his blood, and locked in with his killer."

Here Mrs. Serafin Fairgood lost all control and buried her face in her handkerchief, her shoulders heaving with the rhythm of her sobs.

There was a long period of silence broken only by the splash of whiskey into Quinncannon's glass. Then the Irishman said, "The act needs work, Sally. It went over much better in Cleveland."

The lady slowly raised her head. "Why," she demanded of Captain Walling, "is this man permitted to intrude on my grief?"

"Cleveland was seven years ago," Quinncannon said, not unkindly. "Forgive me, Sally, but I doubt a jury today would swallow the notion of a matron stirring up uncontrollable, lethal passions in a lad half her age." He looked toward Walling. "Have I won our bet, George?"

"It's a drink I owe you, Mr. Quinncannon, and I'll be damned if I know how you figured it." He threw three items on the table: a piece of wire, a pair of nippers, and a spool of thread. "There's the lot, all found in her luggage. The tools of the trade."

Mrs. Fairgood and I both stared at the articles, she in dread, I in confusion.

"The problem is, George," said the Irishman, "that the divorce laws in this country are too stringent. It's almost impossible for a woman to liberate herself legally from an unhappy marriage, and even if she manages it she becomes an outcast among her own sex. Sad but true, George, a divorcée is almost as much a pariah to her respectable sisters as a common prostitute, whereas a widow is embraced by her friends with sympathy and affection." He shook his head. "Small wonder, George, if thousands of unhappy wives choose a widow's weeds over the scandal of divorce."

"Small wonder, sir," the captain echoed, "though it hardly makes my job easier."

I said, "Excuse me, gentlemen. . . ."

"I'll wager," Walling said, "we turn up more than one insurance policy naming her as beneficiary."

"In Cleveland she had four."

"Damn me, sir! *Four?!*"

"Totaling six thousand dollars."

I said, "I wonder if I may ask a question."

"Six thousand!" Walling whistled softly. "And she got away with it?"

"She was never suspected," Quinncannon answered. "Of course, the young man was hung."

The captain regarded Mrs. Fairgood with genuine admiration. "By God, lady, but you're a cool one."

"*Damnation!*" I exploded. "Will somebody tell me if I'm still under arrest?"

Walling seemed surprised to find me still there. "Never did arrest you, lad. You're in the clear. Just be certain you're here for the trial." He took Mrs. Fairgood's arm. "Come along, madam. Step lively there." At the door he turned back to the Irishman. "You'll give the evidence to one of the constables before you go, sir?"

Quinncannon nodded and the captain left with his prisoner. My head was spinning. He lit his pipe and settled back into a fog of tobacco smoke. At last I said, "What happened?"

"The Fairgoods had a domestic dispute."

I leaned forward, elbows resting on the table, massaging my

temples with my fingers. "Please, Mr. Quinncannon, it's not that I'm ungrateful, but nothing that's happened makes any sense to me."

"The lady is Serafin Fairgood, alias Sarah Jane Ashton, alias Samantha Warren, alias Worcester Sal—born Sally Mae Hoyt in Worcester, Massachusetts in 1812—erstwhile shoplifter, hotel thief, and blackmailer. I thought in the coach that she looked familiar but I didn't place her until I learned of your predicament. Dr. Fairgood, like her first husband, was a peddler of snake oil and several years her senior. She worked the same game with each of them while she purchased enough insurance to render them more valuable dead than alive."

"What *was* their game?"

"Blackmail," he answered. "She lured the mark into a compromising situation. Then her husband pretended to surprise them and demanded satisfaction. The victim, either married or a young man of expectations and prospects, would pay anything to preserve his reputation."

"And I was the dupe."

"You were one of them. The doctor was the other. She actually *did* drug his coffee, and then she drugged your wine. With both of you unconscious she simply lugged him into your room and drove a knife into his back."

"But my room was locked from the inside. How did she escape?"

Quinncannon smiled. "That is the question they couldn't answer in Cleveland seven years ago. Unfortunately, as a result, an innocent man was hanged." He stood. "Bring those items on the table and come upstairs."

Officer Fincher was on duty outside the murder room. When he saw me he tightened his grasp on his stick but the Irishman waved his hand. "Relax, Pete. Mr. Brendon's not the murderer."

Fincher thought that over. "The *wife?*" and then, "But how did she get out?"

Quinncannon motioned us into the room. Entering, he removed the key and tied a piece of thread from the spool around the bit, the small metal tongue near the tip of the key. He drew the thread through the keyhole and left the key hanging inside. With the nippers he bent one end of the wire around the pin on the slide bolt—then thrust the other end through the keyhole and closed the door, leaving Fincher and myself inside. By means of the wire the slide bolt was drawn through the nosing until it was in place. Then, by a deft twist, the wire was freed and withdrawn through the keyhole. As Fincher and I watched, the key was pulled up by the thread and, on the third flip, the bit hooked the lip of the keyhole and was drawn into the keyhole. A moment later the nippers, inserted from outside, had gripped the key's pole and turned it, throwing the dead bolt into position. We were locked and bolted into the room. Another moment passed. Then, from the corridor, Quinncannon knocked quietly.

"Well I'll be damned," Fincher breathed.

I unlocked the door.

Quinncannon relaxed against the wall and sipped his whiskey. "It's a variation on an old trick of hotel and boardinghouse thieves, lads. Mrs. Fairgood knew it well when she worked under the name of Worcester Sal:" He tossed the nippers, spool, and wire to Fincher and led the way downstairs.

It was past 5 A.M. and the kitchen staff was already scurrying about preparing for the morning trade. The desk clerk informed me that another room had been readied for me. I shook the Irishman's hand warmly. "I owe you, sir," I said.

"That you do, Toby," he replied.

I was as exhausted as I was relieved. I fully intended to sleep the day away. When I reached my new apartment, however, the door was ajar. The pink-cheeked little barmaid gave me a dimpled smile.

"May I turn down your bedclothes, sir?" she inquired prettily.

It really is a curse.

I locked and bolted the door behind me.

5

The Associates

I awoke alone in the bed with the grandfather of all headaches. My mouth tasted like a swamp. I extended my lower lip and blew upward toward my nose to confirm that my breath would have done justice to a camel. To remain as I was, was agony, and the mere thought of moving was agony. My bones seemed already bleached and sprawled on some parched ground. One by painful one I moved my limbs to assure myself that I was still in working order and, at last, by a supreme effort of will, I unshut my left eye.

There was someone else in the room. Dizzying shapes of him swirled in fuzzy fashion before me and it was a full minute before they coincided into one image and I could make him out. He was a young man, about my own age and build, slim, clean-shaven, with a shock of curly brown hair. For a brief moment I felt the strange sensation of looking into a living mirror.

"May I assume," he said with a good-natured grin, "I have the honor of addressing the late Mr. Brendon?"

"If you are the mortician, sir," I replied with a groan, "you are an hour before time. Do but return in sixty minutes and you will find me entirely at your disposal."

For answer he picked up my dressing gown and flung it at my head. "Come, Mr. Brendon, this won't do at all. You have been on salary since nine o'clock this morning and here you are still abed and nearly comatose. This is hardly the way to ingratiate yourself with The Firm."

I managed to sit up and torturously maneuver my legs off the bed. I hadn't the least idea what he was talking about and, while I wrestled with the robe, I said so.

"Then," he said with surprise, "you never received Mr. Hoffman's last letter?" He took a chair. "Well, then that explains it, you see."

"I'm afraid I don't see at all."

"Of course you don't," he answered with an agreeable smile. "You didn't know and therefore you couldn't be expected to . . . but never mind. It will all be clear to you sooner or later."

I took that in. "If you don't mind, sir, I prefer sooner."

He reached into his pocket. "Here is my card, Mr. Brendon."

I read: "JEREMY TODD ESQ. ATTORNEY AT LAW," and below his name: "OGDEN HOFFMAN and ASSOCIATES. 28 REEDE STREET, NEW YORK CITY."

"I have been corresponding with Mr. Hoffman," I said.

"Mr. Hoffman is in court and I am his ambassador. You've been, I should tell you, quite thoroughly investigated, Mr. Brendon, and the decision is made to offer you a position with The Firm. Mr. Hoffman wrote to you but the letter must have been waylaid. I've had the devil's own time finding you and might be searching yet if I hadn't run into Mr. Quinncannon at the courts."

I looked at him sharply. "You know Quinncannon?"

"Hoffman's closest friend." He lowered his voice. "Have you ever heard of the Jewett-Robinson murder case?"

I shook my head.

"Somewhat before our time, Mr. Brendon. Hoffman and Quinncannon collaborated on the defense. It's a tale for a stormy night before a fire with a bottle or two." He consulted his watch. "But it's nearly three o'clock. We've still to get you ambulatory and fit for polite society." He was on his feet, full of energy and plans. "I've engaged some rooms for us, on Cedar near the river. Not exactly opulent but comfortable. It's three flights up but the view is worth the climb. The landlady is a charming crone—you'll love her at first sight but, fair warning, I saw her first. She reads cards but I advise you not to make inquiries for she perceives nothing but dark forebodings, a veritable Cassandra—"

And on he rattled in his easy, good-humored way while I shaved and dressed and did the best I could to render myself fit for polite society and came to the conclusion that if I had to be turned loose in a strange city and forced to earn my own bread I could not be in better company than that of Jeremy Todd, Esq.

When at last I completed my appointments, Mr. Todd surveyed me sole to crown before nodding his approval. "You'll do," he said, extending his hand. "Welcome, Mr. Brendon, to Hoffman and Associates."

I accepted his hand. "You haven't told me. Who are the associates?"

"Why," he responded, "you and I are the associates, my friend." He retrieved his hat from the highboy and picked up one of my valises. "Now, Mr. Brendon, suppose we go home."

To describe, as Jeremy Todd had, our apartments in Cedar Street as "not exactly opulent" was a masterpiece of understatement. Our two bedrooms, which opened off the sitting room, were not much larger than prison cells and furnished sparsely but practically with a bed, a chest of drawers, and a chamber pot. The sitting room, however, was spacious and remarkably bright as the windows had been recently scrubbed—not, I suspected, by a woman's hand, for streaks of smeared grime were evident despite the scrubber's best intentions. There was a round table, attended by four small captain's chairs, which served for dining, writing, and gaming. A dry sink stood against one wall, and a large, well-stocked bookcase rather slouched against another. But what drew one's attention immediately upon entering were two identical wingback chairs which were positioned vis-à-vis before a great fireplace in which a fire had been laid but not yet lit. Each was provided with its own footstool and tiny, circular sidetable. These chairs were of wine-red leather and wonderfully comfortable— well broken in by numerous former owners who had left their imprints clearly in the indentations of the backs and cushions. To some, I suppose, the wingbacks would have seemed worn and shabby, but to me they appeared as twin thrones and, settling easefully into one of them, I was conscious that, like my predecessors in that chair, I was about to make my own mark on, so to speak, posterity.

"The place has been for some time past abandoned to the rats and the roaches, neither of which did much to keep it up," Jeremy said, "but I have made some headway against them and now that reinforcements have arrived I don't doubt but we shall rout them in a fortnight at the outside. Scotch or bourbon?"

"Bourbon, thank you."

He poured at the dry sink, then relaxed into his own wingback and raised his glass. "To friends and associates," he said. We drank and smoked our pipes as we were to do on many an evening in that threadbare, cheerful chamber, which, from that first moment, became for each of us a place of sanctuary and fraternity and independence—above all, independence—from parent, guardian, tutor, housemaster, and all other species of creature whose single purpose in life is to frustrate freedom of thought and action in the young.

I never recall that night in Cedar Street without smiling. The windows were open, admitting the sounds of clopping hooves and children playing. A pleasant breeze from the river mixed with the more pungent aromas of nearby coaching stables.

The city spread all around us—the old city, venerable when Greenwich Village was a village and Canal Street was still a canal —built and burned and rebuilt with quaint, chimnied, gabled, gnarled houses, each with its little shop—apothecaries, tobacconists, potshops, greengrocers—fronting on twisting, narrow, cobblestoned streets that zigzagged crazily across one another at odd angles. The upper city was being planned with geometric precision: numbered avenues north and south intersected by numbered streets east and west—blocks and plots all neatly, rectangularly logical. But a map of the lower city resembles the aimless pattern of sticks spilled from a cup in the child's game of pick-up. To wander through it is to chance losing one's way, perhaps permanently, but to conquer its narrow intricacies is no small triumph and worth both the effort and the risk. To venture forth daily into that mindless maze of contradictions, in danger at any moment of turning a sharp, unanticipated corner and traveling a strange, unexplored thoroughfare, and yet to know that at day's end you will find your way back to home and hearth —*there* is an achievement.

"Allow me to point out, Toby, my friend," said Jeremy Todd, "some pertinent features of this establishment. The door to your bed chamber sticks in damp weather but can be dislodged by a sharp kick aimed exactly eight inches up and five inches over— I've marked the spot with chalk until you get the hang of it. And always begin climbing the lower stairs with your right foot."

"Why?"

"The sixth step is quite rotted through on the right side and the ninth almost as bad on the left, so you'll want to tread on the right side of every odd-numbered step and the left side of every even-numbered step . . ." He caught my look of bewilderment. "Well, never mind why. Take my word for it. Also, the next-to-top shelf of the bookcase is precarious so store as few volumes as possible on it and be tender in removing any item or the whole thing will come crashing down on your head. I have already enough lumps to make my skull a phrenologist's curiosity. Then, too, the dowels in two of the captain's chairs keep popping out of their sockets despite all that sawdust and glue can achieve. . . ." And on and on he recounted the treacherous pitfalls of our bachelors' quarters, concluding, while refilling our glasses, with a particularly nasty trick of the privy lid.

These warnings dispensed with, he went on to inform me on the topic of the firm, or, as he pronounced it, The Firm! I found he had invented nicknames for most of his acquaintances. Ogden Hoffman was "the Governor" and Quinncannon was known simply as "Himself." He spoke of them with great affection, and of the Irishman in particular with a deep and honest respect which I frankly envied. Quinncannon and, to a lesser extent, Hoffman appeared to have served him as surrogate uncles. He told me with relish of being taught to ride and shoot by his late father, then Hoffman's law partner, and Himself, and of how, as a boy, he would be allowed to stay up long after his usual bedtime in the company of the men, sprawled before the fire in his father's study or perched on the edge of an ottoman, ankles crossed, eyes bright and straining against sleep, listening to tales of adventure and mayhem, of heroic exploits and hairbreadth escapes. The heroes of these tales, of course, were always the tellers. Watching him glow in his reminiscences, I thought I could see him as he had been at fourteen, luxuriating in the special pleasure a boy must feel at being accepted as an equal into the company of men he admires, mesmerized by the wonder of their marvelous escapades, perhaps imagining himself and his young cronies in the leading roles.

It is a bloody crime against a boy to deprive him of that experience.

As Jeremy rambled on about his boyhood I discovered myself becoming increasingly resentful of my new friend and the warmth of his memories. When he spoke with sadness of his father's death I wondered how he might feel had he never known his father at all—had he been deserted in infancy, robbed of his charming recollections, his heritage, his very name. Could he even imagine being raised in the loveless chill of the orphanage, always hungry, always too cold or too hot, where a sound thrashing is a child's only notice that the adult world is ever aware of him. Could he have guessed at the bitter loneliness of the pauper boy in the boarding school, the charity case taunted by his wealthy classmates and despised by his masters?

I consoled myself with the thought that, now that I was in New York, I had drawn very near the end of my quest. Soon I would meet the one man, perhaps the only man, who knew the truth of my paternity. Patience, patience. However horrible the secret, it could not be worse than this agony of ignorance.

"Well, Toby, old boy, since you force me to support both ends of the conversation, I shall carry on as best I can (though I trust you will not prove so reticent on other subjects as you are regarding yourself) and commence by informing you that the bourbon supply is exhausted."

I expressed a willingness to accept Scotch but he waved his hand. "I've a better notion," said he, rummaging about under the dry sink and producing a box full of metal tubing, rubber hose, glass beakers and retorts, and other assorted paraphernalia which he busied himself assembling on the table, concluding by attaching the rubber hosing to one of the gas jets. Content with his arrangements, he went to the fire, which had then been burning for an hour, and ignited a long match. With this he touched off a blue flame above an upright metal tube. He watched my surprise with amusement. "Brand new invention, Brother Brendon, by a Prussian professor named Bunsen. Ingenious device with countless uses. We own one of the few yet seen outside Europe."

He mixed up a concoction of some sort and began cooking it above the flame, at the same time attaching a rubber balloon to the neck of the retort until it was inflated. Then he removed it and invited me to inhale its vapors.

"Trust me," he said.

I returned his grin. "The most callow undergraduate cannot pass his chemistry examinations without learning the formula for nitrous oxide, Brother Todd."

"Do you imply that someone in this room passed his chemistry examinations, Brother Brendon? Do but identify this scholarly rascal, or, alternatively, this rascally scholar, and I shall straightaway pitch him downstairs."

This remark struck me as outstandingly clever and I laughed heartily. He joined in my laughter. The balloon again began to inflate.

Shortly we commenced to exchange confidences respecting our intimate relations with the opposite sex. This turned rapidly into a contest to determine which of us had been the more precocious. He opened with an entertaining exploit of his eighteenth year. I countered with a charming—I flatter myself to say erotic

—memoir of my seventeenth. He saw my memoir and raised me with a ribald remembrance of when he was sixteen, and I favored him with a downright lurid exposé of my romantic feats at fifteen. It was while listening to his wonderfully sordid confessions of his prowess at fourteen that I foresaw his trap and neatly sidestepped it by bypassing my thirteenth birthday and dropping immediately to my twelfth-year adventures, anticipating, correctly, that even he would not claim conquests at age eleven. In the best sporting spirit he acknowledged himself fairly beaten, "outlied and out-laid" as he phrased it, sending both of us into paroxysms of laughter. Of course, throughout the competition we had regularly exploded into gales of hilarity set off by such witty remarks as, "Oh, yeah?" and "The devil you say!"

When, finally, the Clinton Hall clock sounded the hour of three, we extinguished Dr. Bunsen's burner and knocked the last ashes out of our pipes and went wearily and happily to our beds. I remember the chill of the early spring night and crawling under two thin blankets and throwing my coat over me to keep out the cold of that Spartan little cell, and falling asleep almost at once. In all of my life I had never felt so warm.

6

The Governor

Number 28 Reede Street, where the offices of The Firm were located, was a pleasant, compact, two-story structure with a large bay window of spotless, lead-lined rectangles of glass to admit the sunlight of a bright April morning, and a newly painted white door with green trim to admit the clientele—not at all the dismal, foreboding place I had anticipated. A bell above the door announced our arrival and I found myself standing before a mahogany rail with a swing gate beyond which three small desks could be seen, two nearly buried under a clutter of documents. The clean desk, one of two at the rear, I surmised as intended for me, while the one adjoining it proved to be Jeremy Todd's. The one remaining was occupied by the law clerk, Mr. Leggett, a gaunt, angular man in somber garb, who perpetually cleared his throat so that his briefest speech was punctuated by "hem-hem." I took him in while Jeremy made the introduction and I noted that Mr. Leggett's attire, though perfectly fitted, was unraveling and appeared secondhand. He was so stolid a character that I found myself watching his eyes closely to see if I could catch him blinking.

Having made the acquaintance of this gentleman, I was ushered upstairs by my associate and given a brief tour of the law library, which served also as a conference room. We then knocked respectfully at the office of our employer, Ogden Hoffman.

The Governor was seated behind a massive mahogany hunt table. Upon our entering he removed his spectacles, put down his pipe, and rose to greet us. Smiling broadly, he took Jeremy's hand and then grasped my own. "And this is Mr. Brendon," he boomed. "You are most welcome, my boy, most welcome! I trust," with an eye on Jeremy, "that your every comfort has been attended to since your arrival. Ah!" He squinted at each of us. "But I observe the telltale signs. Red rims around the eyes—dark circles beneath." He threw back his great head and laughed heartily. "Well, I remember my own bachelor days, boys, and bachelor nights too. Just this minute I believe I can remember them more clearly than I can recall what Mrs. Hoffman said to me this morning at breakfast."

Ogden Hoffman was then sixty-three and in the twilight of a brilliant legal career. He had spent part of his life in politics, first as a Democratic member of the legislature and later, after quarreling with Andy Jackson, as a Whig in Congress.

But politics had always played second violin to criminal law. For a quarter of a century he had been counsel in virtually every important criminal trial in New York, usually appearing for the defense, save for his term as district attorney. In several of these cases he had collaborated with Quinncannon—Hoffman's skills as an orator complimenting the Irishman's gift for clever, sometimes scathing cross-examination.

In his heyday Hoffman had been reputed to be one of the two most eloquent speakers in the nation. Only Daniel Webster was his peer. His masterful summations were required reading for every student of law, combining as they did majestic language with an almost poetical precision of phrasing. Merely reading these addresses was a pale substitute for the privilege of having actually heard them delivered, but that morning, as I shook his hand and felt the magnetic dynamism of his personality jolt into me like an electric current, I thought I could imagine the power that had fueled his orations and brought generations of jurors to their knees.

Under any circumstances meeting such a celebrated man would have been a great honor and a great curiosity. For me the encounter held a special significance. I was convinced that Hoffman knew the secret of my paternity and I was determined to use whatever means were necessary to discover, at last, who I truly was.

We ate dinner that afternoon at the Union Club amid the finest legal minds in New York, prompting Jeremy to observe under his breath that, should a bomb explode in the dining room at that moment, the courts must needs be instantly shuttered and every felon expelled from the Tombs. The meal, featuring veal and venison washed down with an exquisite port, was both excellent and generous, and I attacked it voraciously. Afterward we lingered over drinks, our conversation interrupted often but pleasantly by the parade of noted attorneys who made a point of paying their respects to our host. Eminent men who had been legends to me became, upon my being introduced as Hoffman's associate, familiar friends. I quickly garnered half a dozen invitations including one to supper in the bosom of the family of Sigfried Camphausen where I would, I was assured, be completely charmed by Squire Camphausen's daughter, Leticia (known, according to Jeremy, as "the great unwed"). "You won't be able to take your eyes off her," proclaimed the proud papa. "You won't dare," whispered Jeremy.

I very much admired Hoffman's popularity. These men of splendid reputation and achievement deferred to him as their superior with an affection that was unfeigned and spontaneous. He accepted their adulation with a graceful ease. For each of them he had a particular concern—an inquiry about a favored relative; a word of congratulation for a recent courtroom triumph. To one, a venerable clergyman, he recounted a delightfully dirty story, and no one joined more heartily in the laughter than the gentleman of the cloth, who went away giggling uncontrollably.

I made a mental calculation. Hoffman would have been forty-one the year I was born.

When the other diners would leave us in peace Hoffman endeavored to draw me out. He impressed me with the feeling that he was immensely interested in me and my affairs, and that, despite my youth and inexperience, he attached much weight to what I thought and considered me a valued addition to the firm. "Snaring you is quite a coup, Toby," he said. "Henry Clinton, either of the Jays, Blatchford, any lawyer in this town would be glad to employ a young man of your gifts and promise."

Modesty, a quality so becoming in the young, was not one of my failings, but I made a stab at it, aided somewhat by the high regard I felt for Hoffman. I managed to mutter a few words of self-depreciation and concluded by observing that my joining his firm was natural enough given the circumstances.

He looked at me sharply. "Circumstances, my boy?"

"Yes, sir. I expect you understand my meaning."

"Do you?"

Jeremy turned from one of us to the other with a puzzled expression.

With a wave of his hand, to my great annoyance, the Governor terminated the discussion and ordered another round of drinks. "My physician tells me I am to consume all the whiskey I can manage, boys." He winked broadly. "Of course I consulted sixty-four doctors before I found him."

Neither of us laughed. Jeremy broke the awkward silence with a reference to Quinncannon and Hoffman smiled. "Ah, the Celtic fox. There, Toby, is a man worth knowing."

I said we had already met and narrated the story of my narrow escape from a murder charge. Hoffman nodded. "That sounds like the Irishman. I saw him this morning—he knew I had offered you a position—and he never said a word. He wouldn't, of course, out of respect for your privacy, my boy. It is an excellent trait, particularly for a lawyer. The folks who consult us are troubled, often desperate. If we succeed in helping them, you will find invariably that they thereafter shun us, not from ingratitude but because we observed them in their most abject moments of agony and shame. The very sight of us reminds them of their former misfortune and that we have seen them at their most vulnerable and most frightened."

"That is as may be, sir," I said, "but I hold no such feelings toward Mr. Quinncannon. I can hardly forget that, but for him, I would certainly not be sitting in the Union Club in such excellent company with my prospects stretching before me and an invitation to sup with Miss Leticia Camphausen."

"No man understands better than Quinncannon," Hoffman said, "that the most important thing about doing a kindness for a friend is to refrain from reminding him of it." He put down his drink and leaned forward, elbows on the table, bearded chin resting on folded hands. "I need not say this to Jeremy for he has known the Irishman all his life, but you, Toby, have as yet only glimpsed him. If you wish someday to become a great attorney you must study him closely. Observe him, emulate him when you can, but, for a time at least, keep your distance from him. He burns with a bright flame, lad, and the heat could consume a young man with more ambition than experience. You have a confidence that borders on arrogance—"

I began to protest but he held up his hand. "Arrogance is a useful quality when controlled and not paraded. Your greatest temptation will be to overestimate your abilities—to seek out challenges before you are prepared for them. For a nature such as yours a premature association with Quinncannon could be fatal."

"You mean professionally?" I asked.

"Among other things," he responded. "Quinncannon is a dangerous man—that is, he attracts danger. He thrives on it. He stands astride this city like a colossus with one foot planted on Fifth Avenue and the other on the Five Points, and the reverberations of his brogue rattle cages in Centre Street and Wall Street and Broadway and Park Row."

Hoffman reached out and gripped my wrist. "Already you are

fascinated by him, Toby." He put his other hand on Jeremy's shoulder. "A word of advice to you both. Be wary of Quinncannon. He is at once the most decent and the most Machiavellian man I know. He may lie quiescent for weeks, even months, but when some special matter stirs up his faculties," he shook his white mane and finished, "he gives as much quarter as a cobra."

If this profile of the Irishman was intended to diminish my interest in him it was poorly aimed. If, as I suspected, its purpose was to divert my attention from the matter of my father, it also failed of the mark. Hoffman's evasiveness on this topic both puzzled and angered me since I had assumed that his invitation to me to associate with his firm was part of a design to make at least partial restitution to me for my dismal childhood.

In the end I concluded that he was simply reluctant to discuss the subject in Jeremy's presence, and that he would soon select a more private place and time. I would be patient, I thought, but *not* much longer.

7

Mr. Brendon Has a Client

Two days after my introduction to the Union Club elite I had my first case. "Normally we wouldn't accept a divorce matter," Hoffman explained, "especially one which promises to be as nasty and sordid as this one, but the girl's cousin is an old client, a respectable dentist of means whose affairs we have long managed. He's brought her to us and he's paying the fees. I could hardly refuse him." He looked from Jeremy to me. "I want you to take her on, Toby. It's a good case to cut your teeth on—complex enough to be testing but one where the odds favor our side. I want Jeremy to sit in with you, but the matter is in your hands."

We were to confer with our clients in the law library. I opened the door and absolutely froze. I was barely conscious of Jeremy bumping into my back. I suppose my expression must have been absurdly foolish to judge from the look with which the lady regarded me. Lady? Say, rather, goddess. Goddess? Pah! Aphrodite was a fishwife. Never mind the details. I shall linger over them later. It was the total effect that stunned me. I was struck deaf, dumb, everything but blind. She smiled. She rose. She offered her hand. I could not move. My feet were rigid, then my ankles, then my legs, and irresistibly on I felt this uprising calcification.

Jeremy shoved me into the room, none too gently, and my hearing returned.

"How do you do?" said she. "I am Mrs. Demis Hubbard."

"How do—that is, I am—" I felt like a blithering idiot. "I am honored to make—uh, your acquaintance." I managed to take her hand.

"My name is Jeremy Todd," my friend said, "and this is my associate, Tobias Brendon."

"So pleased," she said, gently attempting to extricate her hand from my grasp. To complete my embarrassment she succeeded in freeing her fingers but left me gripping her glove. I stared at the damn thing for an inane moment before returning it. She received it with another pretty smile. "May I present," she said, "my cousin, Dr. Harvey Burdell."

And there he was, a sturdy, dark-eyed, well-dressed man in his middle forties of average height with a full, dark beard and moustache, high forehead, straight nose, and thin, compressed lips. Even now, after years, I can visualize him as clearly as if he stood again before me. Strange to say, his features are etched more indelibly on my memory than even those of the beautiful Demis.

But there are excellent reasons for that.

The sight of her companion broke the spell into which the vision of Mrs. Hubbard had cast me. Her faerie, ethereal loveliness was more than counterweighted by his physical, undeniably solid presence.

One particular recollection still stands out vividly in my mind. Though the room was cool, Dr. Burdell was sweating.

On being presented to us Dr. Burdell grunted and gave a short nod. He made no effort to shake hands and plumped down as abruptly as he had stood. Jeremy said, "Shall we be seated and discuss your difficulty, Mrs. Hubbard?"

"By all means, Mr. Todd," she replied. She was just twenty-three. Her hair was lustrous and blond and arranged in delicate curls which fell to her shoulders. There was a daintiness about her—about her little hands and feet, her features, her tasteful and stylish dress. Her liquid blue eyes looked up into mine. "As you are to represent me, Mr. Brendon, perhaps you should sit here beside me. I fear this affair will be terribly unpleasant but I shall feel ever so safe with you near me to protect my interests."

It must be understood that I was already a man of considerable experience with women, not given to bashful awkwardness, always in control, prepared for all contingencies, equal to any situation. I stress this because my performance on this single occasion was so irritatingly adolescent. It was particularly annoying that it happened in Jeremy's presence and so soon after I had defeated him for the boasting rights of Cedar Street. He made absolutely no attempt to hide his amusement at my confusion, but sat openly smirking in the most infuriating manner. ("I was not smirking," he later protested, "I was simply smiling." "Smirking!" I insisted. "Smug, snide smirk!" "Nay, I categorically deny smug," he smirked.)

I took the chair next to hers—the lady left me little choice—and became gradually aware of another pair of eyes. Dr. Harvey Burdell glared at me with a smoldering, jealous hostility so powerful that I was at a loss to say which of the cousins unnerved me more.

"Dr. Hubbard," Demis explained, speaking of her husband, "has some decidedly strange theories regarding the maintenance of good health about which he is not only adamant but unbending. At first I endeavored to live by his principles as I thought befitted a young wife, but, alas, of late I have found his attitude and his demands quite insupportable."

"The man has made her life a goddam, living hell!" Dr. Burdell exclaimed. This, and all his other interruptions, were directed solely to Jeremy. The dentist made an elaborate point of ignoring me.

"Perhaps, Mrs. Hubbard," I said, "you could be more specific."

Burdell answered my question, as if I had addressed him, by speaking to Jeremy as if he had asked it. "Have you ever heard of Vincent Priessnitz, Mr. Todd?"

My friend shook his head.

"A lunatic, sir, I assure you. An Austrian peasant from Silesia —a man utterly without education who presumes to pass himself off as a doctor and claims hundreds of miraculous cures attained without physick or the consultation of medical professionals. In the Middle Ages he would have been burned, and rightly so, but today he is taken seriously by the wealthy, fashionable blockheads of Europe who flock to his Grafenberg asylum, flinging money at his feet and begging for his restorative. Now he has begun to make converts in this country. Do you know, sir—have you any idea *who* his principal American apostle is?"

My friend shook his head.

"Bronson Alcott!" Burdell announced with ringing disgust, as though the patronage of the notorious radical alone demonstrated what an ominous character Vincent Priessnitz was. "This Austrian maniac calls his wonderful system Hydropathy! Hydropathy, Mr. Todd! Have you the slightest notion of what panacea this Silesian wizard offers in place of medications and time-tested remedies; in place of professional, licensed practitioners —my God, sir! In place of *SURGERY!"*

My friend shook his head.

Dr. Burdell screwed up his face into a grotesque mask of unimaginable disdain and spat out the word. *"Water!"*

"Water?" I echoed.

"Water, Mr. Todd," the dentist affirmed. "Water inside and out. Water sprayed on and wallowed in and slopped around and splashed about and squirted into and streaming out of every conceivable cavity, crack, crevice, crater, and chuckhole in the human body!"

"Show some delicacy, sir!" I exclaimed. "There is a lady present."

"Mrs. Hubbard is a doctor's wife, Mr. Todd," Burdell returned. "She is quite used to plain speaking. What she could not become used to was the outrageous treatment to which she was subjected by her husband in the name of 'preventive sanitation.' "

The dentist leaned forward and lowered his voice. "My cousin, Mr. Todd, in her desire to be an obedient wife, has submitted to every depraved abomination forced on her by her husband's mad superstitions—to every degrading form of the Aqua Pumpi treatment. Plunge baths, sitz baths, half baths, wave baths, immersions, emersions, douches of every grade of intensity—and, lastly, 'packing'! Not a pleasant way to pass an hour, sir. Do you know what a packed patient looks like, Mr. Todd?"

My friend shook his head.

"A packed patient, sir, resembles nothing so closely as a gravid female white ant!"

I had never seen a gravid female white ant, but it did not conjure up a pretty picture. Demis Hubbard gave me a pathetic look of doe-eyed helplessness. No one could possibly have appeared less like a gravid female white ant. I smiled at her protectively and felt her hand on my knee.

I don't think my expression changed. "Ah, Mrs. Hubbard," I said. "It must have been a dreadful experience." I put my hand on her hand.

"It was perfectly horrid, Mr. Brendon," she returned, a slight tremor in her voice. "And that is not the worst of it." She squeezed my knee ever so slightly.

I ran the tips of my fingers softly over her hand.

"Indeed," I said, "I cannot imagine a situation more trying, Mrs. Hubbard."

"Oh, Mr. Brendon," said she, "if you put your mind to it, I'm certain you can."

Jeremy Todd's eyes shot from my face to the lady's to Burdell's purple complexion and, to my great annoyance, he smirked. "There are some papers which must be signed, Doctor," he said. "Perhaps you could come with me, sir?"

The dentist eyed me with ill-concealed suspicion. His attitude surprised me, considering that he was first cousin to Mrs. Hubbard and old enough to be her father. For that matter he was old enough to be my father.

He followed Jeremy with obvious reluctance and turned at the door. "Demis, are you coming?" His tone was remarkably plaintive.

"In a moment, Cousin Harvey," she responded.

"Demis!" he repeated in a louder, harsher voice which carried with it something like a threat.

She gave him a sweet smile. "I shall be coming shortly, Cousin Harvey, as soon as I have conferred with my attorney. You run along with Mr. Todd."

The dentist scowled at each of us in turn.

"Really, Cousin Harvey," she purred, "you're not going to be a naughty boy and make a scene."

He took a half-step toward her—then hesitated in some confusion. "Demis, I've warned you," he said in what was nearer a whine than a warning. She did not respond. At last he went out and Jeremy closed the door behind them.

Instantly the lady and I were on our feet.

"Mrs. Hubbard!" I gasped.

"Mr. Brendon!" she cried.

We were in each other's arms, locked together, kissing wildly, madly, passionately. "Mr. Brendon," she breathed, "Mr. Brendon, Mr. Brendon, Mr. Brendon, Mr. Brendon, Mr. Brendon, you're—you're strangling me!"

I released her and sprang back. "Forgive me, Mrs. Hubbard! I have behaved abominably. I am the foulest of scoundrels, the vilest of blackguards!" I seized her hands between my own. "Only think, you came here despairing and defenseless, seeking comfort and succor—"

She looked at me strangely.

"Succor," I repeated.

She nodded.

". . . seeking comfort and succor," I went on, "and I, base villain that I am, was so blinded by your beauty, so enchanted by your grace, so enthralled by your charms—"

I drew her to me and kissed her violently.

She yielded to me for a long, rapturous moment—then gazed dreamily into my eyes.

"So enthralled . . .," she said.

". . . by your charms, lovely lady, that I could think of nothing but the magical pleasure we might share here, together, in this very room—"

She looked around her. "On the *table?*" she exclaimed.

I turned away, my head thrown back, the back of my wrist against my forehead. "I confess it, Mrs. Hubbard! To my everlasting shame, madam. I can never ask you to forgive me, I know, but may I dare—" I faced her again. "May I *dare* to hope you can find it in your heart to forget?"

"On the *table?*" she repeated. She looked at me and her eyes melted. She reached up her soft hand and touched my fevered face tenderly. I held my breath. At last she smiled. "I have never," she confessed shyly, "done it on a table."

8

To Whom It May Concern

Rather than tire the reader with a tedious recitation of the complex negotiations that preceded the final dissolution of the marriage of Demis Hubbard from her husband, Dr. John Hubbard, I have chosen to reprint portions of the statement that the doctor himself authored and published in June 1856, after the affair had been settled in the courts, greatly, I may say without boasting, to the advantage of my client. The document speaks for itself and I will make no comment except to note that at one point John Hubbard made a particularly ugly, not to say libelous, charge against his former wife which I then thought utterly without foundation and believed to be the hallucination of an unbalanced mind.

JOHN HUBBARD'S STATEMENT:
TO WHOM IT MAY CONCERN

It seems to be a duty which I owe, not only to myself, but to my friends and the public, to make the following statement.

I was married to Demis Ward in the year 1854. Previous to and at the time of this marriage, it was well and distinctly understood, by the friends of both parties, that I was what may be called a strict vegetable eater, a practitioner of the Graham system of diet, and also that I entertained many views and doctrines contrary to the popular and received opinions of the day. Under such circumstances our matrimonial career was commenced, and, at the onset, was only interrupted by a malignant disease seated in the nose or head of my wife, causing an extremely fetid and noxious breath, by which I was compelled to turn my face from her when she wished to bestow a token of affection; this she appeared to construe into a want of affection on my part. It is evident to those who may have lived upon an organically grown vegetable diet that their sense of smell is much more acute than when they lived upon the flesh of animals, especially when it arises from matter issuing from a diseased action in the human body. This offensive breath began to subside when she adopted my universal practice of bathing every morning and submitted to certain other treatments of preventive sanitation in accord with my hydropathic convictions.

At this time I consented conditionally to facilitating my wife's desire to commence bearing children, with the express proviso that henceforth she should adhere strictly to my dietetic principles. I explained patiently that, should she fail in this charge, there was a possibility that, the seed once sown and taking root under less than ideal circumstances of good health, she would not only be subject to a miscarriage, but, should this not occur, it would tend to injure the physical energies of the embryo, and hence an imperfect or delicate offspring would in all probability be produced; consequently I expressed a disinclination in being instrumental in bringing about such a result, but this did not coincide with her views or inclinations and she said, "it was absurd to entertain such erroneous notions." Soon after she did suffer a miscarriage. I then told her I had expostulated with her in reference to what I considered an impropriety and what if heeded would have prevented the unhappy occurrence, an injury to herself, and the guilt we had perpetrated which I considered next in degree to murder.

I reasoned with my wife and declared to her that hereafter we ought to proceed on scientific principles of good health in these matters as we had had sufficient experience to test the necessity of it, and, as we both profess to believe in divine revelation, why not admit the assertion of the apostle, who says, "whatsoever ye do, do all to the glory of God"; in reply she said that I "ought never to have been married and every sensible woman would make the same remark, under similar circumstances, if their husbands would not act as other men do." I told her, "my mind was made up on these subjects, and I should act accordingly, and risk the consequence—that she might as well attempt to turn the course of the river as to change my mind when I knew I was right." She declared she "would have no children of mine if I was determined to pursue such a course." I then repeated to her the intention of the marriage revelation as taught in the Bible, where the Lord speaks and says: "Be fruitful and multiply and replenish the earth." I have spoken at large upon these subjects in the Health Almanacs of 1851—2 and 3.

In the spring of 1855, my wife's first cousin, Dr. Harvey Burdell, a prominent dentist of Bond Street in this city, began to make numerous calls at my home, at such times as my practice compelled me to be absent from my house. Soon after, I was attacked with a diarrhoea which ought under simple treatment to have subsided in a week or two. Poisons were given unknown to me, among which was arsenic, my wife having charge of me and, by the advice of Dr. Burdell, employing homoeopathean physicians who administered doses of this odious drug without my awareness or consent.

During my sickness money had to be made out to pay my creditors, and Dr. Burdell proposed to advance it, and take a mortgage on my furniture to secure the same, which I consented to. As soon as I was able to be removed, I spent the remainder of the summer out of the city.

Upon my return, Dr. B. seemed to feel somewhat uneasy in relation to the mortgage, and expressed a desire to have his claim more fully secured, and I told him to do so in a way satisfactory to himself, as I wished him to lose nothing by me. I felt at this time much discouraged and desired as much peace and harmony as possible. In a short time I was called away to treat a patient in Elizabethtown, New Jersey, but could find, upon my arrival, no patient answering to the name and description given. Once back in the city, I was informed by Dr. B. that he had during my absence made his claim safe, and was satisfied, and I signed the bill of sale, which I supposed was for the purpose of satisfying him, and I did not even examine the schedule at the time. Subsequently, however, Dr. Burdell takes the house, and re-lets it to me, reserving certain rights and privileges to himself. Dr. B. now assumed considerable authority and acted "like the man of the house," and soon after I find him seated at my supper table every night, and on multiple occasions remaining in the house throughout the night, he pleading his fear of garroters as his excuse.

My wife now began to act and speak in relation to Dr. B. with great tenderness and affection, stating that he was "very much of a gentleman," that "he acted more like a man, and had more feeling than Dr. Hubbard," that Dr. B. "would not let people tread upon him, for he would assert his rights and maintain them." At various times she declared that she "hated me with a perfect hatred," and that "it would be better if I was dead"; that "she was sorry she had ever married me," &c. &c. Dr. Burdell returned it as kindly, stating "that Mrs. Hubbard was too good for Dr. H., that it was a great pity she ever saw him, that he was a disgrace to his profession and had ruined his business by his ultra views, that he was a crazy Millcrite and Priessnitzite," whose "brain was waterlogged with his own Aqua Pumpi nonsense," and "a maniac who ought to be put into the darbies and thrown into the lunatic asylum."

I now concluded it would be wise to take certain steps, and I requested the bill of sale, or schedule of the articles of furniture, which I had not examined until this time. The schedule comprised articles which cost between three and four thousand dollars, and which were sold by myself to Dr. B. for less than nine hundred. I will here state that the money with interest loaned by Dr. B. was subsequently offered to him, but he refused to receive it, saying that he "owned everything in conformity with the law," and that he "had me bound," and "he would not give back any of the articles at the prices he had purchased them at." He is now in possession of the whole, a part of which, however, he has since sold.

At this time I commenced to suffer with symptoms similar to those I experienced while subjected to the treatment of doctors recommended to my wife by Dr. B. on the occasion of my first illness, and I refused to take my meals at home, fearing that something might be put into my food. For sometime my wife had made up a separate bed for me, and soon after I abandoned dwelling in the house. Previous to leaving, I gave my reasons for so doing, and handed Dr. B. a printed affidavit as a part of those reasons; however, Dr. Burdell commenced a suit against me for the recovery of rent, on the ground that my wife still inhabited the house, but after long and patient investigation the jury decided that Burdell had forfeited the right to recover rent by his intimacy and familiarity with my wife.

My divorce from Mrs. Hubbard is now final and she is free to marry Dr. Burdell although somewhat after the date originally projected, for I believe *their initial calculation was that I would have died in 1855. I have always contended that no person has any right or business to interfere with the domestic relation of a man and wife, or in any way to attempt to put asunder what God hath joined together, and those who do so will surely bring the curse upon their own heads. If Dr. Burdell has coveted his neighbor's wife he will receive his reward, for He who said "thou shalt not covet" will bring every secret thing into judgment whether it be good or evil.*

DR. JOHN HUBBARD

New York, June 10th, 1856

9

The Dentist

Although I have attempted to describe the beauty and charm of Demis Hubbard, I despair of doing the lady justice. Had I the pen of Shakespeare, the brush of Leonardo, I would fail in the endeavor—yet in letter after letter through the spring of 1856 I poured out my adoration to her in a torrent of miserable metaphors and idiotic iambics. The greatest curse on my poetic efforts has always been my ineptitude with rhyme, although, on one occasion, I recall being rather pleased with the result:

> As to a cat a bowl of cream is,
> So to me, my lovely Demis.
> Be true to me as stars above.
> Prithee, Demis, be my love.

> What to a trout a mountain stream is,
> Thus to me, my sweetest Demis.
> To warm thy hand I'll be thy glove,
> If you will only be my love.

> Think what to a full moon its beam is.
> And this, to me, are you, my Demis.
> It's you I'm always thinking of.
> Oh! Darling Demis! Be my love.

As to a bunco man his scheme is,
All that and more are you, my Demis.
If you say you eschew my love,
O'er a cliff my heart you'll shove.

So have a care for what my dream is.
Say you're mine, my beauteous Demis.
Oh! Gentle as a turtle-dove.
Break not my heart, but be my love.

I seriously considered publishing that one. But all the rest, my word on it, were trash—utterly unworthy of the lady. Of course, a major problem arises when one must write in English. The wretched language has but five rhymes for love. Small wonder the French are so much more accomplished in lyrical wooing.

Nevertheless, I had ample evidence that the fair Demis did not find my verses displeasing. The preparation of her suit for divorce brought us close together for long periods, often extending into the evenings, and I found myself increasingly bewitched by her. She was so utterly helpless, terrified of her husband, and wholly dependent on me to rescue her from his matrimonial clutches. To me she was the distressed damsel of whom every young man dreams, and I played the role of knight in shining armor to perfection.

I suppose it was inevitable that our first romantic encounter in the law library was not to be our last. I own it was unethical as well as unwise for me to use her dependency on me to press my advantage with her, but, upon my oath, I could not help it. Naturally we were careful not to be seen together publicly under any but the most innocent circumstances. For all my painstaking precautions, however, it was not long before the truth was suspected by her cousin Harvey, the bicuspid extractor.

From our first meeting Dr. Burdell had made no secret of his enmity toward me. It seemed to stem entirely from Demis' attraction to me. The man was wildly jealous for reasons which, initially, I found inexplicable. He was twice her age and the lady's first cousin. Yet he was behaving like a moonstruck adolescent.

Surely, thought I, the old fool couldn't delude himself that Demise felt anything more for him than a daughterly affection.

On the afternoon that Demis' divorce became final I awaited
her arrival at my rooms in Cedar Street. I had arranged for
champagne and a supper of cold lobster to celebrate her freedom. Jeremy was spending the night with friends. My plans were
laid.

The footsteps I heard ascending the stairs, however, were not
the soft tread of the lady, but the heavy trudging of a large man,
and moments later Burdell, without bothering to knock, burst
into the room.

His face above the thick beard was a florid crimson and his
black eyes smoldered. "She will not be keeping your rendezvous,
Brendon," he growled. "She will never come to you again. I have
forbidden her."

"It seems to me," I returned coolly, "that the decision is properly the lady's."

"Where men are concerned, the lady's judgment is hardly to
be trusted," he replied. "If her disastrous marriage has not
proven that fact, her foolish dallying with you, young man, has
certainly done so. It is plain that she requires protection."

"From *me*?" I laughed aloud. "May I ask, in what guise, sir, do
you assume this authority to select Mrs. Hubbard's friends and
dictate her behavior? Am I to see you as an outraged father
figure, or," I smiled at the notion, "are you playing the jealous
rival?"

He was fidgeting furiously. I tried to imagine him as Paris in
Romeo and Juliet, all got up in a short cape and tights with a bodkin
and not a cane in his hand. In any costume he cut such a ridiculous figure, this lecherous Senex, that I laughed again.

It was a tactical error. He raised his cane and came at me. I
dodged his blow at the last second. His stick crashed against the
table, spilling my supper onto the floor, and, with a snarl, he
again uplifted the cane, wheeled around, and commenced to stalk
me.

I gave ground slowly and adjusted my opinion of him. He was evidently a man of explosive temperament, quick to anger, dangerous when provoked. Clearly I must defend myself. My own cane hung by a leather thong from a nail beside the door. I seized it and, feeling the wall grazing my spine, I advanced on Burdell. To my surprise he took a step backward and I caught a momentary glint of fear in his eyes. My God, I thought, the man's a coward. Steeled by this revelation, I continued to move toward him until I saw his grip slacken and his stick start to waver.

"I suggest," I said, "that we lower our weapons, Doctor, before one of us is injured." I took my own advice and, with some hesitation, he followed suit. Visibly shaken, he edged around me on his way to the door.

"I have determined," he said, "that my cousin shall vacate her present quarters at once and make her home with me. I lease my house, with the exception of two rooms which I occupy, to a respectable window named Cunningham. Demis will share Mrs. Cunningham's apartment. I consider it in my cousin's best interests that she should have the guidance and companionship of an older matron. You will find, young man, that these arrangements correspond exactly with Demis' desires."

That, I seriously doubted, and said so.

"I warn you not to attempt to interfere between my cousin and myself," Burdell concluded darkly and closed the door.

My head was swimming. I sank into one of the wingbacks and stared at the ceiling, trying to make some sense out of the scene the dentist and I had just played. Though at first I'd spoken it in jest, I now thought it very likely that Burdell had far more than a fatherly interest in Demis. That same suspicion, I now remembered, had haunted her husband in the last months of their marriage. But I could not believe that Demis shared these unnatural feelings or even suspected their existence. That she'd consented to live in her cousin's house must be true—Burdell was too sure of himself on that count—but her reasons could be nothing more than gratitude for his support during her divorce proceedings and a naive, misguided sense of obligation to subjugate her wishes to his.

As for the dentist, I had to confess I had underestimated him. He now appeared to me a man of intense emotions and, perhaps, of enormous appetites—obviously a man used to getting his own way. Yet I had seen in him an essential weakness, a tentative, insecure quality. He would bear watching. Meanwhile, I must speak with Demis at the earliest opportunity.

10

The Landlady

As she explained them to me, Demis' reasons for residing at Burdell's house in Bond Street were plausible enough. "It is only that I can live so much more economically there, and really, Toby, the house I shared with Dr. Hubbard holds so many unpleasant memories for me."

I remained unconvinced. "What is to become of us, I should like to know. Your cousin has made it quite plain that he hates me, my love. He'll balk at nothing to keep us apart. He's even managed to chain you to a chaperone—this elderly widow who leases the house."

At the mention of Mrs. Cunningham, Demis frowned. "Oh, she is not so elderly as you imagine. In that matter Cousin Harvey has broken faith with me. My companion was to be the former landlady, a terribly sweet, half-blind old biddy who rented the rooms to only the most immaculately respectable people and loved her glass after supper. This Cunningham woman has upset all of that. At first she convinced Cousin Harvey that she was destitute and moved her whole brood, two daughters, two sons, into the house without paying a penny of rent. Then, on the first of May, at her insistence, he simply refused to renew poor old Mrs. Jones' lease and let the house instead to Widow Cunningham." Demis shook her head. "It seems foolish I know, Toby, but I almost suspect Cousin Harvey is actually frightened of her."

I could not have been less interested in Burdell's affairs. My own were keeping me busy enough. "I hardly care whether the name of your jailer is Cunningham or Jones," I said. "Either way you are virtually the doctor's prisoner. Will you please tell me how the devil we are to go on seeing each other?"

She took my hand. "Alas, dear Toby, I fear we cannot, at least for the present. Cousin Harvey, you see, has forbidden it."

"Oh, for God's sake!" I exploded. "Who the hell is Cousin Harvey to order us about?" I attempted to pull my hand away but she held it tightly.

"Only give me some time with him, Toby," she pleaded. "I'll bring him around. He's been so kind to me and I really don't feel I can defy him in this. He's so . . . so *adamant* on the subject. But I'll make him see what a wonderful young man you are—how goodhearted you are—and then he won't mind at all. You'll see, Toby. It's only that I *did* go against his wishes when I married Dr. Hubbard, and I made such a dreadful botch of *that*—and now Cousin Harvey's terrified that I'll choose the wrong man again, but that's only because he doesn't know you as I do."

"As far as Cousin Harvey is concerned *any* other man is the wrong man."

She looked at me as though she understood me perfectly and didn't want to. "Whatever do you mean, Toby?"

I brought it out with some vehemence. "Burdell is in love with you, Demis. Your ex-husband knew it. Surely it must have occurred to you before now. Why else should he have spent so much time with you, so many evenings in your home, while you were still married? Can't you see that he did everything in his power to destroy your marriage? For the love of God! Why do you think he's so determined to have you under his roof and tied to the Cunningham apron strings?"

She released my hand and stood, scowling down at me in a queenly temper. "You are quite wrong, Toby! You don't know Cousin Harvey as I do, and you *assuredly* don't know Emma Cunningham. Do you suppose I'm to sleep in Mrs. Cunningham's room so that *she* can protect me from you?" She barked a laugh. "And you think *me* naive! Toby! My poor, innocent Toby, don't you see? It is *I* who must protect Cousin Harvey from that . . . that adventuress . . . that *woman!*"

To demonstrate to good old kindly "Cousin Harvey" that Demis' residence under his roof would not prevent me from visiting her, I accompanied her when she moved her belongings from her former dwelling to 31 Bond Street.

I wish I could write that, from the moment I first saw the house, I had a dark foreboding, but my only impression of the place was that it could stand a coat of paint. Like all of its neighbors it was a narrow building of three stories with an attic lighted by two gable windows and a cellar partially above but principally below the level of the sidewalk.

No alleys separated these houses so that all windows were either at the front or the rear. Aside from the attic gables, eight high windows with shutters fronted the tree-lined street—three across each of the upper two stories and two at the right of the ground floor, well above the eye level of passersby. The street door at the left was reached by ascending seven concrete steps. Other steps to the right of the stoop took tradesmen down to a smaller door opening on the basement.

Emma Cunningham met us at the threshold. She was in her mid to late thirties and taller than most women, perhaps five-foot-seven. She was full-busted and narrow-waisted—possibly a bit too broad in the hips, but I recall clearly admiring her figure, which I thought very good for her age.

Her face was oval with high cheekbones and slightly sunken cheeks, and it was wonderfully framed by dark brown hair which, if let down, I imagined would fall below her waist. She parted it in the middle and it swept down the sides of her face to be done up in the back. A tight braid formed a tiara effect at the top of her head while another braid, much looser, swirled over her left shoulder and draped itself on her bosom.

EMMA CUNNINGHAM

She was not beautiful, nor had she ever been, but she was handsome and her features, while not individually attractive, formed a striking composite. Her nose was a tad too long, her eyes set a bit too wide apart; her lips were decidedly too thin and firm. When she was not speaking those lips compressed into a rigid line like a cord stretched taut. They suggested firmness, dignity, and determination, but not unmixed with arrogance and stubbornness. By contrast her eyes were mild, a light charcoal color, and her voice, even when she rattled on and on (as she was wont to do), was always soft and low.

The reader may well remember her—may have glimpsed her as she walked, head held high, between the bridewell and the courtroom, escorted by the marshals—may even have seen her at one of her hearings or trials. To the very end I found her to be prepossessing when animated, which was most of the time. Only in repose, in her unguarded moments, did the sparkle fade from the eyes and the cheeks draw in and become shallow. Then, when her soft voice could not be heard, her lips would draw down and tighten at the corners, and the lids of her eyes narrow, and her whole aspect harden as mortar hardens.

The landlady and her boarder embraced with syrupy insincerity, each careful not to touch the other's back with her hands, each kissing the air at a safe distance from the other's cheek.

"My dear Demis," oozed the widow, "how welcome you are and with what joy your arrival has been anticipated!"

"Darling Emma," Demis returned, "how warm your greeting and how very gracious your hospitality!"

I'll take my oath, the air fairly crackled.

"And this," said Mrs. Cunningham, "must be the young man of whom," her teeth locked behind her smile, "Dr. Burdell so *often* speaks."

I acknowledged her with a bow. But the mention of the dentist had already set her off on one of what I came to call Emma's soliloquies. "The doctor *has* been extraordinarily kind. I'm a widow, you know. I lost poor George just two years ago. He was a distiller, actually—in Brooklyn. Poor George did leave me *some* money, still, since his death it's been very difficult. I have four children, you see, two boys, delightful children, but much too young to contribute to our little family's resources, and two daughters, quite grown-up though one is still in school. I'm a firm believer in schooling for young women as well as young men, but I really can't imagine how I could have managed it without the generosity of Dr. Burdell—" and here the widow cocked her eye toward Demis. "Why, he has paid their tuition at the seminary as well as opening his house to us. He has showered his affection on us all, particularly the children. Already they think of him as if he were their own dear papa."

There is no telling how much longer this paean to Burdell might have continued had it not been interrupted by a violent shout from upstairs. "Help, ho!" a man's voice cried. "Help! Police! Robbery!"

The benevolent filler of molars himself materialized at the top of the stairs in some disarray. His coat, cravat, and collar were off, his shirt sleeves open and dangling. His pantaloons drooped about his knees—his braces hung to the floor like nooses. His hair was tangled, his beard bristled, his face was livid, and his eyes bulged angrily when they fell on Mrs. Cunningham.

"Witch!" he bellowed, fumbling for his braces and trying to yank up his trousers. "Hellion! THIEF!" He began to stumble down the stairs, never leaving off yowling. "You've stolen it, you bitch! You've STOLEN it! I'll have the law on you, woman—nay, disgrace to the name of woman! Help, ho! Police!" He stopped to wag his finger under the widow's nose. "Never think to escape the consequences of your crime, madam! I'll see you clapt in the Tombs for this spiteful act of vengeance, mark me!" He rushed out into the street still crying for a constable.

For me the image of domestic bliss at 31 Bond Street was somewhat shattered. Demis stared after her cousin for a moment before turning to Mrs. Cunningham, a slight, malicious smile playing on her pretty lips. As for the landlady, she flushed scarlet and hurried into the parlor.

In a few minutes the dentist was back with a bewildered policeman in tow. Mrs. Cunningham chose this instant to reemerge from the parlor and Burdell again thrust his finger into her face. "The note! The note! She's taken it, I tell you. Arrest her!"

The poor officer threw a dumbstruck gaze around the vestibule. "Don't you believe him, Constable!" the widow yelped. "He's a congenital liar and a moral wretch!"

"Venal leper," he screamed.

"Blasphemous scoundrel!" she cried.

"Triple apostate!"

"Pestilential monstrosity!"

Burdell seized the policeman's coat. "I had a judgment against my brother for eight hundred and thirty-six dollars. Not wishing to take him to court in my own name, I signed the paper over to this—this *Jezebel!* In return she gave me her note for the amount, and *now*, this very afternoon, while I lay napping in my apartment, the treacherous bitch *sneaked* into my bedroom and rifled my pantaloons pockets for my safe key, and *stole back her note!*"

"Oh! Damn your soul for a liar!" The widow was in a fury. "You wicked, wicked man! You have ruined me. You have ruined my family. But I'll have my satisfaction of you, Harvey Burdell! Do you hear me? I'll have your heart's blood! Oh! I can't bear it that you should mistreat your wife so shamefully!"

"You are *not* my wife, nor shall you ever be, scheme though you will, woman!"

"I *am* your wife by *every tie that could be!*" she retorted, thumping on his chest with her fist after every word.

He threw back his head and laughed, after the fashion of a deranged, operatic tenor. "That I—*I* should take to my bosom a woman who has been seen consorting with depraved men of the town in the vilest of debauched houses of assignation! It is to laugh!" And to prove his point he laughed again.

She coiled as if she were about to lunge for his throat and the policeman, at last recovering himself, stepped between them. "Here, now," he growled, "I'm of a mind to haul you both down to the Police Office and let one of the magistrates untangle you."

At this point I intervened. "One moment, Constable. This matter is not as complex as it appears." I addressed Burdell. "Who obtained the original judgment against your brother?"

For the first time the dentist noticed my presence. His humor did not improve.

I asked the officer to instruct Burdell to answer.

"Mr. Edwards Pierrepont, an attorney of this city," Burdell said sullenly.

"You see," I told the constable, "Mr. Pierrepont obtained the judgment and assigned it to Dr. Burdell in blank, and the doctor in turn assigned it to Mrs. Cunningham and took her note, but the note, now alleged as stolen, is really of no consequence whatever, since the doctor can easily have the judgment *re*assigned to himself by Mr. Pierrepont at any time. Therefore, regardless of the disposition of the promissory paper in question, no crime has been committed."

The minion of the law regarded me as though he'd understood at least one word in ten and repeated two of the words he was sure of. *"No* crime?" I nodded. He gave a huge sigh. "Well, then, I'm leaning to the notion of letting you off with a warning. It appears that nothing has happened, *and it better not happen again!"*

He spun around and stalked out into the street while Burdell stalked upstairs and Mrs. Cunningham stalked into the parlor.

What I couldn't predict was that this skirmish was merely the first exchange of shots in an all-out war between Cunningham and Burdell. Nor could I know that my small role in the squabble had already convinced the widow that I should be her legal representative in the battles to come.

11

Special Sessions

I spent one early June afternoon in the Hall of Justice, commonly called the Police Office, collecting affidavits from various officers in connection with certain criminal prosecutions in which The Firm had an interest. I did not finish until almost sundown and, having missed my dinner, I determined to take supper at the Broadway Oyster House and retire early to my bed. The Court of Special Sessions was still sitting and, as I passed the chamber, the door burst open and I was almost bowled over by a frantic bailiff.

"Are you a lawyer?" he demanded without apology.

I confessed.

"You're wanted," he said, seizing my arm and pulling me unceremoniously into the nearly deserted courtroom. On the bench squatted, according to the plaque beside the door, the Honorable Rufus Alburtis, an unkempt, unshaven, grossly obese mound of a man—his robes undone, his neckcloth untied, shirtless except for a soiled dickey and frayed, unlaundered collar and cuffs. In one of his fat cheeks, along with his tongue, was wedged an enormous wad of tobacco which he worked continuously in bovine fashion, pausing periodically in mid-pronouncement to spit brown juice in the general direction of a cuspidor located not quite close enough to his chair.

At the prosecution table perched one of the assistant prosecutors, one Mr. Sylvester Slido, a particularly greasy citizen who had been pointed out to me that afternoon as a rising star, if not a comet, in the office of A. Oakey Hall, the district attorney. Lawyer Slido was a skeletal youth of cadaverous complexion with the lasting scars of aggravated acne on his face and darting ferret's eyes.

Seated beside Squire Slido and in obvious bad humor was an immaculately tailored and groomed gentleman in, I guessed, his late thirties, probably a professional man. His hair, dark brown, was brushed up into a sort of cock's comb above a broad forehead. His nose was long and slightly aquiline—his lips thin and, at this moment, compressed with annoyance. His upper lip and chin were shaven but neatly trimmed side-whiskers extended along his jawline and met in a beard nearly long enough to conceal the knot of his cravat. His eyes were his most striking feature, set wide apart under brows that suggested mink fur. The lashes were long and the lids were dark and sleepily half-closed. Though he was clearly a robust and manly fellow, those eyes had a feminine, almost seductive beauty. Only one touch spoiled the picture. He managed always to turn his head at such an angle that he was forever peering at people out of the corners of his eyes instead of confronting them squarely. It gave him a furtive, cunning expression that his features otherwise belied.

His name was Samuel Catlin. He was a physician from Brooklyn. He was the complainant in a charge of theft. He drummed his fingers impatiently on the prosecution table, looking for all the world like a tired man who'd missed his dinner. I knew the feeling.

At the back of the room sat—I should say loomed—a tall, rawboned, grim-visaged man in his mid-fifties, outfitted in the somber drab of a preacher. As he was evidently not an actor in the drama, I did not then pause to notice him, except for a vague curiosity over his interest in the proceedings.

I have a tendency to imagine people as beasts in a fable. Probably I read too much Aesop as a child. I could not forbear seeing the magistrate in the guise of a great hog; Lawyer Slido as a weasel; the sour clergyman as an impassive, imperturbable vulture. The doctor I envisioned as a cat, not alley-smart but of the sleek, pampered, aristocratic class. So strong was the image that I enjoyed the irony when I learned his name. In that dingy, foul little courtroom Dr. Catlin was grievously out of his element.

As for the youthful defendant, as I watched him struggle in the bailiff's clutch, his soft features simultaneously terrified and defiant, I recalled once checking traps I had set out for rats and finding instead that I had caught a young squirrel. It was a devil of a task to free the panicky creature without being bitten and when I finally succeeded I found the helpless thing's legs were broken. I exhausted on that squirrel all the healing arts a nine-year-old can command and when, at the end of a week, it died, I wept like an infant.

I recognized the accused as my erstwhile on-too-rage, Zachariah Lamentations Hasty.

"Young man, are you an attorney?" grunted the Honorable Rufus Alburtis.

"I am with Hoffman and Associates, Your Honor. My name is Tobias Brendon."

"Well, the charge is pocket picking, Mr. Brendon, brought by Dr. Catlin here against this little street scum, and you got one minute to confer with your client."

The boy caught my eye and hung his head.

"I have no need for a conference, Your Honor," I said.

Slido put Catlin on the stand. He'd left Niblo's Garden that afternoon on his way to the Brooklyn ferry when the defendant bumped up against his person, at the same time offering to summon a hansom for a penny. The physician, having once before been victimized, was alert to the danger. He had caught the boy in the act of liberating his purse and forthwith summoned a constable. He'd remained in Manhattan at, he insisted, considerable personal inconvenience so that he might press the charge and "rid the streets of at least a fraction of their hoard of fuzzy-cheeked banditti." Mr. Slido approved of this public-spirited sacrifice and said so, Judge Alburtis joining in the acclaim.

I rose to cross-examine. This needless delay in the speedy dispensing of justice did not please the magistrate. So certain was he of our guilty plea that he had forgotten to request it. "Keep it short," he oinked.

"Dr. Catlin," I began, "please explain to the court precisely what your wallet contained at the time of the alleged theft."

"Objected to as irrelevant," said Slido.

"Sustained," burped the judge.

"Dr. Catlin," I continued, "will you tell the court what, if anything, about the defendant's demeanor first aroused your suspicions?"

"Objection. Incompetent," said Slido.

"Your Honor," I said quickly, "it has been established that Dr. Catlin has, at a prior time, had his purse stolen by a street boy. I submit that that unfortunate experience may have so operated on his mind as to prejudice him against my client and induce him to put the worst possible interpretation on certain actions of my client when these actions may well have been entirely innocent."

Alburtis stared at me as if I was crazy. Then his little piggy eyes narrowed. "Went to Harvard, did you?"

I quickly assured him I had not.

"Nevertheless," he said, "objection sustained. Ask your next question. Be pithy."

"Dr. Catlin," I persevered, "say again what, in your perception, were the actions of the accused."

"Objection," said Slido.

"Oh, hell, let him answer and get it over with," the judge snapped.

Catlin's glare said he could cheerfully have murdered me. "The boy slammed into me and stuck his hand in my pocket. I grabbed his wrist just as he lifted my wallet."

I gave the physician a cool, steely look, then turned my back to him and sauntered casually toward the table. "Mr. Witness, how can you be certain my client was *removing* the purse from your pocket?"

"What else could he have been doing?" Catlin responded evasively.

I spun around and sprang the trap! *"Might he not have been putting it back into your pocket?"*

The courtroom, for a long moment, was as silent as a tomb. Then Justice Alburtis said, "Oh, for Christ's sake! Guilty!"

The bailiff yanked Hasty to his feet. The youth's frightened eyes fixed on mine, then on the judge. "Is Reverend Edward Cowley present?" Alburtis asked. The gaunt, hawk-faced cleric in the last pew stood and came forward. Alburtis glowered down at the boy. "Now, Hasty, or whatever your name is, you have been tried and found guilty of petty theft and you could be sentenced to five years in the workhouse; however, the court takes note of your deprived circumstances and tender years and is inclined to be"—the judge paused to belch—"merciful. You are therefore sentenced to five years at hard labor, sentence suspended on condition that you immediately be placed in the custody and under the strict authority of Reverend Cowley here, keeper of the 'Shepherd's Fold,' One Fifty-seven East Twenty-third Street, which institution is incorporated under the laws of the state of New York to receive and adopt children and youths of both sexes, between the age of twelve months and seventeen years, who are orphans, half-orphans, or otherwise friendless. There you will be kept and supported at the public dole, to be educated, apprenticed, or placed out to service in whatever manner Reverend Cowley deems fit. Do you understand this? *Look at me, boy!"*

I stepped up beside Hasty and pried him loose from the bailiff. "He understands, Your Honor," I said.

"Let the boy say it."

"Hasty," I said, "tell the judge you understand."

The lad was shaking violently. I put my hand on his shoulder to steady him. His body was feverish to the touch even through his ragged coat. At last he managed a choked whisper: "I understand."

"Then, boy, understand this also. Any attempt to challenge or subvert Reverend Cowley's authority, by running away or by any act of disobedience, will be swiftly reported to this court and punished by remanding you at once to the workhouse, there to serve the full five years of your term. If you comprehend this, look me in the eye and say, 'Yes, Your Honor.' "

Slowly Hasty raised his head. "Yes, Your Honor," he said in a flat, dry tone that stopped just short of impertinence.

Alburtis squinted down, uncertain whether or not he was being defied, then concluded that he was. "Gratitude is a quality as pleasing in the young as subservience and respect for authority. I want you to assure me, boy, that you are properly appreciative of Reverend Cowley's willingness to undertake your moral regeneration, *and* I want you to convince me that you are thankful for the"—the judge paused to spit—"mercy which this court has shown you. I want you to say, 'Thank you, Your Honor.' "

Hasty had stopped shaking. With my hand still on his shoulder I could feel his every muscle tense. He stood at attention, fists clenched at his sides, jaw set, eyes steady and fixed on the magistrate's own. He was ready to die—ready even to take five years at hard labor—rather than say, "Thank you, Your Honor."

I was about to intercede when, to my surprise, Alburtis coughed uncomfortably and averted his eyes. "Suit yourself, you little gangster. The brat is in your charge, Reverend. You know your business, but my notion is there is nothing like a sound beating with a stout stick for breaking an insolent spirit and promoting docility."

"Shepherd" Cowley smiled unpleasantly and wrapped long, bony fingers around the boy's arm. I noticed that his fingernails were filthy.

At the door Hasty broke free for a moment and took a step toward me. *"Please,* Squire Brendon, ain't there *nothing* you can do?"

I couldn't answer him. I couldn't even think of a lie to comfort him. I watched the preacher lunge for the youngster and drag him away. I told myself I had done everything possible in his cause. I reminded myself that he was, after all, guilty—that he *was* incorrigible—that I *had* predicted his downfall. The boy was fortunate, I reflected, that I had been present. Another lawyer would certainly have pleaded him guilty without making any effort to defend him, whereas I had struggled valiantly against impossible odds. By the time I emerged from the Hall of Justice I was convinced that there was no reason to upbraid myself. The city's streets were swarming with urchins like Hasty. It was regrettable, of course, but there it was. The lower classes spawned like rabbits. Abortions were not only illegal and dangerous, performed by back-alley butchers, unlicensed quacks, and drunken midwives, but the fees of even these slaughterers were beyond the means of the poor. Thousands of unwanted children crawled over New York like cockroaches in a squalid kitchen, filling the orphan asylums and spilling over into the prisons. They lived by their wits or they died, of starvation, of exposure, of violence, of disease. In this glut of human misery the life of one boy really mattered very little.

I had lost my appetite. I passed the Oyster House by and stopped instead in the taproom of the American Hotel. The waiter served my Scotch at a table near the window and I sat, absently rolling the tumbler between my palms and staring mindlessly out at the street under the marquis where a battalion of tattered boys worked the line of cabs and coaches much as they had the afternoon I arrived at the Metropole.

In my mind I could hear Quinncannon's smooth sophistry.
Why not let the boy go, Mr. Brendon? He wasn't stealing your wallet.
And what, sir, would you say he was doing?
Putting it back.

Very clever. A sample of the verbal acrobatics by which he obtained acquittals for his felonious clientele, no doubt. Well, I'd tried it and the strategy had failed dismally. It wasn't my style. I told myself I was too noble a fellow. *Sans peur et sans reproche,* I thought. It sounded more credible in French.

I sipped the drink and brooded darkly over it, and suddenly I felt a pair of eyes staring in at me through the glass. I looked up and, to my horror, there stood Hasty. His cheeks were no longer full and ruddy but hollow, and his skin seemed gray parchment.

The light in his eyes had gone out. Sunken, dilated, and rimmed with red, they gaped at me out of coal-black sockets. It hit me with a sickening swiftness that what I saw was not a living being but some tortured wraith risen out of a lidless hell. It stood at attention, fists clenched at its sides, and in my mind's ear I heard the whisper: "I will not say, 'Thank you, Squire Brendon.' "

I dropped the whiskey and turned away. When I dared to look again, the apparition had vanished.

12

The Hoffmans at Home

Ogden Hoffman lived with his wife and two daughters in one of the more modest homes on upper Fifth Avenue, if the word "modest" can be applied to a mansion complete with carriage house and stables. On the last Sunday in May I received an invitation to dinner.

"You'll love Mrs. Hoffman," Jeremy told me. "She's the soul of grace. And the girls are enchanting, particularly the elder, Emily. She's just turned seventeen and as ripe as an apple." He tossed me a wink. "You'd better keep a rein on your charms, Toby, or she'll tear your clothes off before the cherries jubilee is served."

But that, I thought while riding uptown in Hoffman's carriage, I must not permit to happen. It would never do to become romantically entangled with my employer's daughter, particularly not now when affairs with Demis Hubbard were complicating my life so thoroughly. No matter how attractive Miss Hoffman might find me, *this* time I must stand firm.

I was admitted by an ancient family retainer and ushered into the main parlor where a handsome woman of about forty rose to greet me with a warm smile and a charming drawl that reminded me pleasantly of home.

"My husband informs me we are fellow Virginians, Mr. Brendon. Having lived so long among the Yankees, I cannot tell you how I've looked forward to meeting you."

"Your servant, ma'am."

I bowed and kissed her hand and she gave her husband a triumphant smile. "How very gallant. You may have noticed, Mr. Brendon, that a northern gentleman never bows unless he has dropped his cufflink."

Ogden Hoffman roared with laughter. "You must excuse my wife, Toby. She is the same shameless coquette I abducted from her father's cradle twenty years ago. Now behave yourself, m'dear. You're embarrassing the boy."

"Oh, Ogden," replied the lady, again smiling at me, "I hardly think so."

Ginny, the younger daughter, told me that she was ten and one-half, that she'd been named for her mother, that her real name was Virginia, that her father called her mother Ginger, that her sister's name was Emily, that Emily was not home because she was out riding, that Mama was angry with Emily because she was so late, and that Emily was seventeen and had never had a beau and "Mama says she doesn't know whatever will become of Emily."

Ginny, on the other hand, did have a beau. His name was Herman. Some day, when they were older, Ginny was going to marry Herman and he was going to be a lawyer like her papa and they were going to have three children, two boys and one girl.

This information was imparted to me with great solemnity while the little girl conducted me on a grand tour that led us through the house and grounds and down to the stables. While we stood there admiring the coach horses I heard the clopping of approaching hooves on the gravel drive. "That's Blue Boy," Ginny announced. And, trying to sound as much like her mother as possible, even to the drawl, she stamped her little foot and added, "Emily's *finally* come home."

I was not eagerly anticipating this meeting. God knows what it was that drew women so irresistibly to me. A dozen young men of my acquaintance were, in my estimation, quite as handsome and dashing as myself, yet they did not suffer from my affliction. Surely my near-fatal encounter with the black widow Fairgood had taught me to be wary. Yet, despite that brush with the gallows, I had allowed myself to become involved with Demis Hubbard under the most complex circumstances. This time, moreover, I was not dealing with an experienced woman but a mere girl, barely seventeen, naive, sentimental, bursting, no doubt, with unrealized fantasies—I shook my head vigorously. This time I must resist all temptation—I must be strong enough for both of us. I took a deep breath and turned and, upon my word, my heart sank like a stone.

The girl was lovely.

She dismounted gracefully, a delicate, Dresden doll, tiny beside the huge roan stallion that pawed the ground next to her. She handed the reins to a groom and stroked the horse's neck affectionately. As he was led away she removed her hat and rich, raven-black tresses fell over her shoulders. Her eyes sparkled like jade and her skin was the color of ivory.

I took another deep breath.

"You are *very* late, Emily," her little sister scolded. "Mama is *ever* so peeved."

"Mama will survive." Her voice was surprisingly throaty where I had expected a bell-like treble. I liked its husky sound. She took off one glove and extended her hand to me.

"You must be Mr. Brendon," she said.

"Your servant, Miss Hoffman." I bowed and kissed her hand.

She observed me quizzically. "How very quaint. I suppose southern girls enjoy it." She looked at her sister. "You may run up to the house now, Ginny, and tell Mama I'm back and she can stop being peeved."

The child scampered off. Miss Hoffman's mouth was playing with a slight smile. "I must ask, Mr. Brendon, are you suffering from some sort of cramp?"

I assured her I was not.

"I only inquired," she said, "because I have an uncle who sometimes is plagued by a cramping in his hands so that, when he clasps my hand, his poor fingers lock, you see, and he can't, for the life of him, let go of me."

I instantly released her hand.

She slipped her arm into mine and began steering me toward the house. "Papa is so pleased that you are his clerk."

"Excuse me, Miss Hoffman. I am not his clerk."

"Oh? I thought you worked for him."

"I work with him. I am an associate in his firm."

"You're an attorney *already?*" She stopped walking so I stopped. "That's wonderful. You must be quite a prodigy to be admitted to the bar at only nineteen."

"I am not nineteen," I said. "I am twenty-two."

She gave me a long, thoughtful look. "Are you really?" She commenced walking so I commenced walking. "Well, then, I imagine you're not such a prodigy after all."

"Evidently not," I muttered. I was feeling extremely discomfitted. It was strange to be so close to a beautiful girl without feeling her hand on my knee or in my bosom. Miss Emily, I reflected, had remarkable self-control.

"I suppose," she said suddenly, "you have been told you're a handsome young fellow. Doubtless a dozen little maidens are quite dizzy over you."

It was an astounding remark and very forward. I was at a loss to reply. To agree would sound fatuous, yet I could hardly deny the obvious. While I hesitated she eyed me and smiled. "Yes," she said, "I rather thought as much."

I decided to respond in kind. "Frankly, Miss Hoffman, a girl as attractive and delightful as yourself must have no end of admirers. I fancy you've received your share of proposals already."

"I *do* count several silly, headstrong boys among my acquaintance," she conceded. Again she stopped walking, forcing me to halt beside her. "Truly, Mr. Brendon, I am ashamed of how foolishly romantic and immature so many people our age seem to be today. They stumble in and out of what they call 'love' and declare, on a moment's notice, their undying affection for one another when, indeed, they have no more notion of real love than they have of flying. Don't you agree, Mr. Brendon?"

"With every word, Miss Hoffman."

"As an example," she continued, "let us take two imaginary people such as, for the sake of argument, you and me. We have just met. We are complete strangers. We know absolutely nothing of each other, except, let us say, only for the purpose of this discussion, that we find one another . . . engaging. Would we not be utter idiots to rush into each other's arms, to exchange vows of eternal devotion, to bind ourselves, each to the other, for life? Can you honestly imagine, Mr. Brendon, proposing marriage to me on such slight acquaintance?"

"Not for a minute, Miss Hoffman," I said.

"There you are! Yet how many young people today display the same good sense that we do?" We had begun walking once more. "What is most disheartening, this childish sentimentality is actually encouraged by parents, especially mothers. They suffer from the absurd conceit that if a girl is not wed before she's eighteen, she's doomed to be an old maid. I really should warn you, Mr. Brendon, you are exactly the sort of young man Mama would want for a son-in-law."

A cold chill ran the length of my spine. "Really, Miss Hoffman?"

"Oh, yes. You have all the qualifications, I'm afraid. You're good-looking. You have a profession. Papa thinks the world of you, you know. Then, too, you're a southern gentleman. That will impress Mama above all. I suspect she'll be off on one of her matchmaking binges. We really must be on guard at all times."

I nodded rapidly. "Yes, we must, we really must." It was a very strange conversation.

"After all," she said, "we're quite in agreement on how witless it would be to rush pell-mell into something so confining as marriage."

"Totally addlepated!" I concurred with some vehemence.

She ceased walking abruptly. "Need you be *quite* so adamant, Mr. Brendon?"

"Why," I said, "we've just been speaking of how ridiculous marriage would be."

"Ridiculous?" she echoed. She withdrew her arm from mine. "I did not realize you found the idea of falling in love with me so *very* ludicrous."

"Oh!" I cried. "For God's sake, I'm *agreeing* with you!"

"Not two minutes ago," she said icily, "you admitted thinking about marrying me."

"I simply said, Miss Hoffman, that I could not *imagine* being married to you."

"Honestly, Mr. Brendon, this is the most *insulting* proposal I've ever received!"

"Proposal!" I exploded. "Miss Hoffman, you are the damnedest impossible woman I've ever met!"

Without deigning to reply, Miss Emily spun on her heel and stormed off toward the house, leaving me to stare after her in helpless confusion.

The remainder of my afternoon at chez Hoffman is, to this hour, a jumble of fragmentary recollections, none of them pleasant. I had come expecting to corner my host after dinner and force from him, if need be, some intelligence regarding my father's identity, but the gentleman remained as irritatingly elusive and uncommunicative as ever, managing to dodge my every effort to maneuver him into a private interview. In this he was joined, for entirely different motives, by his wife, who, true to Miss Emily's prediction, never let up in her determination to throw her daughter and me together in the hope of setting off some spontaneous amorous combustion. As for Miss Emily, though I expected her to be cold and distant, she confounded me again by seeming to fall in with her "mama's" wishes. Seated beside me at dinner, she was forever casting dreamy gazes up at me, apparently mesmerized by my every word, emitting breathy, schoolgirl sighs until, to speak my mind, I wanted to slap her silly. No woman had ever treated me so shabbily. There were no means by which I could retaliate and well she knew it. At one point, while laughing too heartily at one of my feebler jests, she reached up and actually stroked my neck.

It came to me suddenly. The same gesture of affection she had bestowed on her horse. And that's what you are to her, Toby, my boy, thought I. A horse's neck. I looked long at her lovely face and gave her my warmest smile, and plotted my revenge.

Ogden Hoffman saw me to the carriage and I seized the opportunity to at last confront him. "Forgive my bluntness, sir, but you have left me little time to press my case. I must know what information you have concerning my father. I will tell you candidly, I cannot understand your reluctance to discuss a matter of such importance to me."

He took out his pipe and pouch, keeping his eyes on mine. "I see, Toby, that Orion Small has betrayed my confidences to you. He had no right to do that."

"He had no right to conceal from me even the little he knows," I answered, growing angry. "Nor have you, sir."

"I swore an oath, lad," he said.

"Your oath be damned!" The issue was far too sensitive for me to stand on polite ceremony.

He struck a match and touched off his pipe. "I suppose I knew it would come to this," he said between puffs. "You're right, of course, lad. If you insist on it I have an obligation to tell you the truth. Only consider this, Toby. There are some truths a man is better off never learning. You are comfortable now. You have education and position. Nothing you could wish for is beyond your reach. For God's sake, boy, let the past die. Whatever I could tell you would only cause you pain."

"I can't believe that," I said. "It is far better to know the worst than to fear it."

"You think so only because you are young." He shook his great lion's mane and put his hand on my arm. "I will strike a bargain with you, Toby. Today is Sunday. I want you to think carefully about what I have said. Next Friday evening at six o'clock I shall go to the Whistling Pig tavern and occupy a table at the back of the room. If you still wish to know about your past, I will

tell you then what I have kept from you. I pray to God, Toby"
—his grip on my arm tightened—"that you will heed my warning."

In a Whistling Pig's eye, thought I.

13

The Lie Direct
and the Retort Pugnacious

I left Hoffman, thinking it likely I would find Quinncannon in the taproom of the Astor House. There, at a round table near the hearth that commanded a full view of the room, the Irishman often presided over a circle of intimate friends like a slim Dr. Johnson at the Mitre Tavern. I directed my hackman down Broadway to the block between Barclay and Vesey opposite the southern tip of City Hall Park and strolled through the ornate gilt and velvet posh of the hotel's magnificent lobby into the mahogany and leather sanctum of the taproom. Quinncannon's table was unoccupied but one of the waiters informed me that he was expected. I decided to wait and sat down, not in the chair with its back against the wall—that was reserved for Himself—but in the chair to its right.

Shortly after the waiter brought my bourbon, I noticed two gentlemen approaching me. One was a stranger to me, tall and thin but not slight, fashionably dressed in a dark suit and matching waistcoat, high, starched collar, and wide cravat done up in an outlandish bow. He was perhaps thirty-two with a full head of curly black hair untinged by gray and he wore a full moustache and thick beard which together covered the whole of his face below the cheekbones and long, straight nose, and which hid his mouth save for the lower lip. He had a high forehead and gray

eyes which, though not keen, gave him an expression of thoughtful intelligence. His forehead was furrowed but there were no
lines at the corners of his eyes, suggesting a man who frowned
often but seldom smiled.

I recognized his companion as Dr. Samuel Catlin, the Brooklyn
physician who had prosecuted the boy, Hasty, for pinching his
pocketbook. As he drew nearer to me, he looked every bit as
unhappy as he had on that occasion. It struck me that, except that
Catlin had no moustache and wore his beard below his jawline,
the two men were remarkably similar in appearance. They were
also both intoxicated and in a mood to be quarrelsome.

"Your name, young man, unless I am much mistaken, is Brendon," said Samuel Catlin. Without invitation he and his friend
took seats at my table.

I considered the term "young man" as offensive as if he had
addressed me as "boy." "Your error, sir," I returned, "lies not
in your assumption but in your presumption."

"Touché," said Catlin with a canine smile. "Did I not tell you,
David, that the young man has wit?"

"You did, Samuel, but tell me, Samuel, what is the term for a
young wit?"

"Why, a witling, to be sure. But, David, we forget our manners.
Allow me to introduce Mr. Tobias Brendon. Mr. Brendon, this
is Dr. David Uhl. Dr. Uhl is a celebrated physician, Mr. Brendon.
Mr. Brendon is a calibrated witling, Dr. Uhl."

"Nay, Samuel, I think you misspeak. Surely you mean 'celebrated witling.' "

"Calibrated! I insist, David."

"Explain, Samuel."

"Why, David, to calibrate is to take the measure of a bore. And
surely your witling is your greatest bore."

My anger was the more intense for the fact that I could not
think of a single suitably clever retort and the certainty that a
dozen would occur to me before breakfast. Then, too, I had no
idea what grievance these men had against me. One I barely
knew; the other was a complete stranger.

"Look here, gentlemen—"

Each of them hunched forward in eager anticipation.

"Now, David, attend and be educated," Catlin grinned. "We have given Mr. Brendon the 'Quip Modest.' Let us note well his reply that we may learn the better how to quarrel by the book from this rare witling."

"I cannot guess the reason," I said, "why you two gin-soaked quacksalvers have chosen to play the fools at my table. I can only hope that your scalpels are sharper than your wits. If you wish to continue this conversation I suggest we do so in a locale more convivial to your manners—such as the garbage pits behind the hotel kitchen."

I was quite ready to take them on, one at a time or both together. Uhl was shaking his head in apparent confusion. "Tell me, Samuel, did we just receive the Countercheck Churlish or the Reproof Valiant?"

"Neither, David. I fear me we have only heard the Retort Sub-standard. Mr. Brendon, I looked to you for drollery and find mere irascibility. Your humor is not a talent but a malady. As a doctor I diagnose an overabundance of bile in the system. If you will visit my office I will prescribe a purge. Here is my card." He turned toward Uhl. "And *that*, my dear David, is what is known as the Reply Regretful."

I was on the edge of losing control. My hands, resting on the table, clenched. I could feel my arms and shoulders tense and my neck and face grow warm. Uhl watched me with some concern.

"I think, Samuel, we have taken enough of Mr. Brendon's time and perhaps presumed too much on his good nature. Why don't we return to the bar? I'll buy you a whiskey and we'll send one to Mr. Brendon's table."

"I think not, David. The gesture might be interpreted as an apology." I studied Catlin and abruptly I realized that, though his manner was calm, the man was furious. His thin lips stretched across his face, tightening at the corners. His eyes glowed strangely. Momentarily I forgot my own rage in my intense curiosity. What in the name of God did the man hold against me?

"Possibly, Samuel," David Uhl said, "we owe Mr. Brendon an apology."

Catlin kept his burning stare on me. "I think not, David," he said again. "We have not insulted you, young man, have we? Nor offended you either. Certainly it was not our intent. We have treated you with just as much courtesy as you deserve, I assure you, but we never intended to insult you."

"Ooooh"—from a quiet brogue behind me—"sure you did."

Both doctors looked up at the man standing at my back.

Damn it, Quinncannon, I thought, stay out of this! I can fight my own battles.

The Irishman remained behind my chair. Uhl put his hand on Catlin's arm. There was real fear in his demeanor. "Come, Samuel, I think we should take our leave."

"Not yet, David. Not until I have said what I came to say."

"Yes," I said. "I *would* like to know exactly what inspired this verbal ambush."

"You are a . . . friend"—Catlin had a nasty way of pronouncing the word *friend*—"of Mrs. Demis Hubbard."

"I am."

"Well, Dr. Uhl and I are friends of Mrs. Emma Cunningham. I was her physician when she and her late husband lived in Brooklyn. Since his death and her removal to Manhattan Dr. Uhl has attended her and her children."

I waited for what seemed a reasonable interval. "What is your point, Doctor?"

"We each have a deep and sincere interest in Mrs. Cunningham's welfare. We find it inexplicable that you, as one who presumably has an even stronger concern in Mrs. Hubbard's affairs, have continued to permit her to abide under the roof of her first cousin in circumstances which seem less than . . . decorous."

I leaned back in my chair, watching him. "Would you care to clarify your concerns, Doctor?"

"You must be aware, sir, that Dr. Burdell and Mrs. Cunningham are betrothed."

"I am not aware of it, sir, but if it is true they have my blessing."

"Have they indeed? Your behavior does not support your assertion, sir."

"Kindly explain yourself, sir."

"Permit me to speak plainly, Mr. Brendon. The engagement of our friend, Mrs. Cunningham, to the man she loves is being slowly, deliberately undermined by Mrs. Hubbard's constant, unseemly efforts to seduce Dr. Burdell."

I was on my feet and livid. "That is a lie, sir, and you are a liar!"

He sprang to his feet. "I say to you, sir, Demis Hubbard is a common slut!"

I hit him full in the face. He staggered back against his chair. The chair overturned and he crashed to the floor.

All conversation in the taproom ceased. Every man's head was turned toward us. Uhl was attempting to help Catlin to his feet. There was blood at the corner of Catlin's mouth and blood streaming from his nose. The sight of his blood served only to infuriate me more. Again I raised my fists. Uhl had managed to prop Catlin up against the table. I took a step. Quinncannon seized both my shoulders and held me back.

"Let me go, damn it! I'll kill him!"

"So the possibility's crossed your mind, has it?" The Irishman tightened his grip.

Catlin was swaying, trying to regain his equilibrium. He gave me a lethal glare and lurched toward me, drawing back his hand as if to slap me with the back of it. When he swung Quinncannon caught his wrist and held it inches from my face. Catlin was heaving for breath. He managed to gasp out, "My seconds will call on you, young man." Then his eyes glazed over and he collapsed, unconscious, into David Uhl's arms.

14

The Code Duello

For over twenty-five years (I was informed by Jeremy Todd) Quinncannon had maintained the same rooms in Broadway on the second floor of a house facing the American Hotel and separated from St. Paul's only by the cathedral's small cemetery. An opulent Oriental rug covered most of the sitting room floor, its deep wine reds and golds reflected in the draperies and leather wingbacks and ottomans. On three walls bookshelves rose to the ceiling, jammed to capacity with worn, well-thumbed volumes. Against the fourth wall stood a sideboard and drysink which served also as the bar. There was a small gaming table attended by captain's chairs and a gigantic secretary at one corner. The furnishings were predominantly leather and maple and the overall effect was one of agreeable clutter and hospitality.

Into this room I walked on the morning after my encounter with Samuel Catlin to find the Irishman settled in a chair near the hearth with a pot of steaming coffee on the sideboard, a pipe in his teeth, and a slender book in his hand. He glanced up and said cheerfully, "Well, Toby, you've really stepped in it this time."

I poured a cup of coffee and sat down.

"This," he continued, indicating the book, "is the Code Duello, the international code of honor governing the conduct of duels. For the next two days it will be our Bible."

I repeated the title. "Is it Spanish or French?"

"Neither, lad. It is Irish—aside from fine whiskey, the most important contribution of my native land to world culture."

"You know, sir," I said, "I'm not as angry by half as I was last night."

"Neither is Dr. Catlin. What difference does that make?" He eyed me sharply. "You're not thinking of backing down, are you, Toby?"

"Well. . . ."

"Because when a man retires from l'affaire d'honneur he brands himself a coward for life. Surely death is to be preferred to a life of shame."

Not by much, I thought. I stared moodily into my coffee while my resentment against Quinncannon burgeoned. That I was in this fix was, after all, entirely his fault. He must have realized last night that I had lost control. He must have seen the explosion coming. Why had he not prevented it?

"Toby," he said quietly, "you would have been highly indignant if I had intervened in your quarrel."

The warlock could read my mind.

"You had better," he went on, "be thoroughly familiar with the code." He adjusted a pair of gold-rimmed spectacles. "Rule 1. 'The first offense requires the first apology, although the retort may have been more offensive than the insult; example: A tells B he is impertinent. B retorts that he lies; A must make the first apology, because he gave the first offense, and then B may explain away the retort—' "

"Then," I interrupted, "there is my solution. Since Catlin gave the first offense it is he who must apologize!"

Quinncannon raised one eyebrow, then finished reading the sentence: " '—after one fire.' "

"Oh. We have to shoot at each other first." I brightened. "But Catlin must then beg my pardon."

"I'm surprised, Toby, that these things must be explained to a Virginian. There are three degrees of apology: the explanation, the apology, and the begging of pardon. The first is not considered demeaning as the gentleman does not admit to error but simply gives cause for his remark. The second, while embarrassing, is not degrading. The gentleman merely acknowledges that he was mistaken and intemperate. But the third is intended to be humiliating. Now, in your case, normally Rule 1 would apply, but matters are more complicated. Your situation is covered by Rule 6:

" 'If A gives B the lie direct, and B retorts by a blow (being the two greatest offenses), no reconciliation can take place till after two discharges each, after which B may beg A's pardon for the blow and then A may explain simply for the lie—because a blow is never allowable.' "

"Does that mean," I asked, "that we must exchange two rounds before anybody can apologize for anything?"

"Not necessarily."

"Then there *is* a loophole."

"Yes, Toby. Catlin may kill you with his first shot."

"But— What if I kill Catlin?"

"Ah, lad, that would be unacceptably dishonorable. The man who gave the graver offense must never shoot to kill."

"Then what *may* I do? Shoot to wing?"

"Well, as Catlin gave the *first* insult, you might shoot to maim."

There was a momentary gleam in the corner of his eye. I half suspected he was laughing at me. But a second look convinced me otherwise. His expression was as somber as a mortician's. The simile made me shudder.

"Evidently, sir, there is no alternative to firing away at one another." I was getting resigned to it. "Who would have thought that bloodying one drunken lout could be so complicated?"

The Irishman freshened our coffee. "There are other circumstances peculiar to this affair, Toby. Rule 10: 'An insult to a lady under a gentleman's care or protection is to be considered as, by one degree, a greater offense than if given to the gentleman personally, and to be regulated accordingly. Offenses originating from the support of a lady's reputation are to be considered as less unjustifiable and as admitting of lighter apologies by the aggressor; this is to be determined by the circumstances of the case, but always favorable to the lady.' " He caught my eye and smiled.

"What in hell does all *that* mean?"

"Why, it's simple enough, lad. Catlin's offense was the lie direct but, as it insulted a lady's honor, it is the more obnoxious by one degree. That is, it is as indefensible as a blow, while your offense, though a blow, and as such unallowable, is nonetheless mitigated by one degree, since it was struck in support of a lady's reputation, making it the equivalent of the lie direct, so that, as Catlin's offense was given first, all other factors being equal, his offense is the more severe and thus he is required to make the first apology. Do you understand?"

He was filling his pipe and still smiling.

"Mr. Quinncannon," I answered, "I suggest that explanation is comprehensible only to you and to God." I paused. "Possibly to God."

He touched a match to his pipe. "The point is that Catlin may not shoot to kill while you may. Shots must twice be exchanged after which, if you are both still standing, he must beg your pardon and you will then give him simple explanation. Unless. . . ."

"Unless?"

"Unless he declines to appear." He was now completely enveloped in tobacco smoke. I could barely make out his features.

"Why would he dishonor himself?"

"As the challenged party, Toby, you have the choice of weapon. Rule 2."

"And what weapon will we choose?"

"We have already chosen, lad. I met with Catlin's second, Dr. Uhl, earlier this morning and gave him your terms. You insisted on squirrel guns at twenty paces."

Though I couldn't see his face, his voice suggested he was on the verge of bursting into laughter. I couldn't imagine what was so funny. "Squirrel guns at twenty paces! We'll blast each other into kingdom come!"

"Dr. Uhl made the same point," Quinncannon returned, "but

you were adamant, Toby. There was just no talking you out of it."

Quinncannon engaged a rowboat and oarsman. At five the next morning we slipped away from the pier at Barclay Street and cut swiftly across the current of the North River toward the sheer, jagged cliffs of Weehawken Heights. A dismal, murky fog had rolled in from the harbor and seemed to settle over the boat, enfolding us in a clammy embrace the more disheartening for its mucid dampness, which saturated first our garments and then ourselves. The fog not only soaked us, it blinded us. A few feet out from shore and the lights of the great city were obliterated. I could hardly make out even the eerie glow of the lanterns stowed in the bow. I took some small comfort in the rhythmic, orange incandescence of the Irishman's pipe, burning in defiance of the gloomy obscurity into which we were rushing.

All my senses seemed dulled by the glutinous vapors. I heard only the slapping of the river against the gunwales and the distant, haunting cries of seagulls. For a time I could smell the sulphuric stench of the Quarantine, the island fort where plague victims were exiled.

To keep my mind off our destination and our errand, I concentrated on watching the smooth, seemingly effortless motions of our pilot. He dipped and rotated his oars almost without disturbing the surface of the water. We were gliding rapidly toward an unseen shore, an uncertain fate, guided through an impenetrable darkness with supreme confidence by a boatman who kept his back always to his destined harbor, pulling away relentlessly, never doubting his course, while I, though facing straight ahead, had no more notion of my future than a blind colt on a treadmill.

"At least," I said to Quinncannon, "tell me the fellow's name is not Charon."

"The fellow's name," replied Quinncannon, "is Egbert."

We left the ferryman at the base of the cliff and climbed the long, steep, rugged path that led to the dueling grounds where once Aaron Burr had put a fatal bullet into Alexander Hamilton. For more than half a century the blood of gentlemen had seeped into this rocky shelf which jutted not more than twenty feet below the poplar-lined crest of the Weehawken scarp. When we were within forty paces of the infamous ledge our heads suddenly emerged above the soupy fog. By the time we reached the grounds the whole skyline of the lower city was visible and I could see the entire, magnificent diorama from the lush, wooded green of the upriver palisades, from the fertile fields and grand manors of the patroons to the pavilion at Castle Garden and the masts of the tall ships moored at South Street, their decks teeming in anticipation of voyages to every ocean and continent of the globe.

At length I said, "You know, it's very strange."

Behind me I heard the clicks as Quinncannon broke the guns to load them. ("The seconds load in presence of each other, unless they give their mutual honors that they have charged smooth and single, which should be held sufficient." Rule 18.)

"What's very strange?" he said.

"Oh, only that, standing here, being able to command such a remarkable view of life, so many men should have willingly turned away instead to face death in the muzzle of a gun."

"Uh-huh." Two more clicks told me the guns were loaded. ("Firing may be regulated first by signal; secondly, by word of command; or thirdly, the parties may fire at their reasonable leisure—but second presents and rests are strictly prohibited." Rule 19.)

"Well," he said, "there is certainly no question that the code is ridiculous."

I spun around and confronted him. "You—*you* think so?"

"Naturally, lad. No sane man would dispute the point."

"But—! But—! Then. . . ." I fought for coherence. "Then *why* did you let me come here? Why are you risking my life? My God! This is madness!"

He suddenly raised his finger to his lips, a gesture for silence. In a moment I could hear it—footsteps ascending the path toward the dueling ground.

I turned away from Quinncannon. Absurd ideas raced through my head. We should have arranged for a surgeon, I thought—then almost laughed. We would have two doctors in attendance. No doubt Dr. Catlin would exert all his skill to save my life after he wounded me to death. I remembered reading that Hamilton had survived for hours—had been carried to his home and died in his own bed. I wondered how difficult it was to carry a man back down the cliff. Probably easier if he died first.

The footsteps were closer. ("In all cases misfire is equivalent to a shot, and a non-cock is to be considered as a misfire. No dumb-shooting or firing in the air admissible in any case. Children's play must be dishonorable, and is accordingly prohibited." Rule 20.)

Barely audibly I muttered, "Good God, if I get out of this alive. . . ." It was either an oath or a prayer. I left it unfinished. The bushes at the top of the path parted, and David Uhl, ghastly pale, stepped onto the ledge and stood, swaying uncertainly. His eyes were fixed on Quinncannon. I tensed and searched behind him for a sign of Catlin. Uhl took a step forward and gave the Irishman a slight bow.

Quinncannon regarded him under an arched eyebrow. "Where is your principal, Doctor?"

Uhl seemed breathless from the climb. "My principal, sir, declines to appear on the grounds."

"On the grounds that he is a coward, I assume, Doctor." One corner of the Irishman's mouth tugged up in a grim smile. "And yet, Doctor, you have kept his appointment."

Uhl returned his smile with the same grimness. "It is Rule 25, Mr. Quinncannon. When one of the principals declines to present himself, his second is honor bound to tender himself to his opposite second in his principal's stead." He sucked in a deep breath. "I am at your disposal, sir."

The Irishman took a minute to extract his tobacco pouch and fill his pipe. "You understand, Doctor, that in these circumstances the choice of weapon, time, distance, and ground are all rightfully mine."

"I do, sir."

"Uh-huh." Quinncannon lit the pipe. He kept his eyes on Uhl and I kept my eyes on him. "You realize, Doctor, that in all probability I will kill you."

"I am aware of your reputation, sir," Uhl replied.

A long moment passed during which again I thought I observed a gleam of amusement in the Irishman's eye, but, as before, on second glance it had vanished. Then Quinncannon relaxed against a tree and folded his arms. "No, no, Doctor, it is quite impossible. Rule 14, my friend. 'Seconds must be of equal rank in society, insomuch as a second may choose or chance to become a principal and equality is indispensable.' "

Uhl flushed with anger. "I have behaved toward you as a gentleman of honor, Mr. Quinncannon. I see no need for you to insult me. My rank in society is, I venture to say, quite as high as your own."

"Higher, Doctor, higher. You, I perceive, are a man of breeding, a respected professional. On the other hand, I am considered, I fear, rather a disreputable and shady character. It pains me to admit it, but the fact must be faced. Any exchange of fire between us would be a blatant violation of Rule 14 and that would never do, sir, never do at all." He exhaled a billow of tobacco smoke before adding, "You will have to withdraw your offer of combat, Doctor. Life before dishonor."

It took some time for the physician to comprehend Quinncannon's meaning. At last he replied with profound relief, "I appreciate your courtesy, sir."

"I appreciate your courage, sir," the Irishman returned.

Uhl nodded. "May I ask one last favor, gentlemen?"

"You may ask, Doctor," Quinncannon said, "but the answer is no."

"You insist on publishing Dr. Catlin as a coward?"

"No, no," I said quickly. "There's no need for that. The whole stupid matter is over and best forgotten."

But Quinncannon held up his hand. "Dr. Catlin will be posted."

"Why, sir?" I asked. "You, yourself, said the code is ridiculous."

"And so it is, Toby. As is war. As is any set of rules by which man regulates the risk of his life for the proof of his honor. But honor is not ridiculous, lad. Courage and decency are not ridiculous."

At the edge of the cliff he turned back with a slight smile. "Dr. Catlin," he reiterated, "will be posted."

After a moment Uhl and I followed him down to the boats. The fog had burned off and the sun was up.

15

Mr. Brendon Reveals
Something of His History

On the Friday following my dinner engagement with the Hoffmans I strode resolutely to the Whistling Pig.

Not for a single second had I seriously considered not keeping
my appointment with Hoffman. I dismissed his dire warning that
the truth of my past would bring me pain as so much twaddle—
the whining of an old man who had lived too long and learned
fear too well. Or, perhaps, it was for him a last-ditch effort to keep
his ill-advised vow of silence with a man who had proven himself
unworthy of either loyalty or friendship.

I entered the taproom as the Clinton Hall bell tolled six. It was
a minute or two before my eyes became accustomed to the half-
light. The bar was deserted except for two stragglers in their
cups. I made out the figure of a man seated at a table at the back
of the room and approached him but, within a few steps of him,
I stopped short. The man waiting for me was not Ogden Hoffman.

"You'd better take a chair and have a drink, Toby," Lon
Quinncannon said quietly.

I did neither. I felt my face grow warm with anger.

"I suppose this means that Hoffman isn't coming."

"Hoffman isn't coming," he said.

"He gave me his word he would be here. He'd better have a damn good reason."

"He has a good reason. I'm very tired, Toby, and running short on the social graces. My options are reduced to two, lad. Either I pour you a drink and conduct a calm, civilized conversation with you, or I knock a few of your teeth down your throat and go home to bed."

I took a deep breath and dropped wearily into the chair facing him. I heard the cork pop out of the bottle and watched him fill two glasses. "He's dead," I said, "isn't he?"

"He's dead," Quinncannon said.

"When and how?"

"At four-eighteen this afternoon. It was his heart."

I leaned back and rubbed my eyes—then suddenly slammed my fist on the table. "Damn! I almost had it. *Damn* it! I came *that* close!" An idea—a suspicion—flashed into my mind. "How did you know he was going to meet me here?"

"He told me."

"Did he tell you what I wanted to ask him?"

"No."

"Maybe he didn't have to."

"He didn't tell me what you wanted to ask him."

"Maybe you already knew."

He struck a match and lit his pipe slowly, methodically. I watched his features become alternately illuminated by the orange glow and cast back into shadow. The process was typical of the man. Now you see him—now you don't. *Ah, I see you have located your timepiece, Mr. Brendon. Now, would you be good enough to return mine?* Substance and shadow. *It's an old trick of hotel thieves, lad.*

I studied the Irishman, trying to read him. "Did Mr. Hoffman ever speak of me to you, sir? Surely he must have said something of my background."

"He said he'd found a bright young fellow somewhere in Virginia and he intended to take you into the firm."

"Nothing else?"

"Nothing else."

I finished my drink and decided to assume he was telling the truth. "Mr. Quinncannon, may I confide in you?"

"This is my day for it," he replied cryptically.

I poured another whiskey. "My mother died when I was two," I began. "I have no memory of her, not even a picture. What little she may have left for me was taken from me while I was an infant. As for my father—" I smiled bitterly. "Only God knows who or what or where he is . . . or *if* he is. I know nothing of myself, not even my true name. My mother called me Tobias. The 'Brendon' I took from the first 'home' of which I was conscious: The Colonel Matthew Jackson Brendon Memorial Orphans' Asylum in Richmond. The colonel was with Washington at Yorktown. There was a painting of him in the dining hall in full military regalia, mounted on a rearing white horse with his sword upraised. When I was four I was absolutely convinced the colonel was my father."

Quinncannon leaned back in his chair, smoking, watching me. "Go on," he said.

"When I was ten I was suddenly removed from the orphanage and placed in a boarding school in Charlottesville. It was a very exclusive academy, extremely expensive, attended only by the sons of Virginia's finest families. I could form no theory to account for the abrupt change in my fortunes. My benefactor preferred to remain anonymous and everything was arranged by an attorney named Orion Small who became my legal guardian. He was an old bachelor, Mr. Quinncannon, a kindhearted man but uneasy with boys. I'm afraid he never quite knew what to make of me. For that matter neither did my masters. I was beaten more regularly than a drayman's nag. At college the tutors eschewed the cane and levied fines instead—the worst infractions being whiskey and gaming. Poor old Orion was forever paying for my indiscretions." I smiled, in spite of myself. "I remember once being caught playing cards for a bottle of wine. When asked what the stakes were I answered that we played for fifty cents—not strictly a lie for that was the value of the wine. I wrote to Orion that only my quick wits had spared him the payment of a penalty for drinking along with the fine for gambling."

Recalling the story, I laughed lightly. "I do have a talent for getting into scrapes, but then, sir, I don't have to tell *you*—" I stopped suddenly, remembering something Quinncannon had said the night he cleared me of the murder charge. *There is a fond belief that bad boys grow into good men. Your recent exploits, Mr. Brendon, may cause some rethinking of that theory.*

He *did* know more of my history than he admitted to. Perhaps Hoffman had confided in him after all. Or . . . was it the Irishman who had confided in Hoffman?

He refilled both our glasses. "You have not explained what this all has to do with Ogden Hoffman," he said.

"After I took my degree I read law in Orion Small's office and served as his amanuensis for two years before passing the Virginia bar examinations. I expected to stay with Small but he insisted I must also be admitted to the New York bar—that it was the wish of my benefactor I should commence my practice with Hoffman—that everything had been arranged by Mr. Hoffman himself—"

I leaned forward on the table, listening to the growing intensity in my voice. "I had reached my majority. I demanded of Orion that he reveal the name of this benevolent shadow and the nature of his interest in me. At last Orion confessed that he knew virtually nothing of the circumstances. Eleven years ago—twelve now —Hoffman had engaged Orion to oversee my affairs. Every action undertaken on my behalf has been on instructions relayed to Small through Hoffman. Orion does not believe that Hoffman was the principal in the matter, Mr. Quinncannon. He thinks he, too, was acting as agent for someone else, and I agree with him. And what is more"—I sucked in a breath—"I'm convinced, Mr. Quinncannon, that this mysterious philanthropist is my father!"

I tossed off my drink, thumped the tumbler on the table for emphasis, and sat back awaiting his reply to this momentous assertion. I'm not certain what sort of response I expected, but

I didn't get it. He merely puffed on his pipe and observed me under a raised eyebrow.

After a full minute I said rather feebly, "At all events Hoffman can tell me nothing now." I could not suppress my frustration. "If only he had not waited so long before agreeing to speak to me. . . ."

"Damned inconsiderate of him to die at such an inconvenient moment," Quinncannon said without a trace of sarcasm.

"Yes," I immediately replied, and then, after a pause, "wasn't it?"

The Irishman scratched pensively at one corner of his thin moustache. "Let me see if I understand your problem aright, Toby. At the age of ten you were suddenly snatched out of an orphan asylum by some manner of deus ex machina and, instead of the wretched life of grinding poverty you had every reason to anticipate, you found yourself cast down amid the pampered puppies of the aristocracy, provided with a first-rate education, with money in your pockets, your future secure, your every need anticipated and attended to. But your good angel remains unidentified and may, or well may not, be your likewise unidentified sire. And the only man who can identify this elusive philanthropist has had the bad grace to die."

Still there was not a hint of irony in his tone. God! I felt awkward and stupid.

"I . . . I should have remembered, sir. Please, accept my condolences. I know . . . Mr. Hoffman was your good friend."

"Thank you for your sympathy, Toby," he said as though none of our previous conversation had occurred. "The whole city is filled with Ogden's friends. The tragedy of his death is increased by its suddenness. He was a truly great man, Toby. I'm sorry there wasn't time for you to know him better." He paused, slowly rolling his glass between his palms. "I once said of him that his greatness lay in the fact that he never devoted himself to saving the whole human race at once, but gave his considerable skills to helping them one at a time. As a direct result he accomplished more good and committed less evil than any man I ever knew."

I was struggling to say something appropriate—anything to cover my embarrassment. "I suppose it will be hard on his family," I managed and instantly regretted the absurdity of the remark, but Quinncannon did not appear to notice.

"Harder than you realize, lad. I'm afraid Ogden's death has left them paupers."

"But, how can that be? He must have earned huge amounts of money."

"Earned and spent," he answered. "The qualities which made the man so attractive and cordial also rendered him hopelessly impractical. There was an indolence about him, a lack of industry and concentration. He basked away his summers at Rockaway and lounged away his winters at the Union Club, never sowing or reaping, trusting tomorrow to fend for itself, and at the end, when he finally took a thought for his family's future, the shrewdness he had always exhibited in managing other men's affairs deserted him in the management of his own. He was villainously swindled by a corrupt broker named Gideon Welles before his friends could prevent it."

"Surely his friends will stand by his widow," I said. It had not entered my mind that Hoffman might be penniless. "I'll contribute what I can, but my allowance ceased when I became twenty-one; nevertheless—"

He held up his hand. "The Bar Committee is already raising a fund, Toby, and your aid would be welcome, but Ginger Hoffman is a proud woman, a Southard of the Virginia Southards, the daughter of a senator, and a lady of strong practical energy and fierce independence. Put simply, she's as immovable as a mule in quicksand and she won't accept the money."

"There are two girls still at home," I said.

He nodded. "As for the girls, without dowries they're unlikely to make good marriages despite the family's social prominence. Then, too, even if Ginger Hoffman would take charity I doubt the amount raised would accomplish more than to clear Ogden's accounts with the usurous Mr. Welles."

The irony of the situation made a profound impression on me.

The very man who, whether as principal or agent, had directed my meteoric rise in fortune had died leaving his own children in penury.

Despite my sympathetic feelings, at that moment, I'm ashamed to admit, an evil thought crossed my mind. I saw the image of the haughty Miss Emily—stripped of her servants, her fine house, her stables—forced to watch her magnificent roan stallion sold at auction. Perhaps I would buy the horse myself and then return him to her as a gift with a magnanimous flourish. (I wondered where I could borrow the money on good terms and short notice.)

Pride goeth before comeuppance—who could doubt it? To think that less than a week ago she had cruelly played with the emotions of a poor orphan foundling, an employee of her father, one forced to live by his own resources, simply because he had made the foolish mistake of letting her see he admired her—and now she, herself, was reduced to genteel poverty and the spinster burden of her mother's old age.

If there were only something I could do to restore her fortunes. I saw myself tossing a banker's check casually in the general direction of her dainty feet. I observed her stoop to pick it up. I imagined her lovely eyes widening as she read the munificent sum inscribed thereon; then, glistening with tears of gratitude, shining at me in wonder. She would attempt to stammer her obligation—"So generous, dear Mr. Brendon, and after I teased you so mercilessly . . ."—but I would merely withdraw my hand from hers—"Nothing at all, Miss Hoffman, a small debt which I owed your father . . ." Perhaps I would curl my lip ever so slightly.

I smiled at the scene—then looked at Quinncannon. "If only," I said, "there was something I could do to help the family."

One corner of Quinncannon's mouth tugged up. "Oh," he replied, "there just might be something you could do."

"You must let me do it, sir," I said, and then, as I caught the gleam in his eye, "Is it legal?"

"Does it matter?"

I considered that. "No, sir," I said firmly, "not if it will save the Hoffmans." Especially Miss Emily.

For an instant the Irishman smiled with both corners of his mouth at once. "Tomorrow I will take charge of the Bar Committee's relief fund and invest it in gold dust. I'm feeling bullish on gold dust just at the moment. Tomorrow evening I will visit you and your roommate in your chambers on Cedar Street."

He had me curious. "What do you have in mind, sir?"

"I have a suspicion, Toby, that Hoffman's speculations with his broker, Mr. Welles, are not as worthless as was first believed. I see unexpected dividends,"—he downed his whiskey—"windfall profits,"—he stood and put on his hat—"a cornucopia of filthy lucre." He touched his walking stick to his hat brim, bowing slightly.

"A presentiment is on me, my son," he added solemnly. "My crystal ball begins to clear."

16

The Sawdust Game

On the afternoon of Friday, June 11, 1856, Mr. Gideon Welles, broker, rose and came around his desk in his Chatham Street office to greet a gentleman who had called on an important matter of business. "Good day to you, Mr. Holland," he said. "A pleasure to make your acquaintance."

While Welles shook my hand I studied him. He was just past fifty, a tall man in robust health and excellent condition, with handsome, open features and an honest frankness of manner that I found quite disarming. His handshake had just the right firmness and his palm was dry. "How, Mr. Holland, may I serve you?" said he, motioning me to a chair.

"I was informed, Mr. Welles, that you are a man whose discretion may be relied upon."

It was his turn to study me. "I flatter myself I have earned that reputation," he at length responded.

I deliberately held fire, counting mentally, two, three, four, five—"In that case, sir, I will take you into my confidence. To commence, my name is not James Holland, but I see you discerned at once that I was employing an alias."

"I admit I suspected it," answered Mr. Welles, clearly taken aback by my confession.

"For reasons of my own I should prefer to be addressed by that name."

His eyes narrowed. "Of course, Mr. Holland," he said slowly.

Our eyes met briefly, then he averted his glance. I stood and put on my derby. "Sir, I fear I have mistook you. Your doubts in me are evident. It is a great pity for there is a tidy profit for two men in this business, but—"

"Come, Mr. Holland, be seated, I beg you. I am most anxious to hear your proposition."

Now I regarded him with intensity. "I must ask you not to remember my visit, Mr. Welles. I perceive you have some scruples—"

"None, sir," he protested. "None whatsoever."

"Well, sir—" I removed my derby. "There is such a thing as too much caution." I resumed my seat and extracted a leather pouch that I tossed to the broker. The removal of the pouch also dislodged a folded paper which fell from my side pocket to the carpet. I gave no indication that I had noticed the paper and made no effort to retrieve it. Mr. Welles observed this dumb show with acute interest. Then he loosened the drawstrings and emptied three ounces of gold dust onto his desk.

With great effort he suppressed his excitement. "Well, well," he said. Again his eyes narrowed. "May I ask how you came into possession, Mr. Holland?"

"Your pardon, sir. I must say I consider that question lacking in tact."

"My apologies, sir." He pushed the dust around, making tracings in it with his fingers. "I assume you are offering this commodity for sale."

"That and two hundred ounces more, Mr. Welles. I have brought you but a small sample."

"Of course you are willing to leave the dust with me for a time. It must be assayed, you know."

"I am not only willing but anxious that you satisfy yourself as rapidly as possible," I returned.

I caught him staring down at the paper on the carpet. He

nodded quickly to cover his curiosity. "I shall proceed with all speed," he said, approaching me with outstretched hand. As I rose to take it, he slid his boot deftly over the paper. When I turned to leave he must have kicked it under his desk for, when I again faced him, the sheet had vanished.

"Kindly call upon me on Monday afternoon," said he. "If all proves to be as you represent it, we will set a fair price for the remainder." He paused, cocking his head slightly. "No offense, Mr. Holland. You seem very young to be involved in such matters."

I smiled. "I find a boyish face and a guileless manner are worth hundreds a year in my profession, sir." I waited before adding, "I shouldn't wonder your appearance is worth thousands to you."

Again he eyed me—then he broke into laughter and slapped me on the back. "Well, well, you're a shrewd youth, whatever your name is. If I'd had a son he'd have been your double, I'll warrant. I shall have to be very wary of you, my boy. Very wary indeed."

I met Quinncannon that evening at the Whistling Pig. "Hook, line, and sinker?" he inquired.

"He swallowed the pole." I grinned. "I wish you could have seen him trying to conceal that handbill."

"I wish we might both have watched him as he read it," he said. "By now Mr. Welles is aware that the gold dust you are peddling is stolen and a one thousand dollar reward is offered for its recovery. He imagines you to be the thief or, at any rate, a confederate."

I nodded. "He thinks he can name his own price for the dust."

"I would say," observed the Irishman, "that Welles has got you right where you want him."

"Does Jeremy know what he's to do?"

"Thoroughly rehearsed, Toby. He has purchased a threadbare secondhand suit from a pushcart that will just not quite fit him. I want him to exactly resemble a plainclothes policeman." He poured us each a drink and raised his glass.

"I give you Mr. Gideon Welles, friend of the widow and or-phan."

We clinked glasses and drank.

The conclusion of this confidence game can be quickly told. When I called again on Welles he was anxious to buy all the dust I had, provided, he said, we could agree on a price. We haggled and he produced the handbill in imaginary triumph and used the threat of having me arrested to work down the price. I pretended to settle for half the dust's worth and we arranged to meet later at a retired spot uptown.

Welles arrived at dusk with a pair of steelyards and, in the shadows of a dimly lit alley, the crafty skinflint weighed his dust and paid me. I then retreated while Jeremy, who had observed the transaction from across the street, approached the broker, announced himself as a constable, and "arrested" Welles for the supposed bank job.

The poor devil whimpered and whined until Jeremy agreed to go with him to his office and "see if we can't arrange this thing." He accepted a large bribe for allowing the matter to drop. Welles must have thought he could still realize a tremendous profit on the stolen gold. I regret not having the pleasure of watching his face when he discovered that what he had actually bought were very fine brass filings, some covered with a thin gold wash.

The money was given to Hoffman's widow with the explanation that her late husband's speculations had unexpectedly paid off. It settled the debt with Welles and provided her family with a comfortable financial cushion.

A week later Quinncannon sent a note to Welles:

Dear sir,
   I am in the market for brass filings. If, in the course of your quaint business dealings, you should come into possession of a bag of this commodity, I would be pleased to hear that you are still holding the bag.

Q

17

Miss Emily Receives
Two Gentlemen

In my mind's eye I had dreamed a hundred times of the moment when I would again confront the haughty Miss Emily Hoffman— this time as the hero who had rescued her family from ruin—and have the pleasure of hearing her beg my pardon for her high-nosed airs and gush with gratitude for her deliverance. It was a satisfaction I could not long deny myself. On the afternoon following the successful conclusion of the sawdust scheme I called at the Hoffman home.

The servant who took my hat informed me that Mrs. Hoffman was not at home but Miss Emily was and would shortly wait upon me. I entered the parlor and stopped dead. Already seated there was Jeremy Todd.

"Hullo!" I exclaimed. "I thought you had a case in the Special Sessions."

"Postponed," replied he. "I thought you had an important client."

"I lied."

He shrugged. "I also."

Jeremy and I had more or less inherited the law practice although most of the clients had removed after Hoffman's death. We operated as partners but kept the old man's name on the shingle—out of respect for his memory, we said, though the fact that new business occasionally came our way from persons un-aware of Hoffman's passing did not entirely escape our notice.

I took a chair and shuffled my feet. He drummed absently on a side table with his fingers.

He asked, "Do you think it will rain?"

"Sooner or later."

A long pause.

"Must you do that?"

"Do what?" I said.

"Bang your boots about so. The whole room is shaking."

"Sorry." I watched him out of the corner of my eye. "Do you have to drum your fingers in that manner?"

"What manner would you prefer?"

The entire situation was damned annoying. He had no busi-ness being there at all. It was I, if the truth were known, who had carried off the plot against Welles so finely. We could have hired any spear toter from the Bowery Theater to portray the consta-ble. I shuffled my feet furiously.

He drummed thunderously.

The scent of roses suddenly filled the room. Miss Emily stood in the doorway, dressed in a mourning gown of black and gray, her hair swept up so as to frame wonderfully her delicate fea-tures.

"My dear Jeremy," she said, coming forward and taking his hand as he stood, "how very kind of you to come and see me." She gave me her attention briefly. "And are you here too, Mr. Brendon?" She focused again on Jeremy and drew him toward the sofa, where she seated herself beside him. "Did I tell you? I have made up my mind to sell Blue Boy."

Jeremy began to protest but she shook her head firmly. "No, no, all the horses must go and the carriage and grooms also. I shall be sorry to dismiss Enoch and Bill but they will find work and it cannot be helped. It will never do to keep a stable now."

"But not Blue Boy," Jeremy persisted. "You love that roan so much, Emily, and now that your father's investments have paid off so handsomely—"

She laughed lightly and patted his arm. "Father's investments are as worthless as ever. You may have fooled Mama about that but I know better. I don't know exactly what terrible things you did to Mr. Welles but I know Mr. Quinncannon was behind it and I can guess the rest."

That seemed my cue. I leaped to my feet. "Tush, it was nothing, Miss Hoffman. A small debt I owed your father. It is natural that you should feel grateful. The sentiment becomes you, Miss, and I would not insult you by refusing to accept it, but I did only what any right-minded person would do when he perceives an injustice has been committed against those who have a claim on . . . uh, a claim on his. . . ."

They were gaping at me as if I were mad.

I had rehearsed that damned speech before a mirror for hours.

Nothing—ab-so-lute-ly nothing—was working the way it was supposed to.

I repeated, "Tush, tush," and sat down, feeling very angry at them both. What really irritated me was that neither of them even deigned to laugh. I must have looked the perfect dolt.

"Of course I shall have to let most of the household servants go too," Miss Emily was saying to Jeremy, "but the house, itself, must be kept. Poor Mama could never hold her head up otherwise. With the money you and Mr. Quinncannon have wrung from Father's broker we should be able to manage. Naturally I shall have to take a position."

"Position?" he echoed.

"As a governess. I'm to tutor two little boys who board in a house on Bond Street."

I shot her a sharp glance. "The two little boys. Their name wouldn't happen to be Cunningham?"

"It is," she answered. "Do you know them?"

"A slight acquaintance," I said grimly.

This development struck me as a remarkable and disquieting coincidence. Miss Emily in Bond Street. Some evil genius, I reflected, was again meddling in my affairs. I should have guessed the truth. How many evil geniuses did I know?

"I happened to mention to Mr. Quinncannon after Papa's funeral that I would now be requiring employment. Really, governess is the only position I'm suited for, and I was so afraid I should have to leave Mama and Ginny and live with another family. But Mr. Quinncannon by wonderful chance knows an old client of Papa's, a dentist, whose landlady has two children in need of schooling, and they are right here in the city so I shan't have to move after all." She gave me a bright smile. "Wasn't that lucky?"

Fortuitous as hell, thought I.

I was determined not to leave the Hoffman house unless Jeremy left with me, and for his part he proved quite as stubborn as myself. When we were finally in a hansom headed for Cedar Street he said, "What the devil got into you this afternoon?"

"I have no idea what you're talking about."

"That ridiculous oration regarding gratitude and injustice and right-minded persons." He winked at me. "Tush, tush, tush."

I merely stared sourly at the rump of the cab horse.

"You do have a bit of a problem, Toby, old man. Miss Hoffman and the fair Demis together under the same eaves? Rather awkward for you if the ladies compare notes, eh?"

"Look here," I said, "let's get one thing clear. I have no interest of a romantic nature in Miss Hoffman. It matters not a farthing to me if she and Demis 'compare notes' as you put it. In fact, Miss Hoffman has no notes to compare."

I made a promise to myself to get Demis out of Bond Street as quickly as I could.

"So much the better for Miss Emily's other admirers," he said. "Imagine the gumption of the girl. Her father not dead a week and she's taken hold of things with a firm hand. They'll be better run now, I daresay. You have to give her credit, Toby. She's a splendid young woman."

"Yes," I replied grudgingly. "She *is* splendid."

18

The Runaway

Near the close of June New York was inundated with three days of torrential rains. It was almost midnight of the third day when Jeremy and I returned home from a congenial evening at the Whistling Pig. While my friend settled the fare, I stepped down from the hansom and nearly stumbled over what appeared in the gaslight to be a bundle of filthy rags carelessly thrown on my stoop. Closer inspection showed the rags to be occupied by the body of a half-grown boy. I knelt beside him and felt for a pulse. His legs were bare and part of his breast and shoulder were visible through rends in his tattered clothing. His body was covered with ugly red welts.

"Good God!" exclaimed Jeremy. "Is he alive?"

"Just barely." I gathered him up in my arms and wiped the rain from his face. His lips twitched and his eyes blinked open.

"Squire?"

"Don't talk, Hasty," I said. "He won't hurt you again."

"Mr. Quinncannon ain't home, sir," the boy whispered. "I had no place else to go."

"You did the right thing, lad."

"I wouldn't do it, Squire." He managed to grin up at me. "He ordered me to get on my knees and pray for my sins with him but I wouldn't do it if he beat me to death." Though his pain must have been great his grin became impish. Then he lost consciousness.

I carried Hasty upstairs and when we were inside our chambers Jeremy said, "I gather you know the boy."

"He is by way of being a former client of mine."

"You defended him?"

I considered the question. "No," I said at last. "I betrayed him."

The proof of the boy's recuperative powers lay less in his having withstood his brutal treatment at the Shepherd's Fold than in his survival of our blundering efforts to nurse him back to health. We applied cold compresses to ease his fever and hot compresses to stimulate his blood circulation. Jeremy brewed coffee over Professor Bunson's burner while I ladled brandy down his throat. We stopped short only at bleeding him and, had we had a few leeches on the premises, we might have tried that too. Miraculously, by morning the color was back in his face and he was able to keep down a bowl of my homemade soup.

"Jesus! What's in here, Squire? It's *meat!* I ain't had meat since forever." He sat cross-legged on the rug, wearing one of my shirts and wrapped in a blanket. "At the Shepherd's Fold they give us oatmeal mush and water with a bit of milk in it, and if we're quiet and don't rile him, old Cowley lets us have a raw tomato." Again he gave us his infectious grin. "I didn't get a lot of tomatoes, gents."

The grin vanished. "I hated it when he beat those little kids. Some of 'em are only five or six and they don't understand. They cry a lot—'specially at night. I used to jump him sometimes to pull him off the little ones and then he'd wallop me till he forgot which one he'd started on, only—" The grin came back. "Only it got kind of strenuous for me." Another swig of soup. "They keep us in the cellar most of the time. We roll up at night in blankets but it's hard to keep dry. Some days they let us go out in the backyard but it's pretty small and the fences are real high. There ain't much sun. We have to march around—no playing games—no noise." He looked from Jeremy to me. "I got whipped one time for laughing."

I examined the bruises on his legs, remembered the welts and cuts on his arms and back, saw again his terrified face as the Reverend Cowley dragged him from the courtroom, heard again his cry to me for help.

Please, Squire Brendon, ain't there nothing you can do?

But I had not answered him. I was late for my dinner.

". . . old man Cowley was gonna send me to the Orphan's Asylum," Hasty was saying, "so I had to get out. I watched my chance an' jumped the fence, and I went to Mr. Quinncannon, only he's out of the city. I heard his housekeeper say so."

"Hasty," I said, "why did you go to Quinncannon?"

He gave me a puzzled expression. "Jesus, Squire. Everybody knows when you're in trouble you go to Mr. Quinncannon." He appealed to Jeremy. "Ain't that right, sir?"

"That's right," Jeremy said.

"Only he's not around," the boy continued, "so I thought of you, Squire, on account of you standing up for me in front of the judge, and I thought, Squire Brendon's not afraid of that judge and old Cowley. He'll tell me what to do. He'll put things right."

He regarded me with such admiration and trust that my guilt at my shameful betrayal of him became almost intolerable. I caught Jeremy watching me from the corners of his eyes. My own expression must have been particularly grim because a look of alarm crept into the boy's features and he said, "You *will* help me, sir? If I'm caught I'll go to Blackwell's."

That was true. He *was* a fugitive—not a John C. Colt or a Professor Webster—but a fugitive all the same. If I were caught protecting him I might well be disbarred. I was risking my career before it had really begun. And the boy *was* a thief. That was indisputable—and the sentence he'd received was perfectly appropriate under the law, perhaps even lenient.

All these thoughts raced through my mind in a matter of seconds. I determined my answer to the boy and had half opened my mouth when one last idea stole up on me and, like a garroter, seized me by the throat. Were he in my place, I wondered, what would Quinncannon do?

I took a deep breath. "You'll go back to the Shepherd's Fold," I said, "when hell goes Presbyterian."

All the terror vanished from Hasty's face. Jeremy said, "You *do* understand the risk you're taking?"

"It's my problem," I answered. "I don't want you to become involved."

"Be careful you don't offend me, Toby," he said. "I refuse to be left out." His eyes narrowed. "I don't suppose you have a plan."

"I have the kernel of a plan." I turned to the boy. "First, Hasty, we're going to disguise you."

Hasty flopped into a chair, drawing up bare, dirty legs around which he wrapped bare, dirty arms. He crossed his ankles, gnawing on one gritty knee. "What'll I be disguised as?"

"As a human being." I stood. "We're going to have to take something away from you that you've had for most of your life."

"What's that?" He eyed me defensively.

"Dirt," I said. "Dust. Soil! *Grime!*" I strode toward him like an avenging angel. *"Filth! Soot!* MUCK!" I gripped the arms of his chair and loomed above him. "GRIT!" I said. *"ORDURE!"*

He cowered beneath me and gazed up soulfully. He said, "Ordure?"

"I think what Squire Brendon means, Hasty," Jeremy said, "is you're going to have to take a bath."

He was stunned. "With *soap?*"

"With soap," I affirmed. "Yellow soap and boiling water. You're going to march downstairs to the landlady and tell her we want a bar of her laundry soap and a bucket of well water and two kettles of boiling water and the brush she uses to scrub potatoes. And then you're going to give yourself a bath."

He had the most incredibly hurt look on his greasy little face. "What if I won't?"

"Then," I said, "the landlady will do it for you."

He either went ghastly pale or flushed scarlet. There was no

way of telling which. He slid out of the chair and sulked toward
the door.

I said, "Tell the landlady we want some kerosene and her
tweezers too."

"Tweezers! Whadawewant *them* for?"

"If my suspicions are correct," I said, "we may need a pair of
tongs and a rifle."

While the boy bathed I left Jeremy on guard and went out to
Lambert & Son, Fashions for the Gentleman.

"Tsk, tsk, tsk," clucked fastidious little Mr. Lambert, taking
one of my lapels delicately between his fingers and observing it
with dismay. "Oh, Squire, you *have* come to us just in time."

I informed him that I had come to purchase clothes for a boy.
I selected a brown frock coat, mixed drab pantaloons, two shirts,
a cap, small clothes, stockings, and a pair of brown boots. While
the purchases were being wrapped Mr. Lambert called his prissy
son over and they whispered together before standing back and
scrutinizing me with cocked heads.

"Pity," murmured Mr. Lambert pere.

"Pity," responded Mr. Lambert fils.

I gathered up the packages and smiled at each of them. "Thank
you, gentlemen," I said. "I shall tell all my friends I buy my
wardrobe at Lamberts'."

I walked out and headed for the printer's shop, leaving both
Lamberts aghast.

When I returned Hasty was sitting on the floor at Jeremy's feet,
folded in a blanket, while Jeremy worked on his scalp with the
kerosene and tweezers. "Almost done," my friend announced.
"We take no prisoners."

I picked up the boy's grimy clothing and threw it on the fire,
and Hasty stiffened and gave a little cry of anguish.

"It was necessary," I said, "as a matter of public hygiene."

"But, whadamigonna wear?"

I handed him the packages from Lambert & Son. He took them

gingerly, as if they would break, then looked at me with sudden suspicion.

"What do I owe you?"

"Sixteen dollars and twenty-seven cents," I answered. "You can pay me back a dollar a month out of your wages."

"But, Squire," he said, "I *got* no wages!"

I shook my head. "Look here, lad, if you're going to become a respectable member of society you'll require debts and earnings. We've already got you in debt. What's needed is a salary." I addressed Jeremy. "Burdell employs an office boy and he's just dismissed the latest of the lot. You're on good terms with him. . . ."

I might as well own that, in addition to my concern for the boy's welfare, it *had* crossed my mind that it would be useful to have a spy planted in the dentist's household, especially so long as Demis remained there.

Jeremy held up his hand. "I'll speak to Burdell about Hasty."

I nodded and produced a small, brown parcel, holding it out to the youngster. After some hesitation he accepted it. His fingers fumbled at the string and peeled off the paper. Inside was a stack of calling cards I'd had printed. He read the top one aloud:

Zachariah Lamentations Hasty, Eee-ess-cue.

He looked at me. "What's eee-ess-cue?"

"An abbreviation for esquire," I answered. "It means gentleman."

"No kidding," he said softly. He ran his fingertips gently over the smooth surface of the card, feeling the raised letters of the name. Abruptly he glanced up.

"How much I owe you for this?"

"Nothing, Hasty. That's a gift."

"No kidding."

He put the card carefully back in the package. With the parcel held tightly he seemed uncertain what to do. Suddenly he ran toward me, flinging his arms around my waist. Then he backed up rapidly and extended his hand. I shook it as one man to another.

When Hasty went off to try on his new clothes I caught Jeremy smiling at me. "You know, Toby, my boy, you're a good, decent fellow."

"No I'm not," I said with resolution. "But, God damn it, I'm trying."

19

What Hannah Conlan Knew

Word of my aborted "duel" in defense of Demis' honor had reached Bond Street. The lady was appropriately impressed. In defiance of "Cousin Harvey" I visited her and she gushed with gratitude all over me in precisely the reaction I had vainly hoped for from Emily Hoffman. I took advantage of the moment to press again the importance of her removal from the dentist's house, but she refused to budge.

"You may speak all you wish of my reputation, Toby, but I cannot abandon Cousin Harvey in his hour of need."

"That nonsense again." I could not hide my disgust. "If Emma Cunningham is so determined to trap Burdell into marriage, she has, I must say, a strange way of going about it."

Demis regarded me with perfect seriousness. "Yes, Toby, she has. That's just the point. I'm very much afraid if she can't marry him she'll murder him."

"Frankly," I said that evening to Jeremy, "I think Demis is being absurdly melodramatic."

He was dressing to go out and listening with half an ear. He said, "If you mean about Mrs. Cunningham and the dentist, I agree. Going through a man's trouser pockets and prowling about in his safe are the sorts of things a woman only does after marriage."

I watched him from my chair over my newspaper. "I see you have an engagement again tonight."

"Anna Mowatt is playing Mrs. Tiffany in a revival of her own play, *Fashion*, at the Park Theater. Miss Emily and I will take supper later at the Astor House, so don't wait up."

"I shall leave the bunson burner in the window," I said drily.

He glanced at me. "You don't mind, do you, old man?"

"No, no." I returned to my journal. "I have my hands full with Mrs. Hubbard."

There was a pause. "I know what I should do in your place."

I waited. "I suppose you're determined to tell me."

"No," he said.

I took my time packing my pipe and lighting it. "All right, what *would* you do?"

"I'd march over to Bond Street and grab a fistful of her hair and drag her out of there."

I thought that over. Then I decided to take his advice.

But Emma Cunningham beat me to it.

The Fourth of July was a Friday. Demis went off on holiday over the weekend, visiting friends in Brooklyn. When she returned on Monday she found her belongings packed and piled on the front stoop. Emma barred the door with the resoluteness of Horatio at his bridge.

I got the message at my office and took a cab to Bond Street to find Demis perched, demure and downhearted, on one of her trunks, and Widow Cunningham, feet set apart, fists on hips, grim visaged and immovable.

The landlady made herself clear. She would offer no explanations, brook no interference, retreat not an inch. Demis was persona non grata. I made a pro forma protest but secretly I was relieved. Emma had saved me a great deal of trouble. We entered into negotiations and the upshot was that Demis' baggage could remain in the house while I found her suitable quarters. I got her settled at a respectable rooming house in Brooklyn and returned near evening to collect her possessions. The little Irish girl who answered the door informed me that Dr. Burdell was not at home and had been absent for several days. Mrs. Cunningham had gone out but was expected within the hour. The girl knew nothing about Mrs. Hubbard's effects, but I might wait in the back parlor or, if I preferred, the kitchen belowstairs where "Cook" would give me a cup of coffee. I chose the kitchen.

"Cook" was Hannah Conlan, a sturdy, sharp-eyed, no-nonsense Irish woman of about thirty. Flame-red hair was bound up under an enormous, mushroom-shaped white cap. Her face and hands were ruddy and always shiny with soapy water no matter how often she wiped them on a clean, unstarched white apron. Her sleeves were rolled carelessly up to the elbows of fat arms and one or the other was forever falling down around her wrists and being tugged up again. She was the most industrious person I'd ever seen, a study in perpetual motion. She had perfected the art of doing things that did not need to be done. Again and again she wiped a clean table, washed a clean dish, scoured a clean pot, scrubbed a clean stove. Things that did need doing, however, she ignored. A jar, inadvertently overturned, lay where it fell. A small terrier, let into the yard at its own urging, shortly came back and made a messy shambles of one corner of the kitchen, but pup and pile went unnoticed.

Hannah Conlan's natural manner was sullen and taciturn. Such, at least, was my first impression. It has been my experience, however, that household servants, having little time to themselves and little life of their own, live to a great extent vicariously through their employers. They are like patrons at a melodrama being played out abovestairs—most of the time observing from front row center, but now and then permitted to take up a spear and make a brief entrance, carrying a message, overhearing a conversation, discovering a misdirected letter, and retiring again to their seats in the orchestra, or the kitchen.

Like a theatrical audience they develop a rooting interest in the characters, loving some, hating others. They mine for motives, applaud or denounce actions, search out exposition—and eventually they become critics and presume to judge their superiors through a process of inverted snobbery. In the United States the rich have promulgated the idea that wealth corrupts while poverty is morally uplifting, and, aided by the clergy and the sentimental novelists, they have sold the poor on this quaint notion. The result is that the poor are invariably moralists, poor females are great moralists, poor Catholic females even greater moralists, and poor Irish Catholic females are your greatest moralists of all.

Now, the most pleasure to be derived from attending a play is to discuss it afterward, and here Hannah Conlan was doomed to frustration. She was the only servant who lived in, and the only adult. Burdell employed an office boy and Emma a parlor maid, but these were merely children and seldom did they hold their jobs longer than a few weeks. So there was Hannah, hearing all, seeing all, nearly exploding with gossip and scandal—and no one to confide in. It would have been heartless not to ask one or two innocent questions.

"She met the doctor two summers ago, sir, in Congress Hall Park at Saratoga Springs."

"She?"

"Mrs. Cunningham," Hannah replied in a dark, brittle tone that spoke volumes. "The doctor goes up to the spa every August, which well she knew, and there she was, purely by accident, you understand, and her first husband not dead and buried two months together. And there they are until September, and back he comes, and back she goes to Brooklyn, and here she comes again."

"Did she move in here?"

"Not all at once. She oozed her way in like an insurance salesman or honey spilled downhill. She developed, all at once, a mouthful of the most painful teeth this side of Flatbush, such that she's in his chair every day of the week and Lord bless me if her troubles don't spread to her young ones. It was purely an epidemic of bad bicuspids—nothing less, and it did keep the doctor on his toes."

She busied herself washing several clean tumblers. "Was it then Mrs. Cunningham came here to live?" I prodded.

Hannah shook her head. "She was on Twenty-fourth Street for a time, and then she told the doctor she had to move and needed somewhere to stay temporary, just until she could find new lodgings, and he offers her rooms here, poor man, as if it was all his own idea. That's when she moved *in!*" She grimaced at the memory. "I mean to say, sir, she invaded and occupied. I remember telling old Mrs. Jones to mark me well. That widow's established a beachhead and no explosives will blast her loose. I knew that very day that Mrs. Jones had better pack and buy a ticket."

"That would be Margaret Jones," I said, "the lady who leased the house and let the rooms."

"A good-hearted woman, Mr. Brendon. She accommodated Mrs. Cunningham every which way, and Mrs. Cunningham all the time scheming to take the house away from her."

"Emma wanted the house?"

"What she wanted—still wants—is the doctor. Not twenty-four hours after she came I heard Mrs. Cunningham tell the doctor she was so comfortable here she was content never to leave at all. I saw her face, sir. She had the look of a cat with cream. But there was trouble coming."

Demis, I thought. "Another woman?"

Hannah gave me a sharp look. "You don't know the doctor very well, do you, sir?"

"Other women," I amended.

"There's the doctor's divorced cousin," she said, and I braced for Demis' name, but the cook finished, "Mrs. Lucy Ann Williams."

Another divorced cousin? "I suppose she also has trouble with her teeth."

"Something dreadful! Why there were afternoons you couldn't walk down the hall past the doctor's door without hearing her moaning."

"Whatever became of Lucy Ann, I wonder."

"Well, sir, it was very strange. The doctor has a relative in New Jersey, a congressman or something, and one day last fall Mrs. Cunningham takes Mrs. Williams into the back parlor and tells her this congressman has gotten an unsigned letter in the post saying all sorts of nasty things about Mrs. Williams' morals and general deportment. Mrs. Cunningham says how sorry she is and how, of course, she don't believe a word, but she's afraid this congressman will write to the doctor and blacken her character, and Mrs. Williams thanks her for the warning and makes a speech about true friendship."

"You, by coincidence, were standing nearby, Hannah?"

"I'd only then come up the stairs and the door just happened to be ajar." (I'll swear she winked at me.) "Then, a few days later, I opened the street door for Mrs. Williams and in she roars under a full head of steam, and 'Where is that lying witch?' says she. Then Mrs. Cunningham comes down the stairs, like the Queen of England, but not all the way down, so Mrs. Williams has to look up to her.

" 'I've written to Cousin Charles,' she cries, 'and he got that letter all right but he never told you one thing about it. You know what was in that letter, Emma Cunningham, because *you* wrote it yourself!' 'I never did,' yells Mrs. Cunningham and then there was a donnybrook until the doctor came down and got between them. The doctor read the letter and told Mrs. Williams he believed Mrs. Cunningham because, he remarks, 'there's things in this letter, Lucy Ann, that Emma couldn't know.' "

It sounded, I thought, as if some of the letter's accusations were true. "And Lucy Ann left the house?"

"Never came back," Hannah announced. "But," she added, "*she* wasn't the only problem."

I nodded. Now I would hear about Demis.

"There was also Mrs. Sophronia Stevens."

"Not another cousin?"

"No, sir, but Mrs. Stevens is a regular patient, every Thursday afternoon, certain as time and tide. Her husband is Colonel Cyrenius Stevens. He's a retired gentleman, pushing hard on seventy years I should guess."

"And his wife is somewhat younger?"

"It really is a pity, sir, that a woman that young has such bad teeth."

She began vigorously polishing some spotless silverware. I watched her and waited. She shyly inquired, "Is it Mrs. Hubbard you're curious about?"

I told myself I might as well hear the worst, but I also reminded myself that, whatever might be the perceptions of this scandal-mongering biddy, I knew Demis better than anyone alive—knew her virtue, her noble character. Whatever might have been between her and Harvey Burdell during her unhappy marriage, she had been driven to it by her husband's tyrannical bullying and unnatural coldness. I had no doubt that, once she and I had commenced our relationship, she was so completely fulfilled, physically, emotionally, spiritually, that she would have found any further connection with the aging dentist not simply unsatisfactory but superfluous.

"Tell me," I said, "what you know of Mrs. Hubbard."

"Mrs. Cunningham hates her. Just when she'd driven Mrs. Williams away, the doctor started spending his evenings at Mrs. Hubbard's house in Brooklyn. Her husband was sick and the doctor lent him money and somehow he wound up with the house. It got so he didn't come home at all some nights and Mrs. Cunningham simmered like a stew but she was too smart to say anything to him. I'll give her that much. Then last August, instead of taking Mrs. Cunningham back to Saratoga, the doctor shipped Dr. Hubbard up there and moved into Mrs. Hubbard's house."

"What was Mrs. Cunningham's reaction to that?"

"Nothing you could put your finger on. She behaved—I don't

know how to put it—relaxed and restless at the same time, as if she was going to stay calm if it was the death of her. She never raised her voice. She was polite to everybody—even to the servants—even to the hired girl we had then and she was as dizzy as a dervish—but Mrs. Cunningham didn't blink even when the girl started a grease fire in the kitchen.

"I watched her, Mr. Brendon. I can always tell when she's plotting some devilment. Her eyes get hard and cold and her lips barely move when she talks. She was like that all the time she was packing up Mrs. Hubbard's things to throw her out. She was like that last August when the doctor was living with Mrs. Hubbard in Brooklyn. As soon as he came back she started asking him to take her out for a day. So sweet about it she was. He had some property over in New Jersey, near Elizabethtown, and she wanted him to take her over on the train to see it. They went right at the beginning of September and didn't come back till the next day. She said they'd lost track of the time and then they lost track of the train and had to stop over at the hotel. 'Separate rooms, of course, Hannah,' she told me, laughing the whole time. Right off I guessed what she was up to."

For the first time Hannah stopped fidgeting and sat down. Her sleeves fell down. She didn't bother to push them up. She stared past my shoulder at some ugly memory.

"It was Thanksgiving day of last year. She and the doctor were in her bedroom most of the morning, arguing about something. They kept their voices low but I could tell it was more stormy than usual. The children were sent out somewhere—I don't know where. There weren't any other lodgers at the time. There was just the three of us in the house. All at once it got deadly quiet. It was frightening how still it got. I hated to hear them fighting, but the silence was worse. After maybe twenty minutes—no longer—the doctor comes downstairs. I was dusting in the front parlor and I saw him go out the door to the street and turn east, toward the Brooklyn ferry. I don't know why I thought he was going to Mrs. Hubbard. I just thought that's where he was headed.

"I wasn't feeling at my best and I went up to my room in the attic to lie down. I stopped at Mrs. Cunningham's door but it was shut and everything was quiet so I went on up and fell asleep. Some time later I thought I heard Mrs. Cunningham cry out. She said, 'Oh, Doctor, where are you!' Something of that sort. I waited to see if she'd cry out again but I heard nothing more. I was only half-awake and I suppose I thought maybe the doctor had come home and was tending to her, and I went back asleep. The next I knew it was dark and cold and someone was coming up the attic stairs. The footsteps were slow and unsteady, as if made by some wounded thing. Then my door was thrown open and I froze, so terrified, mind you, sir, that I couldn't even scream—"

She shuddered at the recollection. The kitchen had also grown dark and cold. The fire in the stove was almost out. I reached across the table and took one of her hands to steady her.

"I couldn't scream, but *she* did. I thought she'd never let off screaming."

"Mrs. Cunningham," I said.

"She screamed and screamed and then she cried, 'My God, Hannah! Are you going to let me die here!' "

She shook all over violently for a moment and then regained control. "There was blood smeared all across her face. There was blood on her hands and clothing. Her nose was streaming blood. She had fallen against the stove in her room and cut herself— that's the first story she gave me. I helped her back down to her bed, then got a basin and tried to wash her but she grabbed the cloth angrily and said she would clean herself. She guessed she was capable of cleaning herself! I looked at her stove and there wasn't any blood on it. Then I ran outside and went for Dr. Woodward. He had to dress but he said he would come straightaway, and, as I didn't want to leave Mrs. Cunningham alone too long, I ran back to the house. I went up to her room and that's when I saw it."

I thought I knew but I asked anyway. "Saw what, Hannah?"

She looked steadily into my eyes. "There was a foetus in the chamber pot. Mrs. Cunningham said to me, 'Take a good look, Hannah, and don't ever forget what you saw. Dr. Burdell seduced me at Elizabethtown with lying pledges of devotion and false promises of marriage, and *that* is the fruit of his deception and depravity. *That* is his bastard spawn!' "

20

Mrs. Cunningham Goes to Law

After my interview with Hannah Conlan I would cheerfully have lived the rest of my days without once hearing again the names of Emma Cunningham and Harvey Burdell, but on this score I was out of luck. Hasty, whose infiltration of the Bond Street house I had myself arranged, brought home dozens of tales of violent quarrels followed by long, simmering silences between the pair, almost all of which arose out of disputes over money or marriage. The dentist had actually made a confidant of the boy and would deliver to him interminable lectures on the "insidious perfidy" of the female sex. I comforted myself that at least the lad's vocabulary was being expanded.

To my continued annoyance, Burdell regularly corresponded with Demis and traveled to Brooklyn at least once a week to call on her. These visits unfailingly upset her. She remained convinced that Cunningham had sinister designs on "Cousin Harvey" and his fortune. I remained convinced that the old lecher had sinister designs on Demis. When I discovered, quite by accident, that he was sending her money, she and I had a terrific row. It made her appear a kept woman, I argued, and was totally unnecessary as her divorce settlement had left her comfortably well off. She stated that she did not care a groat's worth for her reputation and I retorted that, evidently, she did not give a rat's fart for mine either. It was almost a month before we made it up.

At the end of August Emily Hoffman began tutoring the little Cunningham boys and at once sided with their mother against Burdell. I saw little of Miss Hoffman but she and Jeremy were keeping company and he, under the mistaken impression that I was interested, repeated her stories until at last I pleaded with him to respect my right not to know.

When, for a week in September, I heard nothing at all concerning Burdell and Cunningham, I began to hope that they and their troubles were behind me once and for all. Nothing could have been further from the truth.

On the morning of September 16 my law clerk, Mr. Leggett, rapped on the door of my office and a moment later was nearly bowled over by the lady who had come to consult me. Emma Cunningham exploded into the chamber.

"Mr. Brendon," she announced in a whirling fury, "I wish to bring suit against Dr. Burdell for breach of promise!"

The charge was then considered a grave matter. Once brought it could result in Burdell's arrest. Bond as high as ten thousand dollars might be required to keep him out of the bridewell. Possibly, I thought, that was more cash than the dentist could raise. I pictured Burdell in a drafty cell in the bowels of the Tombs, vermin scurrying across the granite floor, foul-smelling water condensing on the stone walls, the shrieks of some half-crazed old debtor reverberating through the dank corridor. The image left me smiling.

I calmed Mrs. Cunningham and drew up a chair for her. I offered her tea. She expressed a preference for gin. I sent Leggett out for the bottle and his notepad and joined her in a libation while he prepared to record her affidavit in shorthand.

"Now, Mrs. Cunningham," I leaned back, elbows propped on the arms of my chair, fingers pressed together, swiveling slowly, "just explain, in your own words, your complaint against the doctor."

"I first met Harvey Burdell in August 1854," she commenced. "We were introduced at Saratoga. The doctor paid his attentions to me but I was still in mourning for my late husband and I thought it unseemly to receive him as a suitor. Upon returning to New York, however, he again sought me out, renewed the acquaintance, and pertinaciously and continuously made himself agreeable to me in every way. He arranged to be useful in attending to my business and domestic affairs and insisted upon bringing me and my children into his home and paying for the schooling of the two eldest, Augusta and Helen. I found his attentiveness flattering and not unpleasing, and did nothing to discourage it, and gradually, I would say, an understanding grew up between us, culminating in a contract of marriage in the summer of 1855." She paused and looked toward Leggett. "Am I going too fast for you?"

"No, madam," said the clerk impassively.

The lady was on her second gin. "We were to be wed this past June. That was quite settled on, you must understand, or I would never have permitted him to—"

She broke off abruptly, biting down hard on a word she left unspoken. But another swallow of gin and her narrative resumed. "A year ago, soon after our contract of marriage, Dr. Burdell invited me to accompany him to New Jersey, to Elizabethtown where he had some property in real estate which he wished me to see. We were engaged in inspecting the premises until after the train left Elizabethtown. This was by design on his part and made it necessary for us to remain overnight. Of course I insisted on separate chambers at the hotel, but during the night he came into my room and lay beside me on the bed. Then he began to. . . ."

Once more she broke off, removing a lace handkerchief and touching it to her eyes. I saw no tears but her lower lip quivered ever so slightly.

"You need not describe everything that occurred," I said gently. She was, I told myself, going to make a wonderful witness if we took Burdell to court. "Naturally you resisted."

"With all my strength," she responded, "but, at last, I—I yielded to his persuasions."

That part of her story needed work. A jury was not likely to be too sympathetic to a woman with grown children who had allowed herself to be seduced when she was clearly old enough to know better. I suggested carefully that, as the dentist was a powerful man and she a respectable widow, it seemed likely to me he had resorted to more than "persuasions."

She snatched up the hint. "Oh, yes!" she exclaimed. "The matter was a forcible thing altogether."

In other words, the charge was rape.

"Were there," I asked quietly, "consequences?"

"There were," she responded. "I lost the child on Thanksgiving Day."

The image of the foetus in the chamber pot flashed into my mind. I banished it with a quick wave of my hand.

"Did you miscarry?"

Her eyes burned with anger. "Dr. Burdell *aborted* it," she almost snarled. "He keeps instruments in his office for that purpose."

"Good Lord," I muttered. I glanced at Leggett. He kept jotting, placidly jotting. He might have been taking our orders for dinner.

The marriage was to have taken place, according to our client, in June, just at the time that Burdell invited Demis to join the happy family circle. It now struck me that Demis was correct in believing that her cousin was using her as a barrier between himself and the predatory landlady. In assuming his lust for Demis I might well have misread the situation. By placing the two women not merely in the same room, but in the same bed, Burdell now seemed to me more concerned with banning Emma from his own chamber than with luring Demis into it. Emma's hatred of Demis was as bitter as ever, but I now thought I understood it, just as I understood her eviction of Demis in early July. Emma's theft of the promissory note, coming as it had on the very day Demis moved in, was probably exactly what Burdell called it, an act of vengeance. The note itself was worthless to the thief. Very likely Emma wanted to be detected—wanted to be publicly accused of a crime Burdell could not prove.

I had Leggett draw up the affidavit for the client's signature and, while I was at it, prepare a warrant for Burdell's arrest for breach of promise, rape, and abortion. The accusations were being brought on information, not on indictment. That is to say, the dentist could be arrested and jailed not on the findings of a grand jury, but on Emma's unsupported word, provided we could find a sympathetic justice to issue our warrant. The law allowing arrest on mere information was outrageous but, in this case, convenient. We had Burdell in a tight corner.

But the lady did not want the warrant executed.

I could hardly hide my disappointment.

"I wish to discuss this matter with the doctor before I take further steps," she explained, by which I understood that her intention was to use the threat of the suit and arrest to blackmail Burdell into marriage. With a shrug I instructed Leggett to file the papers and hold them in readiness, adding under my breath, "Be certain you collect the fee before she leaves."

"I procured the fee in advance, Squire Brendon," replied the invaluable Leggett.

But, if blackmail was indeed Mrs. Cunningham's battle plan, it didn't work. I soon discovered that none of Mrs. Cunningham's plots ever worked.

On the evening of September 20 Hasty arrived home bursting with news.

"You'll never credit it, Squire!"

"Try me."

"The doc called the police out on Mrs. Cunningham today!" he proclaimed with a broad grin. The tale simply spilled out of him. "The doc has a safe in his office and he keeps the key in his trouser pocket and this afternoon, things in the tooth business being slack, he slips off his pantaloons to catch a nap and Mrs. C. slips into his office and takes the key and opens the safe and steals—"

"A promissory note," I finished for him.

His jaw dropped. "Yeah. Aw, Squire, you already know."

I assured him I didn't. "A lucky guess. What was the note?"

"Near as I can figure it was for money she owes him on the lease."

So once more Emma had pilfered a worthless paper and manipulated Burdell into making a public charge of theft against her which he could not prove. Her original motive was to substantiate an accusation of slander, should she choose to add that complaint to her other grievances, but why, I wondered, repeat the whole charade? The dentist, I concluded, had remained resistant to the notion of marriage, and the lady was bolstering her evidence of defamation in preparation to swearing out another warrant against him.

In anticipation of Emma's next move I had Leggett draw up the suit for slander the next morning but the client did not reappear at the office until October 10. On that day a second warrant was prepared and Burdell taken into the custody of the deputy sheriff. For four days he languished in the Tombs until the bond—an incredible twelve thousand dollars—was posted by one of his few friends, Dr. Alvah Blaisdell.

I had expected to enjoy the dentist's public humiliation but I found I could take no pleasure in his misery. I even felt sorry for him. In vain did he charge that the suits were designed only to extort money from him. In vain did he deny there had ever been a marriage contract. In vain did he insist that she *had* stolen the notes. The authorities accepted her word on every point. She had him tied in knots.

I began to wish I had not become entangled in Cunningham's machinations. The fees, however, were paid on time. Leggett saw to that. And they were starting to mount up handsomely at a time when other clients were not exactly beating down our doors. I reminded myself that it was my job to argue the case, not to judge it, and I went to work preparing for court.

But we never got to court.

On Wednesday, October 22, Emma Cunningham arrived at my

office to drop all charges. "The doctor and I have resolved our differences, Mr. Brendon. He has agreed to marry me within the week."

She was obviously terribly pleased with herself. She produced two papers for my inspection, both dated October 17, both signed by Burdell, which she evidently felt bound the dentist to her for life. They were the strangest documents I had ever seen and I read them carefully several times.

The first ran:

I take my oath that I have never made a will up to October 8, 1856, and if such a will is discovered, it is a forgery.
October 17, 1856   *Harvey Burdell*

The second was even more peculiar:

In consideration of settling the two suits now pending between Mrs. E. A. Cunningham and myself, I agree as follows:
First, I agree to extend to Mrs. E. A. Cunningham and family my friendship through life;
Second, I agree never to do or act in any manner to the disadvantage of Mrs. E. A. Cunningham;
Third, in case I remain and occupy the house No. 31 Bond Street I now do, I will rent to Mrs. Cunningham the suites of rooms she now occupies 3rd floor, attic and basement at the rate of $800 a year.
October 17, 1856   *Harvey Burdell*

I considered these documents. The first said, in effect, that Burdell had never made a will and if he had he didn't mean it. It was obviously part of Emma's agenda to make certain that, should she wed the dentist, no previous testament existed by which she might be subsequently disinherited. I had to admire the lady's perspicacity. Not yet a wife, she was already contemplating widowhood.

There were, however, limits to Emma's cunning. If she thought the second paper compelled Burdell to marry her, as clearly she did, she was much mistaken.

I looked up at my client. "There is nothing here concerning a marriage contract."

"Oh, that is all right," she responded. "The doctor and I have an oral agreement to wed as soon as the suits are settled."

But she'd thought once before she had an oral agreement. "Mrs. Cunningham, will you take my advice?"

"I pay you for it," she said.

"Then do not settle the suits. Merely *discontinue* them. Once they are settled it may be difficult, perhaps impossible, to revive them, if Burdell does not keep his word to you, whereas a discontinued suit can always be reinstituted. It will give you some protection since you do not have the doctor's pledge in writing."

The possibility of Burdell's reneging was clearly one she did not wish to contemplate. "Very well," she said somewhat sullenly. "Do as you think best."

"I would suggest another change," I added. "In the third clause Burdell promises to rent most of the house to you, but only while he continues to occupy his current rooms. He could move out at any time and free himself to lease your suites to anyone he pleased."

I watched the glimmer of a faint suspicion dawn in her eyes and grow until they almost blazed. "I understand," she said. "The wording was entirely Dr. Burdell's." Her head snapped forward sharply, all concentrated attention. "What would you advise, Mr. Brendon?"

I took up a pen and crossed out the words "in case I remain and occupy the house No. 31 Bond Street I now do." Then I handed her the paper. She nodded slowly with grim satisfaction.

I heard from Mrs. Cunningham only once again in 1856. About November 21 she came to me with a question about a "hypothetical situation."

"If a woman is married can she still do business in her former name—sign documents, I mean, or endorse cheques? That is, Mr. Brendon, would such dealings be legal?"

I took it from this inquiry that Burdell had kept his pledge to marry her. "It would be proper to use the married name," I informed her, "but, if there is no doubt about the identity of the person, the assignments would be valid."

This seemed to content her, but at my door she paused. "Do you still retain the papers I had prepared a month ago?"

I answered that I did. "Why do you ask?"

"Oh," she replied languidly, "I do not know but I shall have to revive the suits."

I was left in confusion. If she were *not* married to Burdell, why should she worry about conducting business under the name of Cunningham? If he *had* married her, why the devil would she consider reviving the suits, especially the one charging breach of promise?

21

The Butcher

On October 15, two days before Harvey Burdell signed the documents that led Emma Cunningham to discontinue her suits, a new inmate joined the cast of characters at 31 Bond Street. His name was John J. Eckel. He had been for many years a butcher and was now a trader in animal fats and hides, employed by Smith Ely & Co. He made Burdell uncomfortable. "The doc calls him 'that damned cutthroat fellow,' " Hasty informed me. "He thinks Eckel and Mrs. C. are in cahoots."

"Cahoots over what?" I asked, but the boy just shrugged.

I learned from Hasty that Eckel's arrival had triggered a considerable shifting of accommodations. Emma had left her room adjoining Burdell's suite and moved into two rooms just above the dentist on the third floor. Eckel was installed in the chamber next to Emma's new quarters; in fact an inside door led directly from his bedroom to hers. The two little boys were sleeping in the attic near Hannah Conlan's room.

Emma now slept directly over Burdell's bedroom and, "The doc ain't very happy about it," Hasty said. "He wants me to help him move his stuff around so his office is under Mrs. C. and his bed is in the front room looking out on the street. That way, he says, she can't lay in her bed at night and listen to see who he's entertaining in *his* bed chamber." He grinned at me. "The doc thinks Mrs. C. crawls about on all fours upstairs with her ear to the floor, spying on him. Maybe she does, too, Squire. They're all crazy in that house.''

It occurred to me that, as Emma lived over both of Burdell's rooms, shifting his furniture would hardly guarantee his privacy, but I let it pass. In early December I discovered from the youngster that the long-planned switch of the dentist's rooms had taken place.

As for John J. Eckel, I first saw him about a week after he began to lodge in Bond Street. Jeremy had promised to call for Emily Hoffman following her day of tutoring the Cunningham boys but a wife-beating case delayed him in Special Sessions and he sent word through Leggett requesting me to stand in for him. Obligingly I hailed a hansom and we trotted along Broadway toward Bond. As we neared the house I observed a young lady being accosted by a man who, viewed from the side with his face averted, I first thought was Harvey Burdell. He was not above five-foot-six, thickset, with a shock of black hair, heavy beard, and moustache. He had hold of the lady's wrist and was exhorting with her while she struggled ever more violently to free herself. I recognized Miss Hoffman at once but, on drawing closer to the pair, I realized that the man, for all the similarities, was not the dentist. This fellow's complexion was bilious, his face pitted by an old case of smallpox. He was about thirty-five, ten years Burdell's junior. His eyes were a pale blue and his nose curved down sharply in the Hebrew manner.

"My dear Miss Hoffman," he said in a nasal whine, "won't you let me see you safely to your mother's door? It will soon be dark and there are garroters about, and worse. The streets are not safe for a handsome young woman."

"Indeed, Mr. Eckel, they are not," she responded with some heat, "and you, yourself, are the proof of it. Once more, sir, I demand that you release me or, I warn you, I shall summon the watch."

I dismounted from the cab and removed the ruffian's hand forcibly from the lady's wrist. He spun angrily to face me. "As

your attentions are clearly unwanted," I observed, "I would suggest you go about your business without delay."

"It is your intrusion that is unwanted, young man." He gripped
his walking stick and waved it about. The gesture, intended as
menacing, was merely ridiculous. I cracked my own cane against
a set of his knuckles and he dropped his weapon with a howl.
While he danced about moaning, I handed Miss Hoffman up into
the hansom and we drove away, leaving the hooligan shaking his
uninjured fist after us.

I explained Jeremy's absence. We rode for a time in silence.
Then she said, "I suppose I ought to thank you, Mr. Brendon."

"It is unnecessary, Miss Hoffman, considering how painful it
would be for you to do so."

To my surprise, she laughed. "Is that your impression? Oh,
dear. What a common scold you must think me."

Well, yes, I thought. "Oh, no," I said. "If I have been of some
small service to you, I am glad for the opportunity."

"It is only," she went on, "that men expect women always to
flutter about so and to be quite helpless and dependent. If a girl
does not have the vapors at least twice a day she is thought to be
callous and unfeeling."

I began to protest but she forged ahead. "Consider, Mr. Brendon, when a young man intervenes to spare a young woman the
unpleasant advances of an obnoxious boor (to select one hypothetical situation for the sake of the argument) how inevitable it
is that the young man should expect the young woman to collapse
into his arms in an absolute stupor of relief and adulation. Should
she fail in this, he considers her a wretched ingrate."

She was so serious that I could not forbear smiling. "It is my
distinct impression, Miss Hoffman, that if I had not happened
along you would have simply dashed out the fellow's few brains
with your umbrella. Indeed, I'm not sure I'd have had the courage to confront him had you not been there to protect me. The
very thought of our recent peril makes me lightheaded. I wonder,
should *I* get the vapors, if you would mind terribly my collapsing
into your arms."

"Should *you* get the vapors?" She regarded me with cocked head and cocked eye. "What an extraordinary notion." She gave the matter solemn consideration. "Well, Mr. Brendon, one hardly ever hears of such a thing, but I suppose I could not in good conscience deny you the comfort of my arms."

She was actually *smiling* at me.

But her smile quickly faded. "He *is* a dreadful man. I wonder Mrs. Cunningham would have him in the house."

The non sequitur threw me momentarily. "He? Oh, the ruffian."

"Mr. Eckel," she said with distaste. "The *butcher.*" Her delicate features screwed up into a mask of abhorrence. "What you witnessed this evening, Mr. Brendon, was not the first time that brute has pressed his attentions on me. Ugh! his abominable breath is still in my nostrils! Do you know, he pretends such friendship toward Mrs. Cunningham, and yet I have it on the best authority that he regularly visits a divorced woman named Rachel Prosser."

She spat out the words "divorced woman" as if she had said "tart." I recalled something Quinncannon had said on the night he cleared me of the murder charge: *A divorcée is as much a pariah to her respectable sisters as a common prostitute. Small wonder if thousands of unhappy wives prefer a widow's weeds.*

"Poor Mrs. Cunningham. She is so trusting—so *naive* where men are concerned." Her gloved hands tightened into tiny fists of frustration.

"So trusting is she," I said with a taut smile, "she's even installed Eckel in a room communicating with her own."

My irony was wasted on Miss Emily.

"I feel such sympathy for Mrs. Cunningham," she went on. "Why, she actually imagines that miserly misogynist will marry her!"

"The butcher?"

"No, Mr. Brendon," she said patiently, "Dr. Burdell."

Her capacity for changing the subject was dizzying.

"It is queer," she said, with a shake of her pretty head, which loosened a few strands of raven hair. I thought the effect most attractive. "It is queer, but I have the feeling Mrs. Cunningham has known him for some time."

"Dr. Burdell?"

"No, Mr. Brendon. The butcher." Her lips tightened slightly at one corner. "I do wish you would make an effort to follow the conversation."

"My mind wanders," I replied by way of apology.

"He," she looked at me sharply, "that is to say, Mr. Eckel, claims to have taken his room in response to an advertisement in the papers, but I'm quite sure Mrs. Cunningham never placed such a notice at all. Isn't that strange?"

"Decidedly."

"He—" Again the sharp look. "I refer to Dr. Burdell. He seems especially annoyed at Mr. Eckel's presence in the house. He makes an elaborate point of leaving a room whenever Mr. Eckel enters it."

It crossed my mind that Eckel might be a confederate of Cunningham's in some new scheme to trap the dentist into matrimony—possibly her intention was to make Burdell jealous—but of this I said nothing. I had no desire to kindle a new quarrel with Miss Emily. I confined myself to remarking that I could conjure up no explanation for the dentist's hostility.

"Nor can I," she answered. "For it cannot be that Dr. Burdell has any interest in Mrs. Cunningham. *His* only concern is for that wanton cousin of his."

Miss Emily's ungenerous reference to Demis cut me deeply. I choked down a stinging reply and reminded myself that Miss Emily had no notion of any relationship between Demis and me, and no sense of either the bad taste or the injustice of her remark. I ventured to suggest that Burdell's only connection with Demis was paternal.

At this she gave me a soft smile of pity and patted my hand as though she were patting my head. It was damned irritating.

The cab had arrived at the Hoffmans' door. She gathered up her skirts in preparation to descend—then her dark eyes met mine and held them. "I am very much afraid, Mr. Brendon," she confessed, adding quickly, "not for myself, of course," as if I could possibly misunderstand her so completely. The self-reliant, self-possessed, self-directed "new woman" afraid for herself?! The idea was pure absurdity. The mind reeled.

"But I am afraid for Mrs. Cunningham—" Mrs. Cunningham, thought I, was every bit as independent as Miss Hoffman and in even less need of protection. I said nothing, however. I was becoming quite accomplished at suppressing my thoughts in the vicinity of the "new woman."

But perhaps she read them anyway, for she said, "I'm really very serious, Mr. Brendon. There is something ugly and hateful in that house. It is as though the people there were rushing toward some prefigured horror which no one can prevent. That man—I have such a strong sense—that man is the devil himself!"

This time I knew she was speaking of John Eckel, the butcher.

22

Mrs. Hubbard Entertains a Gentleman

Her own prospective marriage was not the only one on Emma Cunningham's mind. She was encouraging the visits of a nineteen-year-old youth named George Vail Snodgrass who came to Bond Street often in the evening to strike up a lively tune on his banjo and entertain the Cunningham daughters, particularly the younger, sixteen-year-old Helen. The boy had a winning charm and, though he had no visible means of support and whiled away his days in the saloons of the Fifteenth Ward, he was the son of a Presbyterian clergyman whose Brooklyn church Emma had attended with her late husband, and George was available. There was evidence that Emma had young Snodgrass marked out for her eldest, Augusta, but he had an eye for the younger, far more attractive Helen, and the feeling was mutual.

Hasty liked "Georgie." He was pleased when Snodgrass was invited to move, baggage and banjo, into the attic to live rent-free. This was on November 12. Eight days earlier another boarder, Daniel Ullman, had been ensconced in a room at the rear of the second floor. Ullman, a respected attorney and recent, unsuccessful Know-Nothing candidate for governor, kept pretty much to himself. He took his meals at various Broadway hostelries, as did Burdell, who had now abandoned Emma's table. The remaining inmates, including Snodgrass and Eckel, formed a sort of household, often gathering in the back parlor after supper for banjo-led songfests, "making as merry," Hasty told me, "as pigs in a pen."

"I figure Georgie and Helen are hitting it off pretty good, Squire," Hasty informed me in early December. "This afternoon he sent me up to get something out of his trunk and—I wasn't snooping, Squire—but I couldn't help but find them."

I waited for a decent interval. "All right, what did you find?"

"Lady's undergarments," he almost whispered. "They're all over the place, scrambled in with Georgie's own things. There's a lace handkerchief right on top with the initials 'H.C.' And something else, Squire. She writes him poetry. Want to hear it?"

"You didn't steal it?" I said.

"No! Honest. I got it in my head. Listen:

> 'What would the rose, with all her pride, be worth,
> Were there no Sun to call her brightness forth?
> Maidens unloved, like flowers in darkness thrown,
> Want but that light, which comes from Love alone.' "

He gave me his impish grin. "Really powerful stuff, huh? I'm going to switch some of the words around and use it myself. If you want, you can have it for Mrs. Hubbard." He winked at me as one man of the world to another. "Are you gonna see her tonight, Squire?"

"Not tonight, Hasty."

He shook his head and a thatch of curly hair cascaded over his forehead.

"You should get that mop cut off," I said.

"Oh, I dunno. The girls seem to like it."

"Girls!" I exclaimed. "At your age, Hasty, I was still playing with blocks and rolling hoops." It annoyed me that Jeremy was yet again at the theater with Emily Hoffman while I sat home alone. Even young Hasty had what he called an "engagement."

On his way out the boy turned back. "Did you really mean that,

Squire? About playing with blocks when you were my age?"

"Certainly I did."

"Well, then," he said with a smile, "I guess that explains why Mrs. Hubbard is in Brooklyn and you're still here."

He dodged out the door, his nose narrowly escaping contact with my slipper.

For a few minutes I remained in the chair, brooding into the fire. Then, with sudden resolution, I rose, dressed, and took a cab to the Brooklyn ferry.

Demis' boardinghouse was not many blocks from the ferry slip. There was a crack of light visible behind the draperies in the window of her room. I rang the bell several times before I heard the bolts being drawn back. The street door opened the length of a still-fastened chain and one of the eyes of the little housemaid peered up at me.

"No visitors tonight, sir," she almost whimpered. "Miss Demis is feeling poorly."

"Why, Margaret, all the more reason that I should see her. I'll bring her cheer and comfort."

"I don't think so, sir," the girl answered doubtfully. "Miss Demis most particularly said no visitors tonight." She brightened. "I believe she's got something catching, sir. Why, the whole house is like to come down with it."

The girl's behavior was so peculiar that I became alarmed. "Unchain the door, Margaret. I will see Miss Demis at once!"

"Oh, please, sir," she whined, "please go away or I shall lose my position!"

"The devil take you! Open the door or I shall break it in!"

Ruefully she withdrew the chain, still pleading. "Don't go up, sir. The doctor is with her now."

"So much the better. I will question him directly regarding her illness." I took the stairs two at a time and pounded on Demis' door, my terror for her mounting with every second. Again and again I shouted her name.

At last she cried out in a voice so shrill and fearful that I could barely recognize it as hers. "Do not come in, Toby! Oh, God! As you care for me, I beg you, Toby, be gone from this place. Go home! Go anywhere, but leave me in peace!"

I continued to beat my fist against her door. "Demis, you must admit me. I must know the truth now, this very night!" I paused for breath. "Demis, do you hear me? I know the doctor is there!"

I heard her gasp. "Oh, my God, Toby!" The key turned in the lock and the door swung back. Demis stood before me, her eyes filled with tears, her golden hair loosed and disheveled, her nightdress drawn hastily about her. "How *could* you know, Toby?"

Beyond her, in her bed, the blankets tugged up under his bearded chin, lay Harvey Burdell.

"How could you *know*, Toby," she repeated. "How *could* you know that the doctor was here?"

But, before she had done speaking, I turned away and went heavily down the staircase and into the bitter cold night.

23

An Irish Christmas Eve

Of all holidays I hated Christmas the most. I recollect one Christmas Eve in particular when I was thirteen. The other boys had all gone to their homes and I sat alone in the school library, reading Dickens by the feeble light of a dying fire. I reached the point where Scrooge sees himself as a schoolboy abandoned by his fellows on Christmas Eve. I read it again and again and wept myself into a perfect frenzy of self-pity.

The following year one of my classmates took reluctant pity on me and invited me to spend the holiday with his family. We were driven to a magnificent plantation outside Arlington—it was the first time I was permitted to ride *inside* the coach—and my anticipation of festive pleasure grew with every roll of the carriage. My friend's mother was beautiful. I thought her like a princess in a faery tale. She bent down and swept him into her arms, fussing over him in mock fretfulness and covering his face with kisses. Then she stood back and cast a dubious eye upon me, and at last she said, "And this must be your little friend, the orphan boy."

After that I made it a fast rule never to pass Christmas with someone else's family. The season is hard enough to face on your own, but you are never so lonely as when surrounded by other people's relatives. Thus it was that I refused Jeremy Todd's kind offer to visit with his people, and prepared instead to spend Christmas Eve at work in my office.

The scuttle was empty. I might have sent Leggett for coal but I let the fire burn down to embers. The chill gloom of the chamber suited my mood. I had not even begun to recover from the shock of discovering Demis at fine blankets with "Cousin Harvey." My own gullibility infuriated me. Time and again I reviewed the blatant evidence of their true association—her former husband's accusations against them; her unseemly haste to move into the room adjoining his; his constant visits to her in Brooklyn; the money he had sent her; Emma Cunningham's violent jealousy; even Catlin's nasty innuendoes. Nothing had been wanting to jolt me into awareness, yet my willful blindness had shut out all of it. Fool that I had been! I could forgive Demis for I now saw that she was helpless against the promiscuity of her nature. But I could not make peace with my own stupidity, and, before all, I could not absolve Harvey Burdell. I loathed him with a pure loathing.

I was about to give myself up totally to a good wallow in my misery when I heard Leggett ascending the stairs. He was moving quickly and, when he opened my door without rapping, his face was excited. Leggett never did anything hurriedly. He never became agitated. I stared at him. "It's that boy, Squire Brendon," he said. "He's been taken."

"Boy? Do you mean Hasty?"

"Yes, sir. The lad that works for the dentist. I noticed him through the window, whistling along the street, and I thought he was coming to see you, sir, as he often does, but. . . ."

I knew what he was going to tell me. I said, "Go on."

"A man stepped up behind the lad and seized him by his arm, sir—a tall man, ill-favored and garbed like a preacher. He had Jimmy O'Hara, the beadle, with him. I strode smartly to the door, sir, and said to Jimmy, 'Jimmy, what, if anything, has the boy allegedly committed, that you should take him into your official custody in this manner?' And Jimmy replied, 'Leggett, that is a reasonable inquiry and my response to it is that this reverend gentleman here has preferred charges against the lad as a felon and a runaway, and has called upon me to do my sworn duty, which I am, as any idiot can plainly see.' "

The clerk gave me a mournful gaze. "In brief, Squire, they have dragged the boy away, and I heard the reverend say he will have the youngster up before the magistrate the first day after Christmas. He added, sir, that a certain young lawyer has been harboring a fugitive and will have much to answer for, by which I understood him to be referring to you, sir."

Joyeux Noël, thought I, and a Merry Christmas, Toby, my lad. "Possibly," I said to the invaluable Leggett, "if you have any influence with the turnkey, you can arrange for Hasty and me to occupy adjoining cells."

I walked to the window and looked out over the holiday crowds of shoppers rushing home with armloads of gaudily wrapped and ribboned parcels, shouting and waving to each other. On the corners paunchy, side-whiskered, rosy-faced men in dilapidated top hats and moth-eaten mufflers peddled fir trees from stacks encircling the gas lamp poles. Two small children marched along swinging a huge goose between them. Others had built an ice slide on the sidewalk toward which they raced and leaped into death-defying skids. The snow had fallen through the afternoon and horse-drawn sleighs had begun to appear among the hansoms, their laughing passengers blanket-bundled, their harness bells jangling above the clear chimes and the orchestra of bells that rang from the churches. A vendor hawked roasted chestnuts under my window. I could fancy the festive smell through the frosted panes. The whole of Reede Street seemed to be sitting for a portrait by Currier and Ives.

I stared out at Christmas the way a small boy stares in the window of a toy shop. I came near pressing my face against the glass. Jeremy was in the bosom of his family. Demis was in Brooklyn in God knew whose bosom. Poor Hasty was again in the clutches of Reverend Edward Cowley in the hellhole called the Shepherd's Fold. And I— I was headed for certain disbarment and a possible vacation in the Tombs. As I had on the night the boy came to my door, I wondered what, circumstanced as I was, Quinncannon would do. There was one simple way of finding out. I threw on my greatcoat and pulled my cap down over my forehead and sent Leggett to hail a hansom.

The older reader will remember the outcry set loose in the press by the arrest and trial of Shepherd Cowley and the revelation of the barbarous, squalid conditions that prevailed at his "Fold" and numerous similar establishments, spawned by the infamous "Friendless-Youth" law, which concealed their monstrous abuse of their helpless charges behind a posture of charitable piety. Until now, however, the full story of what I've come to call "Quinncannon's Raid" has not been revealed. In truth, the Irishman insisted on suppressing his role in the affair and it will not please him to have it told here, but the man has a tendency to make a vice of modesty.

When I reached Quinncannon's lodgings he was supervising the loading of dozens of gift packages onto a dray. There were sacks filled with wooden wagons, rocking horses, animals enough to crew several arks, all festooned with bright ribbons of red, yellow, green. His gang of laborers were some of the toughest, scruffiest hooligans I had ever seen outside the bridewell. I recognized two or three of them: Boston Jimmy Burns, the celebrated bank sneak and burglar, known to his fraternity as "The Prince of Thieves" because of his liberality to the widows and orphans of his late associates, and Big Bill Brady, called Bible Billy because he carries a testament over his heart and plies his pickpocketing trade chiefly in Presbyterian congregations. Quinncannon introduced me to others including Charles "Doc" Smyth, the sawdust swindler; James "Red Fitz" Fitzgerald, the bank steerer; and the famous pickpocket Frank "The Hook" Sullivan who, as soon as Quinncannon's back was turned, smiled warmly and shook my hand while my Irish friend, without turning, said quietly, "Give them back, Frank." I watched with astonishment while "The Hook" sheepishly, relinquished my watch, wallet, and belt buckle.

"The cash too," Quinncannon said, still without turning.

Sullivan shrugged and handed me my money clip.

"Frank," Quinncannon said, "you're incorrigible."

"No, sir!" the thief protested. "I ain't had even a wee drop!"

I gathered that the dray's cheerful cargo was holiday gifts intended for the children at a house on Vandam Street run by a couple named Kelly for Irish street boys convicted of petty crimes. The trip to Kelly's had for years been an annual event in which the honor of participation was prized by the dregs of the Irish underworld. Each Christmas Eve this riffraff surfaced from the sewers of the Five Points to perform one decent act. I expressed my surprise to Quinncannon.

"There's an Irish legend, Toby," he said, "of a thief whose life was unalloyed wickedness until one night, having clubbed an old usurer and stolen his gold piece, he came upon a starving child and, in a moment of inexplicable pity, gave him the coin. For that solitary kindness he is allowed out of hell every Christmas Eve." He gave me a wry smile. "Have you not heard of the good thief who hung beside Jesus?"

I nodded.

"Well, he was Irish."

It seemed the right time to tell him about Hasty and the Shepherd's Fold. He listened gravely and then called aside four of his crew. "Go over to Connelly's stables and rent his carriage— then drive to Stewart's store on Fifth Avenue and buy up all the toys and warm clothing you can transport and head up to Kelly's." He pressed two large bank notes into Boston Jimmy Burns' hand. "Let none of that stick to your fingers, lad, or I'll know."

He would have too.

This quartet dispatched, Quinncannon ordered the remaining men into the dray and swung up into the hansom beside me with orders for the wagon to follow us, and in seconds we were sprinting over the cobblestones toward Cowley's Fold. The others fell back farther and farther behind us.

Quinncannon's boots hit the street before the cab had fairly stopped and he strode toward the house while I scrambled after him. When I reached his side he was pounding on the door with the head of his cane. At last the door slowly opened the extent of a chain lock and a little sparrow of a woman peeped worriedly out. Everything about her was gray—her gray hair parted in the middle and drawn back under a gray cap, her gray dress hanging shapelessly about her stooped figure and covered by a gray apron. Even her skin was gray, her face and hands wrinkled and the texture of old parchment. I sensed that the "friendless youths" were not the only ones who had felt the sting of Cowley's wrath.

Quinncannon ordered her to stand clear. I shouted Hasty's name and heard his answering shout, and the Irishman kicked the door in. The splintered fragments flew across the uncarpeted floor and fell at the feet of the demon of the place. Cowley half bent beside a straight chair that Hasty had been forced to strad-dle. The boy's wrists were lashed to the chair's legs. His fine coat lay in a crumpled heap and his shirt was ripped up to the collar, laying bare a back badly cut and scarred with ugly welts. A gnarled cane was gripped in the reverend's upraised hand and wavered menacingly above the youth's slender frame.

I took Cowley in with a glance. His garb was as black as his wife's was gray, with only the glint of a white clerical collar at his throat. His nose was a crow's beak protruding over a pair of wide, bloodless lips beneath which grew a thick prophet's beard. He was tall and powerfully built—though in his mid-fifties, still a man of great strength. He growled, "Get out of my house!"

"Let the boy go!" I cried. I pushed past Quinncannon.

"The boy is in my charge," he returned. "The law is with me."

"Yes," I said, "but if you hit the lad again I will break your head—" I stopped abruptly, realizing I had left my own cane in the cab. "I will throttle you," I amended.

In reply he lifted his stick over Hasty's back and I sprang for his throat in a blind rage. He brought the club down on my shoulder and pain screamed through my right arm into my fingers. I seized his jacket with my left hand and spun him around but I couldn't make a fist with my right—my arm hung uselessly —and he smashed his weapon against my leg. My knee buckled and I went down, trying to pull him with me, but he braced his weight against me and as my grip slipped from his coat he again raised the stick and then Quinncannon drove his fist into the pit of Cowley's stomach and the clergyman doubled over and lay writhing on the floor.

"Damn it!" I shouted in anger. "I could have taken him!"

Quinncannon regarded me under a raised eyebrow. "He'd have killed you, lad," he answered quietly. He was untying Hasty. I managed to drag myself to my feet and stood swaying while the boy ran to me and threw his arms around me.

"I knew you'd come after me, Toby," he said in a strangled voice. "I knew you'd come. I knew it! I knew it!" The tears he had stubbornly choked back while he was beaten now began to roll down his cheeks but he blinked furiously to clear his eyes and manfully fought off the desire to weep openly.

There was a sudden thumping of many boots outside the battered door. The dray had finally caught up to us. Quinncannon's band of desperados trooped into the room and stared at the debris around them while the Irishman issued orders.

"I want you three to come with me. The rest of you watch these two. Be easy with the woman, but if this old sinner even twitches I'll pretend I can't hear him screaming. And you," turning to me, "sit down before you fall down."

With Hasty leading they descended into the basement. When Quinncannon reappeared he was carrying a five-year-old child named Louis Victor. The little waif was in a state of emaciation almost beyond belief. He was literally skin and bones with nothing on his body that looked like fat or muscular development. He was very stupid, unable to talk coherently or make any sound but a constant, piteous weeping. After them came other children ranging in age from sixteen to three, many suffering from severe physical abuse and all in the grip of clinical starvation.*

The police and the ambulance were sent for, the Cowley's taken into custody, and the orphans brought to Saint Luke's Hospital where Hasty's wounds were treated. Quinncannon's gang handed out their treasure of toys to the youngsters in the charity ward right to the last rocking horse. It was near midnight when we adjourned to a saloon in the core of the Five Points where the party roared on well past dawn and I became thoroughly anesthetized.

When the hansom stopped outside my lodgings Quinncannon took the sleeping Hasty in his arms and I stumbled up the stairs behind them. The boy was deposited in Jeremy's bed. During the long night I had somehow gotten on a first-name basis with the Irishman. In the parlor I shook his hand and said, "This was the best Christmas I've ever had, Lon."

He returned my grin with a wry smile. "One night out of hell, Toby. Tomorrow we return to defending the ungodly."

He placed two fingers at the corner of his thin moustache and was gone. I listened to his boots descend the stairs until I could no longer hear his footsteps and then I said, out loud, for no one but myself to hear, "God! but I wish that man was my father."

The following morning I recounted my adventures to Leggett before going to my work. Near noon the stolid clerk returned to my office.

---

*In the interest of preserving this cruel history, that it may never be repeated, I list these unfortunates: Fannie McCurdy, 16; Bessie Lawrence, 15; Minnie St. James, 15; Lillie Hawes, 14; Emma Bowman, 15; Lizzie Hunter, 13; Mary Shaw, 8; Rockwell Macon, 9; Philip Macon, 5; Lillian Anderson, 8; Edith Anderson, 4; George Predeau, 5; Mary Metzler, 11; Gussie Sweeney, 12; Charles Sweeney, 9; Frederick Sweeney, 7; Maggie Sweeney, 3; Lawrence Martin, 7; Robert Wood, 3; Alfredo Lauzi, 9; Estelle Staudenbach, 13; John Staudenbach, 10; Thomas Banks, 10; John Banks, 7; James Fox, 14; John Campbell, 16. The discovery of the Shepherd's Fold horrors led to the establishment of the Society for the Prevention of Cruelty to Children guided by Mr. Elbridge T. Gerry. Edward Cowley was sentenced to two years in prison.

"I have spent much rumination on what action I should take in this matter, Squire Brendon, inasmuch as I was in Mr. Hoffman's confidence for twelve years during which I had sole custody of his most sensitive private papers, and I retain a loyalty to the man which I have honored even after his demise. However—"

He hesitated. I had no idea what he was talking about.

"As I am now in your employ, sir, I have concluded that a transfer of my loyalties to you has occurred and is not inappropriate. In short, Squire, this is properly yours."

He extended a thick file and I received it. It had my name written on it in Hoffman's hand, and it was sealed.

"I shall see you are not disturbed, sir." Leggett closed the door behind him.

The file contained a complete record of the arrangements made for me during my childhood. The voluminous correspondence between Hoffman and Orion Small, my guardian in Virginia, was there before me. There were also several letters to Hoffman from the man who had arranged for my release from the orphanage, underwritten my education, dictated every important event in my history. At the bottom of each letter, by way of signature, was the single initial, *Q.*

When I'd read this far I had no doubt. Quinncannon *was* my father. My first reaction was one of pleasure. To find myself the son of the man I admired above all other men brought me a joy and a quiet satisfaction I lack words to express. But gradually a dull resentment began to stir in me. This man by whom I had set such store, whom I had sought to emulate as the model of all estimable qualities, had sired and then abandoned me for ten bleak years. Even when he deigned to rescue me from the misery to which his own neglect had consigned me it was accomplished behind a cloak of anonymity that afforded him continued concealment and allowed him to avoid what he obviously considered the embarrassment of publicly acknowledging me. That he should be ashamed that I was his son—this was the most painful of all my dark reflections.

Well, Quinncannon was not the only man who could keep a secret. If Leggett knew the truth I could rely on his discretion. In no one else, not even Jeremy, would I confide. The Irishman had chosen to have no son. Very well. I now determined to have no father. What he had done for me was done. We were quits now. I was on my own. I pushed my chair back from the desk with some vehemence, jarring the file, and a slip of yellow paper dropped to the carpet. I picked it up and glanced at it, absently at first. Then, with a start, I reread it over and over, my lips silently forming the words.

Something Ogden Hoffman had said came back to me: *There are some truths a man is better off never learning. For God's sake, boy, let the past die.*

Book II

MURDER IN BOND STREET

24

Murder in Bond Street

The last day of January being a stormy Saturday, I would normally have slept in but a mountain of unfinished work called me to the office. I never arrived there, however, for as I descended from my lodgings at eight-thirty in the morning I met a breathless, ghastly pale Hasty rushing in at the street door. "Mrs. Cunningham's sent me to fetch you, Toby," he gasped out. "Dr. Burdell's been murdered in the night and the police are preparing to arrest her. You're to come at once."

He scrambled back up into the cab which had brought him and shouted to the hackman while I leaped up beside him. As we lurched forward I said, "How was the doctor killed?"

"I don't know for sure, but there's an awful lot of blood." He flung a wide-eyed look of horror at me. " 'Twas *me* that found him, Toby! I went to his room to start his fire and he was lying there, on the floor, just inside the door— There was blood on the wall, on his face, under his head—" An involuntary shiver ran through his slender frame. "He must of put up one hell of a fight."

To steady him I put my hand on his shoulder. "Tell me what happened, lad. From the beginning."

He sucked in a deep breath and stared straight ahead at the gray winter morning, oblivious to the street noises and the clutter of commercial traffic that impeded our progress up Broadway.

"I got to the doc's house at seven sharp, Toby. The doc's very strict about time. I knocked on the door from the street to the basement. Hannah, the cook, opened it like she always does."

"It was locked from inside?"

He nodded. "And bolted. Always is. I heard her turn the key and slide back the bolt. Then she locked it after me again. She does it every morning. The doc is—was—most particular that the doors and windows be kept fastened. Hannah says she never knew such a man for fussing about keys and bolts and locks."

"Go on," I said.

"I went through the cellar and out the back basement door into the yard for a scuttle of coal. That door was locked inside and bolted too. Then I went upstairs to the washroom behind the rear parlor to make a fire. I was looking out the window there when I saw Mr. Eckel go out into the yard. He came through the door on the first floor onto the back porch and down the stairs, dressed like a workday. I thought that funny because on Saturday he usually stays in bed. He had his hands in his pockets—the rain had started up again—and he went into the last of the privies, the one nearest the back fence. I didn't see him come back but Hannah said he went away without his breakfast and, Toby, Eckel *never* passes up breakfast."

He was speaking more rapidly now, as though anxious to finish the story and put it behind him. I didn't interrupt him.

"The next thing I had to do—I had to make up fires for the doc and Mrs. Cunningham. I had to go out twice for more coal—I can only carry one scuttle at a time. I put the first one by the doc's office door and I saw he'd left his key in the outside of the lock." He shook his curly head slowly. "I particularly noticed that, Toby, on account of that key is *always* inside. Every morning I have to knock so he can unlock the door and let me in. Today being Saturday, I figure I'll let him sleep, so I left the coal and went back downstairs.

"By then it must've been near seven-thirty and all the Cunninghams and Georgie Snodgrass were having breakfast in the kitchen. I thought Mrs. C. looked kind of sad towards what she was other mornings—sort of downcast. She asked Hannah if Eckel was down to eat yet and Hannah answers he's gone out already without his meal. That seemed to bother Mrs. C. but she didn't comment on it. I went up to the third floor and built her fire and then I went back to the doc's room and knocked."

The storm had become heavy. It beat down on the roof of the hansom as we turned from Broadway into Bond. Gusts of wind threw stinging sheets of rain into our faces. Hasty's voice was so soft I had to strain to hear him.

"There was no answer and I tried to make out if he was stirring around inside. I guess breakfast was over and they all must have gone up the back stairs to Mrs. C.'s rooms because all of a sudden I could hear Snodgrass playing on his banjo from that quarter and the rest of them singing along like they were having a party. That's when I gave up listening for the doc and tried his door. It was unlocked and I pushed it in but it would only open about six inches. Just enough so I could see—"

"You could see the body," I prompted.

He nodded grimly. "He was on the floor, lying on his belly with his face turned toward me and his eyes just . . . staring . . . you know? He was dead but it was like he was looking at me, and there was so *much* blood—"

Again he shook his shoulders convulsively and the tremor ran through his body. "He was wedged up against the door so it wouldn't open more than six inches. If I hadn't grabbed for the door frame I'd have fallen. I'm gonna see him lying there to my dying day, Toby. I ain't never gonna get shut of him."

Once more I placed my hand on his shoulder and allowed him a minute to recover himself while my mind raced. The basement doors had been locked and bolted from within. If this proved true of the ground floor doors as well, as I suspected it would, the murder would have to be considered an inside job. The most obvious suspect was Emma Cunningham. The antagonism between herself and the victim was well documented, but Burdell was a powerful man and, if the death struggle was as violent as

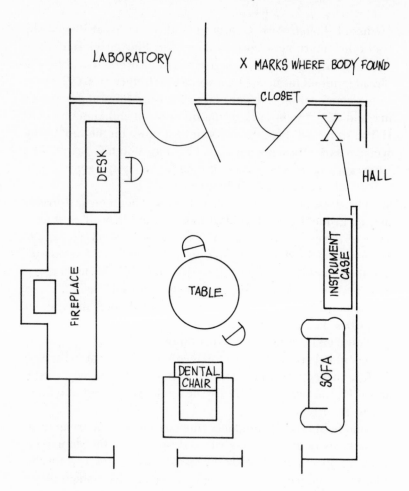

Hasty's observations suggested, it was unlikely she could have killed him unaided. Since the authorities thought her guilty they were probably hunting for an accomplice. My money was on Eckel, the butcher, he of the early departure and the connecting boudoir. As I had done some legal work for Emma in the past, she had now sent for me to defend her on this most serious of charges. I needed every scrap of information Hasty could give me.

I asked, "What did you do after you found the doctor?"

"I ran down to the kitchen and told Hannah. She was kneading dough and she threw her apron up over her head and screamed, 'My God! my God, don't say such things to me.' She tore up to Mrs. C.'s rooms—I never saw her move so fast—and she kicked in the door. They were still playing the banjo and singing, and Hannah cried, 'My God, you are enjoying yourselves all very well, and the doctor is murdered in his room!' "

"How did the others react to that?"

"All hell broke loose," he replied simply. "Mrs. C. cried out and seemed crazy and tore her hair. Helen, the younger daughter, fainted and Georgie Snodgrass had to get her some camphor. Then he sat on the bed and held Mrs. C. while she cried. He was talking to her but I couldn't hear what was said. Helen was moaning. Hannah told her to get control of herself and then ran out across the street to call Dr. Mayne."

"What about the older daughter?" I asked.

"Augusta?" His lips tightened at the corners. "There's a hard case. She sat still through the whole thing. Never spoke or moved. Hardly seemed excited, as though—" His eyes became hard. "As though she wasn't even surprised to hear the doc was dead."

The cab stopped before the murder house. The rain was now pelting down in a deluge but a crowd of the ghoulishly curious stood stoically on the sidewalk, whispering among themselves, their number swelling with each passing minute. A constable was stationed at the street door with another posted at the basement stairs. I seized Hasty's shoulders.

"There's no time left, lad. Tell me the rest of it."

"When Hannah came back with Dr. Mayne I took him upstairs to the doc's room. The office door wouldn't open all the way so we went to the other door, the one to his bedroom in the front, but that was locked. Dr. Mayne had to shove the body back to get into the office. I stayed in the hall. I wasn't going in that room for all the money in the world. Then Georgie turns up and tells me the police are there and Mrs. C. is suspected and he sent me to find you, Toby. That's all I know, and I wish to God I didn't know that much."

With the boy trailing me I pushed my way through the crowd. The officer at the street door blocked my way.

"I've been summoned," I said. "I'm Mrs. Cunningham's attorney."

"Can't be true, sir," he replied. "Mrs. Cunningham's in conference with her lawyer right now."

"Who are you speaking of?" I demanded.

"Why," he responded as though it should have been obvious, "Mr. Lon Quinncannon, naturally."

25

Mr. Quinncannon Investigates

I sent Hasty inside with a message for the Irishman. In a few minutes he reappeared with another policeman. "Mr. Quinncannon says it's all right to pass this young fellow in, Fred." Fred looked doubtful but he stepped aside.

"Himself is upstairs where it happened," Hasty informed me. "You can go up if you're of a mind, Toby."

"How very gracious of Mr. Quinncannon," I said as drily as I could and climbed the stairs to what had been Harvey Burdell's office. Just inside the door, sprawled partially on his stomach, partially on his left side, his right eye still open and gaping up at me, terror-stricken, lay what had been Harvey Burdell.

I'd been curious to see how the sight of the mangled corpse would affect me, but I found I could look at it without recoiling —indeed, with something like bland detachment. The image of the dentist shrinking before me under the blankets of Demis' bed was more clearly fixed in my mind than the sanguine scene that now presented itself. A smear of blood on the hardwood floor showed how the head had moved when the door was pushed against it—from right to left—to allow admittance. I stepped through and noted that the body seemed otherwise in the same position it had assumed at the moment of death.

To my immediate right was the blood-splattered door to a small closet and beyond that, standing open, was the door leading to the tiny laboratory that connected the murder room with the bedroom overlooking the street. This door also opened into the office from right to left, swinging within two feet of a small rolltop desk set against the wall directly opposite the entrance from the corridor. Above the desk a gas lamp still burned. To the left of the desk was the hearth in which the remains of the evening fire had smoldered into ash. A horsehair sofa was backed up to the wall on my left. In the center of the room stood a large, circular table. There were two matching armless chairs, apparently the last survivors of a dining room set, one at the table and one before the desk. To my left, at the other end of the room, two windows with drapes drawn back presented a view of the rear yard. In front of these windows, looking much like a throne, was the dental chair in which Burdell's patients had submitted to his ministrations.

A huge bear of a man, with a thick red beard, in a police uniform sat at the center table, leaning forward on his elbows with a pad and the stub of a pencil in his fat hands. I recognized Captain George Walling. A second man, unknown to me, stood near the fireplace. He was well above six feet, in his early sixties, wiry-lean and white-haired with a great white curling moustache. His squint seemed permanent and imparted a sharp, wise appearance to his thin face. Bright gray eyes darted constantly about the grisly setting, noting and recording the smallest details. His long, deft fingers suggested the surgeon even before Quinncannon introduced him as Dr. Stephen Mayne.

The Irishman, of course, had taken that throne of a dental chair for himself. He lounged comfortably, boots propped on the footrest, a pipe in his hand, and said to me, "You're just in time, lad. Dr. Mayne is about to reconstruct the crime."

The physician smiled slightly. "Hardly that, Mr. Quinncannon," he responded in a clear baritone voice. "An autopsy must first be performed and I have as yet neither assistance nor the proper instruments."

"Nobody can touch the deceased until the coroner arrives," Captain Walling said, doing his duty mechanically.

At the mention of the coroner Quinncannon laughed aloud.

"I *had* to notify Mr. Connery, sir," Walling apologized. "This *is* murder and the law requires it."

"Edward Downes Connery," Quinncannon exclaimed with amused disdain. "Have you met our coroner, Toby?"

I shook my head.

"A paragon of blundering officialdom. A paradigm of inept corruption. The beau ideal numbskull—prototype of the political hack, stooge, and bagman for the Tammany thugocracy. You'll love him, Toby. Not Fielding, not even Dickens could have invented him." He turned back to Walling. "I assume he'll have Connery Junior in tow. The fruit of his loins, apple of his eye, chip off his old blockhead! 'That thou art my son I have partly thy mother's word, partly my own opinion, but chiefly a villainous trick of thine eye and a foolish hanging of thy nether lip.' " Again came his rich, deep laugh. "We're to have a circus, gentlemen. Two Connerys for the pricelessness of one."

I smiled at his joke about fathers and sons, but with an emotion which, I was sure, he could not guess. Nevertheless, he fixed on my eyes with such apparent perception that, for a brief moment, it quite unnerved me. Then he rose from the dental chair and strolled toward the corpse.

"Since the victim cannot yet be moved, Doctor, let us see what can be learned without doing so."

"Well," Mayne began, "the countenance is surcharged, plethoric. The face is fully distended with the eyes obtrusive, the mouth firmly drawn together, and the tongue protruding between the teeth. The appearance suggests garroting, as though he died from a convulsion."

"Only he was stabbed to death," Walling put in, "not choked."

"Not choked *to death*," Mayne agreed, "but choked all the same. Observe, Captain, his throat beneath the neckerchief. There is a distinct line passing around the front of the neck but not continuing at the nape, and not angry enough to have been caused by a cord. I should say the killer approached him from the rear and seized him by the neckerchief, yanking it tight. My guess is this was done while Burdell was seated at his desk at the time the first stab wound was inflicted. You will notice there is blood splattered on the desk top and considerable blood on the left side of the chair."

Quinncannon nodded. "Everything points to the murderer hiding in this laboratory when Burdell came home."

I looked up from my notebook. "What makes you say that?"

He had relaxed once more in the dental chair and was filling his pipe. "Precision of observation and logical reasoning, Toby. Look carefully about you. There were dozens of witnesses to this crime."

He startled me. "I understood there *were* no eyewitnesses."

"Not *eye*witnesses, lad. Never trust direct testimony any further than you can throw the fellow who swears to it. It's always the circumstantial evidence that tells the true story. Our chief witness, for example, is lying at your feet in a pool of his own blood."

"That's a fact," Mayne confirmed.

"The witnesses I speak of," Quinncannon continued, "are the *things* around us. That ring of keys on the desk, for instance, and the key found outside the door. The open safe and the outer garments on the sofa. The very position of the bloodstains reveals more than a battalion of eyewitnesses could communicate. Do you see my meaning?"

I thought I did and said so.

"Then," said the Irishman, "try reconstructing Burdell's murder."

"I'll help you this far, lad," Walling said. "The doctor never took his meals here. The cook says he went out last evening as usual for his supper and she didn't see him again alive. The rest of them—that is, the Cunninghams, Eckel, and Snodgrass—they had something of a party for the girl Helen as she was supposed to go off to school in Saratoga today. They claim they were in bed by eleven and Burdell was still out. The other boarder, Ullman, the politician, was at some testimonial dinner and came in after

1 A.M. He says the house was dark and quiet. If everybody's telling the truth—about that much at least—then Burdell returned between eleven and one." He turned to Quinncannon. "There's one funny thing, sir. My men have been up and down Broadway checking every restaurant the doctor was ever known to frequent and he wasn't at any of them last night. I can't figure where he spent his time."

"Demis," I half-whispered with a bitterness that, after so long, surprised me. Her name had slipped out without warning but Walling heard it.

"Mrs. Hubbard," he said, jotting a note. "I'll check that out." He glanced at me. "Seems to me she used to be a friend of yours, Squire Brendon." His tone conveyed a suspicion I did not care for.

"We're acquainted," I answered and quickly changed the subject. "Suppose Burdell got back about midnight. He let himself in the front door—"

"We found the latchkey in his pocket," Walling interrupted.

Quinncannon's eyebrow went up. "Not on his key ring?"

"No, sir. He carried the latchkey and the key to his bedroom loose. They were both in his trouser pocket."

Quinncannon waved his hand.

I continued. "He climbed the front stairs and unlocked his office—"

"Leaving the key in the lock outside," Walling again broke in.

"Evidently," I said with impatience.

"Only he didn't," the captain said. "At least not according to young Snodgrass. The boy says about ten-forty last night he went down to the kitchen for cider and, the hall on this floor being pitch dark, he lit the gas jet over the doctor's office door. He extinguished it on his way back and he swears he saw no key at that time."

"All that proves," I said, "is that Burdell had not yet returned at ten-forty."

"Yes, Squire, but we've questioned the cook and some of the doctor's friends. They all swear that Burdell had an obsession with keys and locks and was certain Mrs. Cunningham had copies of the keys to his rooms and safe. He told both the cook and Alvah Blaisdell, one of his cronies, that Emma and Eckel and even Augusta used to open his door from the corridor and spy on him while he was at his desk. To prevent this he had a habit of leaving his keys in the locks when he was inside his rooms. They insist he would never have left that key where it was found this morning by the office boy. The boy, himself, backs them up."

Quinncannon was dragging on the stem of a dead pipe. Suddenly he said, "Well, that would explain it."

"Explain what?" I asked.

He seemed not to have heard me. "Doctor," he said to Mayne, "you were the first person to enter these apartments, were you not?"

Mayne said he was. "No one could have preceded me, sir, as the body was wedged against the office door and the door to the bedroom was locked."

"And the key to the bedroom was in the lock inside the door?"

"No, sir. I believe the police found that key in the dead man's pockets. They used his key to unlock the bedroom from inside."

"Good," the Irishman said softly. He caught my eye. "Go on, Toby. You'd gotten Burdell as far as this room I recall."

I gathered my thoughts. "He unlocked the door and did *something* with the key. Then—it had to be completely dark. He'd light a lamp."

"Which one?"

"The closest one—the one over the desk. It's still burning." I cast about the room. "Then he'd light the fire and remove his outer clothes, or maybe he removed the clothes first, and he threw the coat and shawl on the sofa and pulled off his rubber boots. After that he must have opened the safe for the papers that are on his desk. He unlocked the rolltop and put his keys—that is, the ring—on the desk, and sat down to go through the bank ledger. Then the killer came out of the laboratory . . ." I paused for a moment. "Lon, *why* are you so certain that's where he was hiding?"

"The murderer caught Burdell completely off guard. He must have been almost on top of him when he struck. He'd have to come either through the laboratory or from the hall and I think we can be confident Burdell had locked the hall door behind him with the key inside."

"Suppose," I asked, "the killer was someone Burdell brought home with him. Someone he'd never suspect."

"Why would he turn his back on a guest to work at his desk? For that matter, who would he be entertaining at midnight? I think not, Toby."

Another idea struck me. "Isn't it barely possible he *did* leave the key outside?"

"No, lad, not even remotely possible. The murderer put the key where it was found."

"What brings you to that conclusion?" Walling inquired.

The Irishman smiled. "Are you going to arrest our client, George?"

"No decision will be made regarding Mrs. Cunningham until the coroner completes the inquest," the captain replied in his best official manner.

"Well," Quinncannon said, still smiling, "when you've made up your mind let me know and, if you've released her, I'll answer all your questions. Until then you've gotten all the information Squire Brendon and I are prepared to give you."

He stood and I made ready to follow him. "When your examination of the body is finished," he said to Mayne, "we'd appreciate hearing your findings—assuming the authorities have no objection."

"None at all, sir," Walling returned.

"Then excuse us, gentlemen," Quinncannon said. "We'll go out by the route the murderer took."

We walked through the bedroom into the corridor, leaving the door shut but unlocked. "Hasty and Dr. Mayne found this fastened," I reminded him.

"The killer had a duplicate key, Toby."

"Then, it *was* someone from inside the house."

"Very possibly."

"Mrs. Cunningham would have carried a passkey."

"You saw the shambles in there, lad. Do you think that little woman could have wreaked such havoc on a powerful man like Burdell?"

"But, if she had an accomplice? What do you say to Eckel?"

"Don't be so anxious to build a case against our client," he said. "The police are managing that nicely without our help."

I thought that over. It occurred to me that, in accepting this case, I had put myself in a very awkward position. "Eckel," I ventured, "might have done it without Mrs. Cunningham's knowledge."

"Or it could have been someone from outside."

I looked at him sharply. "Why do you say that? What about the duplicate bedroom key?"

"Everyone in New York seems to have had keys to Burdell's doors," he responded. "Someone has left a trail of blood from outside the office down to the basement front door." He watched me for a few seconds. "Come on, lad. I'll show you."

There was a spot of blood on the doorsill of the office. We could hear the voices of Walling and Mayne coming from the room. Quinncannon signaled for silence and motioned me to the head of the stairs. "There's no question that door was closed during the struggle," he explained. "That drop of blood must have fallen later, outside, most likely when the killer inserted the key. And see here—traces of blood on the wall of the staircase— a place where a person going down in the dark would naturally reach out to steady himself."

He led me down and back along the ground floor hall toward the rear of the house. Blood had dripped on the base moulding near the front parlor. There was more blood on the baseboard by the bannister and another stain on the door at the foot of the basement stairs. Yet another spot in the shape of a fingertip appeared on the right side of the door which opened from the cellar hallway into the street. It was close to the hinge as though someone unfamiliar with the premises had fumbled in the wrong place for the knob. The total effect was to suggest the killer had groped his way from the murder room out into Bond Street dropping blood like breadcrumbs.

"It's a false trail, Lon," I said firmly. "The killer wants us to think he left the house but he couldn't have."

"Why not?" he asked quietly.

"Because this door was not only locked but *bolted* from *inside*. Hannah Conlan had to unbolt it this morning to let Hasty in."

"Consider," he said, "the killer, if an insider, might have made these marks to divert suspicion from the inmates, and then bolted the door himself."

"But that destroys the whole illusion," I said. "The murderer would have to be incredibly stupid."

"Well, Toby," Quinncannon replied, "let's hope you're wrong. The intelligent murderer is always easy to trap. It's the stupid ones that get away."

26

Hannah Conlan
Tells Her Story

It was nearly noon when we finished examining the trail of blood.
Returning through the basement, we met one of the battalion of
constables who were now crawling over the house. He carried a
message from Walling.

"The captain says to tell you the coroner has arrived, sir, and
has set about impaneling a jury. The inquest will commence at
three o'clock this afternoon in the room where the murder was
done."

I was astonished. "He's going to hold the inquiry in that bloody
chamber? Good God! What will he do with the corpse?"

The officer shrugged. "The other doctors are here. Mr. Connery wants the cadaver stripped and put in the front bedroom.
I figure they're going to carve on him, or whatever doctors do."

Quinncannon observed my consternation with an ironic smile.
"Don't be surprised at anything Edward Downes Connery does,
Toby." He consulted his watch. "We have three witnesses to
interrogate and three hours to accomplish it."

I assumed our first interview would be with Emma Cunningham but he shook his head and led me to the kitchen.

We found Hannah Conlan sitting alone at the table, grimly
clutching a glass of gin. She brightened immediately when

Quinncannon introduced himself. I gathered he was a hero to the entire Irish community of New York.

"I heard you'd taken the case, sir, though, if you'll forgive me saying it, I don't wish you much luck. I had no great affection for the doctor, but no man deserves a death like his. And them two killed him, sure as our Savior walked on water."

"Them two?" I echoed.

"Mrs. Cunningham and Eckel!" declared the cook as though that settled the matter and rendered the inquest unnecessary. Without my prompting she at once launched into a detailed description of the domestic battles between Emma and the dentist as she had once related them to me. Quinncannon showed, I thought, surprisingly little interest in the alleged abortion performed by Burdell, but the particulars of the lady's lawsuits seemed to fascinate him. I told him what I knew of the affair, concluding with Emma's visit to my office on October 22 to drop all charges.

"She had two papers of the doctor," I explained, "one promising his friendship to her and hers, the other avowing he had made no will. She thought she also had a proposal of marriage."

"In writing?" he asked.

"No, Lon, and that's why I advised her not to drop the charges but merely to discontinue them. If he failed to marry her she could always revive the suits."

"It's odd she didn't take him to court eventually," he observed. "There seems not to have been a marriage."

"Well, that's just what isn't clear," I said. "A month later she returned to inquire whether a married woman could execute legal papers with her former name. I gathered from this that she *was* married, but then she wanted to know if she could still revive the suits, which I took to mean she was *not* married."

The Irishman scratched at the corner of his thin moustache. "I wonder if Burdell realized she could have had him arrested again any time the whim struck her."

"Not," I replied, "until about a week ago."

He shot me a sharp look. "What happened?"

"Burdell dispatched his friend, Alvah Blaisdell, to ask about the suits. I told him they were dormant but not dead—that Mrs. Cunningham could reactivate them whenever she chose."

"Aye, that's true," Hannah Conlan put in, "and the doctor was *furious!* There was a devil of a row between them up in his office that evening, what with them screaming at each other the way that I couldn't make out what all they were saying." Not, I thought, that she hadn't tried. "Once the doctor came running down the stairs and tore around, frantic, pulling at his hair and shouting, 'My God, what am I to do with these people? They will at last have my life!' Then he bounded up the stairs again and the shouting went on and on and at last Mrs. Cunningham came down and saw me standing in the hall and said, 'Hannah, when the doctor was here, did you see him get a gun?' And I said, 'No —no, I saw no such thing.' Then, 'Hannah,' she said, 'the doctor is a very bad man. Do you know that he is a bad, wicked man?' And I said, 'I don't know but there are a great many wicked people in this house.' "

She paused for breath and gulped her gin. Quinncannon observed that discussing murder was thirsty work and Hannah fetched two clean tumblers from the cupboard. "They had another brawl the next day," she said. "That was the 24th."

Evidently a reply was required. "What happened the next day?" the Irishman asked.

This time Hannah had heard some of their exchange. "The doctor wanted her to sign his brother's note back over to him. 'I been waiting for two months,' says he, 'and I'll be damned if I wait another day!' He wanted another paper from her too, a promise that she'd take her children and Eckel and Snodgrass and leave the house when her lease was up on the first of May."

"Naturally she refused," I said.

"She did at the beginning, sir, but the doctor went storming out and came back with three constables and stood outside the house with them, shouting that she was the most horrible woman, very artful, who would stop at nothing to destroy him—and how she had keys to all his doors and would prowl about the house at night, and was a sinful woman who slept with one of the boarders, 'and him a foul-mouthed butcher, not fit for the company of decent folk,' says he. Lord knows what the neighbors would have thought if they hadn't heard it all before. Why, the street was clogged with the carriages of people stopped to listen!

"Once Miss Augusta poked her head out the parlor window and told him he was a fool and advised the officers to take charge of him for a public nuisance. He became so aroused at that that I thought it well the police were there to restrain him. At last Miss Helen went out and said, 'Oh, Doctor, for God's sake come in and go upstairs, and I will get my mother to give you those papers.' That seemed to calm him and he let himself be taken inside." Hannah smiled just a little. "I have no use for the others of that pack, God knows, but Miss Helen *can* be very sweet."

"All this occurred last Saturday?" Quinncannon asked.

"Yes, sir."

"Did Burdell get the papers, do you know?"

She shrugged. "I never heard one way or the other, but there was another furor that night. The doctor went out as usual about five. It was a severe night—no moon at all and the wind howling so that I couldn't close my eyes—and then I heard a noise downstairs that frightened me out of my wits. A terrible hammering banging it was, coming all the way up three flights to the attic from outside the street door—and the doctor himself shouting and cursing so as to wake the dead out of their graves.

"He'd just had one of them new patent locks put on and sometimes it slips and the key won't turn it. There's a partition in the attic between my bed and the place where Snodgrass and the little boys sleep, and I called out to Snodgrass to go down and let the doctor in. I had no doubt of the doctor's mood, you see, and I don't get paid enough to take his abuse when he throws a fit."

I said, "Did Snodgrass let him in?"

"That he did, and Dr. Burdell swore at him and cursed him with language it would be worth my immortal soul to repeat, and cried that the door of his own house had been deliberately bolted against him—that there was a conspiracy against him to drive him crazy and they were all in it together and he would soon be fit for Bedlam. Upon my soul, I think he was crazy already."

This last was said with somber sincerity. I considered that she might be right.

"The next morning at breakfast," she went on, "they were all talking about the words the doctor had had with Snodgrass and what an ugly-tempered man he was. Mr. Eckel remarked that Dr. Burdell deserved a good knockdown if it could be done handy. They all laughed, especially Mrs. Cunningham, and then Eckel said, 'By jingo! Shouldn't I like to be at the stringing up of that old fellow, if I would not have too hard a pull at the cord.' That struck Mrs. Cunningham as a wonderful joke. Eckel leered so lecherously at her, I had to turn my face away."

Quinncannon touched a match to his pipe and puffed thoughtfully. "Hannah, tell us who came to the house yesterday."

The cook, of course, knew the comings and goings of the place as though she'd been collecting tolls at the door. "Miss Helen left at twelve-thirty for her music lesson. About an hour later Dr. Blaisdell called to see the doctor. They went into the parlor. I heard the doctor complaining about Mrs. Cunningham but it was only his usual bellyaching." Meaning, I gathered, that it was not worth her time to eavesdrop.

"Dr. Blaisdell went off a little after two. He and Dr. Burdell spoke for a time in the front hall before he left, and I heard the doctor ask Dr. Blaisdell to come to the house and stay with him until May 1st. I don't know what Dr. Blaisdell answered." Blaisdell, apparently, had a bad habit of keeping his voice low.

"And after that Mrs. Hubbard stopped in," she said.

I looked up sharply from my notebook. Quinncannon was watching me. "Was that unusual?" he inquired.

"Oh, yes, sir. I don't think Mrs. Hubbard has been at the house since July when Mrs. Cunningham threw her out."

"Do you know what they talked about?"

"No, sir. They were in the front parlor with the door shut. It was my day to dust the lower hall, you know, and I was about there a good deal but I couldn't make out their conversation. Afterward—Mrs. Hubbard had just gone out—Mrs. Stansbury rang the bell to discuss taking the house with the doctor."

At this the Irishman showed great interest. "Who is Mrs. Stansbury?"

"An old friend of the doctor's. She and her mother visited him last Wednesday and he asked me to conduct them through the house. I understood he was anxious to rent it to her after the first of May. He said that on that date he would be rid of Mrs. Cunningham and all her brats, and rid of Eckel and Snodgrass too— that he had a paper from Mrs. Cunningham to that effect. Mrs. Stansbury said she must discuss the matter with her husband."

"And the lady returned on Friday?"

Hannah nodded. "She agreed to lease the house and Dr. Burdell said he would draw up the lease and have it ready to sign this morning."

"This morning?" Quinncannon lifted an eyebrow and turned to me. "Why his haste, I wonder, since she couldn't take possession for three months' Make a note, Toby, to check the whereabouts of that lease, if it exists, and also the paper Emma supposedly signed promising to vacate in May." He shifted back to the servant. "Do you know, Hannah, if Mrs. Cunningham was aware of Burdell's arrangement with Mrs. Stansbury?"

"Indeed she was, sir. She came to me after Mrs. Stansbury went out and said, 'Hannah, is that the woman the doctor is going to let the house to?' and I replied that it was and she would return in the morning to sign the papers. Then Mrs. Cunningham said, 'Perhaps he will not live to let the house, or sign the paper either.' "

27

Emma Cunningham's Secret

Though she was not yet under arrest, Mrs. Cunningham was confined to her rooms on the third floor under police guard by order of Coroner Connery. The uniform on duty outside her parlor informed us that she was forbidden to advise with her attorneys prior to the inquest.

"By whose authority?" Quinncannon inquired mildly.

"Coroner Connery, sir. It was his son, Johnny, the deputy coroner, who gave the instructions."

"I see, Sergeant—Davis, isn't it?"

"Yes, sir. Edgar Davis. I worked with you on the McGuinness murder, Mr. Quinncannon."

The Irishman was staring directly into Davis' eyes. It seemed to me the policeman was growing shorter.

"Are you aware, Sergeant, that no one has the right to prevent counsel from consulting with a client at any time?"

Very slowly Davis stepped aside.

Emma was seated on the sofa, dabbing at her eyes with a handkerchief. Beside her a pretty, dark-haired girl of about sixteen sat, holding the older woman's free hand in her own, chafing it gently. This, I soon learned, was the younger daughter, Helen. She was small, narrow-waisted, with large, brown doe eyes and tiny features—in short, she did not resemble her mother in the least.

Augusta, the elder girl, by contrast was the image of Emma but with none of her mother's vulnerability. At the age of only twenty she was already rock hard—hawk-eyed and granite-jawed. Brownish, straight hair was drawn back tightly into a severe knot. A high forehead dropped like a sheer cliff to a browed ridge. The line of her nose and that of her jaw seemed to be honed by nature to a cutting edge. Her voice, when she deigned to reply to our questions, had the rasp of flint on steel. I thought her hideous, but not ugly. She had, time taught me, all of Emma's stubbornness and arrogance but none of her dignity, and while Emma could fly into outbursts of passion ranging from sloppy sentiment to outraged fury, Augusta's rigid control of her emotions seemed never to waver—not, at least, until the very end.

The room's fourth occupant was George Snodgrass, the happy-go-lucky, banjo-plucking, unemployed son of a clergyman whom Emma had planned to match with Augusta but who, for reasons which could hardly be wondered at, had preferred to romance Helen. At nineteen Snodgrass was still baby-faced and fuzzy-cheeked with long, straw-blond hair that curled over his ears and shirt collar. He had a toothy grin and a light step, the sort of ingratiating youngster who charms women of any age, and whom men instinctively detest. The reporters who covered the trial smirked at the fact that frilly lady's nightdresses and undergarments were, on the morning of the murder, found among the articles in his bed, but, in fairness to Snodgrass, I must point out that these belonged, not to him, but to Helen Cunningham. Whatever hobbies the boy indulged in, playing dress-up did not make one.

The police were still dragging the city for John Eckel. Mrs. Cunningham explained that a man she didn't know had come to the house at nine-thirty the previous evening with a message that the butcher's employer wanted to see him "the first thing this morning." She sighed. "Mr. Eckel went off without his breakfast. I'm afraid the authorities find that suspicious."

I congratulated myself that Eckel was not our client. Though there was as yet no actual evidence against him, so far as I knew, there had been bad blood between him and Burdell. He had means and opportunity, a motive was not hard to imagine, and I considered his arrest an inevitability. Our task would be to convince a jury that, if Eckel murdered Burdell, he did so without Emma's aid or knowledge.

In fact it now struck me forcibly that our best chance of clearing Mrs. Cunningham might well be to do all we could to incriminate John J. Eckel.

Quinncannon's interrogation of Emma was lengthy and detailed, but as it covered much ground already revealed, I will not repeat it here. He led her through her relationship with Burdell from their first meeting at Saratoga to the history of her residence in Bond Street. Her version of the visit to Elizabethtown was that he had tricked her into missing the last train home and attempted to "wickedly seduce" her, and, when she resisted, had "used force." As a result of that *single encounter* (she insisted) there had been "consequences," culminating in an abortion from which, she claimed, she had "almost died."

There had followed his promise to marry her the previous June, on which he reneged, and the business of his assigning to her, at his request, his brother's note, and all those troubles with the police until, her patience finally at an end, she had brought charges against him, which she discontinued only after he again offered to make her his wife.

I thought Quinncannon was going to ask if they *had* married, but instead he casually mentioned Demis. Mrs. Cunningham exploded.

"That wicked, scheming slut! That scarlet Whore of Babylon. I have forbidden her name to be uttered in my house!"

The Irishman was studying her closely. "It seems unlikely, madam, that you will be able to prevent it. Why not simply tell us what you know of her?"

All at once her fury was spent. She crumpled back on the sofa and dabbed at her eyes with her handkerchief. She attempted to simulate a sob but she couldn't hide the cold anger in her voice. "The doctor," she began, "brought many women into this house for immoral purposes but none sank so low in iniquity as that— that *harlot!* Her own husband publicly accused her of lewdness and of conspiring to defraud him."

"Conspiring with Burdell, as I recall," he said quietly.

"Dr. Burdell," she replied in an icy tone, "was quite in her power. She cast a spell over him, sir, and bent him to her will at her pleasure. Having no money of her own, she induced him to purchase her freedom from her lawful husband, and then, so soon as her divorce was finalized, she finagled her way into this house—*my* house, sir. He placed her in the room adjoining his own."

"The room you had occupied."

"Yes, Mr. Quinncannon."

"And you remained in that room and shared your bed with this woman you hated."

"I did indeed!" she proclaimed grandly. "The man was a fool. It was essential to protect him from that vixen—to protect him from himself! She was, you must understand, his own first cousin! The arrangement was positively scandalous!"

"Were you successful, madam, in keeping them apart?"

There was a long pause. "I awoke one night," she responded at last, "to find the other side of the bed cold. I knew she was with him."

"How can you be certain?"

She raised her head, her eyes smoldering. "I watched them. Through the keyhole."

Quinncannon took out his pipe and pouch and let that sink in. "Through the keyhole," he echoed quietly. "As a result of this episode did you take any action?"

She squared her shoulders. "I certainly did, sir. I threw the trollop out."

"This occurred on July 7th?"

"It did."

"And what was Burdell's response?"

"The doctor became extremely agitated."

"As a matter of fact, he was furious, wasn't he?"

"*He* had no right to be furious. It was *I* who was the injured party. He had brought that slut into *my* home and paraded her before me—threw her straight into my face—and this in the very month when he had sworn to—"

"To make you his wife," Quinncannon finished. "Did he raise the subject of Mrs. Hubbard again?"

"In September. He told me he intended to have her back. I said I would first see him in his grave!" The phrase escaped her before she realized it. She gave him a startled look.

"Never mind, Mrs. Cunningham," he said gently. "A mere figure of speech, common enough. Of course we must consider carefully before we speak when we are giving testimony." He was lighting his pipe. "After Mrs. Hubbard moved away," he asked between puffs, "did she ever again return to this house?"

She examined the question as though, it seemed to me, she suspected a trap, but apparently found none. "Only once," she replied.

"Yesterday afternoon," he said. "The afternoon of the murder."

"Yes," she said warily.

"What conversation passed between them?"

"I don't know, Mr. Quinncannon, and I could not care less." Her manner suggested that she cared very much.

"Do you know Mrs. Stansbury?"

"She is a friend of Dr. Burdell's."

"Do you know that yesterday afternoon Burdell and Mrs. Stansbury came to an arrangement by which she was to lease the house after May 1st?"

"I do not."

"Do you know that they were to sign the papers today?"

"That is quite impossible," she said firmly.

I watched Quinncannon. "Why is it impossible, madam?" he inquired.

"Because the doctor could not have made such an agreement without my consent." Her thin lips drew back in a smile of triumph. "You see, Mr. Quinncannon, I am Harvey Burdell's wife!"

I wrote in my notebook, "MOTIVE: EXCELLENT!!"

One corner of the Irishman's mouth tightened and he nodded grimly. He took a chair, stretching out his long legs and crossing his boots. "Perhaps, madam, you would favor us with the details of your nuptials."

"Dr. Burdell and I were married on October 28th of last year. That was a Tuesday. The clergyman who officiated was the Reverend Uriah Marvine, who is Dutch Reformed, and the wedding occurred in his home. My daughter, Augusta, witnessed the ceremony. I have a certificate." A small purse lay beside her on the sofa, from which she extracted a paper. Quinncannon examined it carefully, then passed it to me. It was as she had represented it, but at that moment the question that would become one of the overriding issues of her case first struck me. There was never any doubt that on October 28 Emma Cunningham had appeared before Reverend Marvine and gone through the motions of a wedding with a bearded man, but *was that man Harvey Burdell?*

Quinncannon said, "Are you aware of the value of Burdell's estate?"

"It is somewhat in excess of two hundred thousand dollars, I believe."

"Am I correct in assuming that the doctor died intestate?"

"I have a signed document from him to that effect."

"A document which you required of him eleven days before your marriage as a condition of discontinuing your suits against him?"

"He gave it to me freely, sir."

"Mrs. Cunningham, are you at all conscious of the significance of these revelations?"

"Certainly, sir. As the doctor made no will, I, as his legal wife,

will inherit his entire estate, and those jackals who were his relations may help themselves."

Quinncannon shook his head. "You needn't be so smug,
madam. Until now, despite the stormy history of your relationship, you had no motive for murder strong enough to warrant
your being charged with the crime. Now, however, your arrest is
inevitable."

I thought her reaction to this news remarkably dispassionate.
"Oh, dear," she said softly. "But I really am innocent, you know."

"How many people knew about your marriage?"

"Only my daughter, Augusta. Dr. Burdell insisted we keep it
a secret."

One Irish eyebrow slowly elevated. "What reason did the doctor give?"

"Why, only that he had spoken so freely and so vehemently
against marriage that he feared, if it were known, his friends
would make sport of him."

Her answer, to my mind, was ridiculous. "And was that his only
purpose?"

"My mother," Augusta injected icily, "is telling the truth."

I ignored her. "Excuse, me, madam, but you concealed your
wedding, even from your daughter Helen, *only* because Burdell
did not want his friends to laugh at him? How long was this
matter to remain secret?"

"Until June of this year. My husband intended to close up his
office and take Augusta and myself on a tour of Europe at that
time."

Worse and yet worse. I kept imagining what a prosecutor
would do with this faery tale. "If that was his plan, then why was
he preparing to lease the house to Mrs. Stansbury in May? Why,
if you were his wife, did he tell his friends he would have you
evicted on that date?"

"I'm sure I have no explanation," she replied haughtily.

I was pretty sure I knew the explanation. "When you visited my
office on November 21st why did you not inform me you were
married?"

"My husband most particularly requested that I not do so."

"He singled me out as one who must not be told the truth?"

"Most especially you."

"Why?"

"He did not give me his reasons."

I observed her narrowly. "Why did you say on that occasion that you thought you might have to resurrect your law suits?"

"Well, you see, Mr. Brendon, my husband wanted me to reassign his brother's note to him, which had originally been assigned to me in the name of Cunningham. I needed to know if I could do so in that name although I had since married. I feared, by asking you the question, I might arouse your suspicion that we *were* now married, so I raised the issue of the suits to put you off the scent."

Her explanation was glib and superficially plausible, but I didn't believe a word of it. A glance at Quinncannon told me that he, too, was unconvinced.

"Mrs. Cunningham," he said, "will you reconstruct, to the best of your memory, the events of last night?"

"I will try, sir," she responded, "if you will try to remember that my name is not Cunningham but Burdell."

He waved his hand.

"After supper," she commenced, "we came here to my rooms. My daughter, Helen, was to have left for school this morning and I wanted to have a small party for her. My other children were here and George, and of course Mr. Eckel. I understand Dr. Burdell went out at his usual time, around five, but I did not see him after mid-afternoon. Then—it was about eight—I happened to be downstairs when a message came for Mr. Eckel from his employer that he should be at his place of business very early this morning. I delivered the note and he said it was an inconvenience, as he would have to miss his breakfast. Remember, girls?"

"Don't forget, Mama," Helen said, "you were worried about Hannah."

"Yes, I thought Hannah looked pale and tired when she served supper. I went to the kitchen near ten o'clock and suggested she go to bed early—that if anything was needed we would manage for ourselves. Then—let me see—nothing else happened except that we thought it would be nice to have some cider before bedtime and, George, you went down for some."

Snodgrass agreed. "It was so dark that I lit the lamp outside the doctor's office. On the way back with the cider I turned off the light. I'm sure the doctor had not yet returned. There was no key in his door and I saw no blood on the sill." He looked at Quinncannon. "The police asked me that so I figured you'd want to know."

"When did you retire?" I inquired.

"Just at eleven," said Mrs. Cunningham/Burdell. "George and the boys went to the attic and Mr. Eckel to his room. My daughters slept with me."

"In the same bed?"

"We thought, as Helen would be away for four months, it would be cozy, Mr. Brendon, rather like three sisters gossiping together. I slept in the middle."

"So that, to get up, you would have had to climb over one of the girls?"

"Yes, but, you see, none of us *did* get up. It would have wakened the others."

"And none of you heard the struggle in Burdell's office."

"I'm afraid not. If we had. . . ." She let the thought drift away.

And *that,* I reflected, is all we've got for an alibi.

"When," Quinncannon asked, "did you first learn the doctor was dead?"

"It was in this room after breakfast. Hannah came in in a dreadful state and I recall I cried, 'Oh, God, no! Who could have murdered Dr. Burdell?' "

"What made you assume he'd been murdered?"

She gave him a gaze of wide-eyed innocence. "Why, Hannah said so." She nodded her head firmly. "Yes, yes, I'm quite certain Hannah said so."

28

Mr. Eckel's Secretoire

The police had located the elusive John J. Eckel and brought him to the house but we were forbidden to interview him by the coroner's son. "His daddy is all in a twit that you got to Mrs. Cunningham," Captain Walling told Quinncannon, "but at least she *is* your client. Connery says you're not Eckel's lawyer and he'll be damned if he lets you within twenty furlongs of the butcher." His voice lowered. "There *is* something you may find interesting. We've searched Eckel's room and opened up his cabinet."

Walling led us up to the third floor where Eckel occupied a chamber adjoining Mrs. Cunningham's bedroom. Upon entering I observed a small bureau and a fireplace on my right. A lumpy, horsehair sofa was on my left and, just beyond it, the door communicating with the Cunningham suite, now locked. Scattered about the room, and to my mind its most remarkable feature, were twenty-one canaries, in gilded cages, which broke out in sprightly melodies at our party's arrival.

Across from the door and beyond the fireplace stood a large rosewood cabinet (the *Times* would call it a "secretoire"), which proved a most versatile piece of furniture. The top was a bookcase enclosed by glass doors. The lower portion served as both desk and bed, opening into either with the turn of a key. The lid of the desk dropped down and became a work surface. Within were several small drawers and cubbyholes crammed with papers. From these Walling selected one packet to hand to Quinn-cannon, who examined them and passed them to me.

There were Burdell's affidavit that he had not made a will prior to October 8, 1856, and his promise of lifelong friendship to Emma that she had brought to my office when she discontinued the suits. I noted the line I had drawn through the words "in case I remain and occupy the house No. 31 Bond Street."

There also was a release by Mrs. Cunningham of all claims she might have against Burdell, undated, written in the dentist's undoubted hand, and unsigned by the lady—and therefore worthless. I found Emma's lease, which ran from May 1, 1856, to May 1, 1857.

The last remaining document was a reassignment of William Burdell's note for $826 from Mrs. Cunningham to the doctor, which she had endorsed in the name of Cunningham, and dated September 1856, and which she had evidently later stolen back.

Far more interesting to me were the papers I did *not* find. There was no evidence of the paper she had allegedly given him in which she promised to vacate the premises on May 1 at the expiration of their rental agreement. This was the affidavit he had demanded on Saturday, January 24, which Helen had told him she would get from her mother.

Also missing was the new lease that Burdell had informed Mrs. Stansbury on the day of his murder would be ready for her signature the following morning.

Of course it was possible that neither of these documents had ever been drawn up, but Walling volunteered information to the contrary. The police had located Demis in Brooklyn and she was prepared to swear that Burdell had visited her on Saturday evening, the 24th, and showed her Emma's signed release. Furthermore, Demis knew he had drafted the Stansbury lease because he had exhibited it to her when she called on him on the afternoon before his death.

What had happened to these papers? The likelihood was that

Emma had destroyed them. To do so she would have had to obtain them from Burdell, which meant, I thought, that she had rifled his safe sometime on Friday evening. The discovery in Eckel's cabinet of her own lease and her unsigned release—which Burdell had undoubtedly also kept in his safe—further reinforced this conclusion, *and* implicated Eckel in the theft if not the murder.

The question was, had Emma stolen these documents *before* or *after* the dentist returned home to face his killer?

While I pondered this another idea struck me. Emma and Eckel now had in their possession her reassignment of William Burdell's note, the very note Harvey Burdell had accused her of stealing from him back in September. On that occasion the doctor had made such an ass of himself that I had assumed he was mistaken. Now, however, his charge against her began to seem credible. In fact, Dr. Burdell was starting to appear less and less paranoid, and the case against Emma and her butcher boyfriend was growing stronger by the minute.

In defending Mrs. Cunningham, I reflected, I would need to be extremely careful not to misstep.

While I returned the papers to Walling he said to Quinncannon, "We went through Eckel's trunk too, sir. Didn't find anything except a vial of capsules." He winked broadly. "Balsam of copaiva."

I looked at the Irishman quizzically.

"It's a drug, lad," he explained, "used to treat gonorrhea."

I was getting an ever clearer picture of the butcher's habits.

29

The Unsuspecting Suspect

The committee of physicians had completed their examination of the victim and Quinncannon was anxious to speak again with Dr. Stephen Mayne. I rose to follow him and felt the restraining hand of Captain Walling on my arm.

"A moment, Mr. Brendon, for a word or two."

I regarded him with curiosity. The Irishman watched us both.

"You may go ahead, Mr. Quinncannon," said the policeman. "Mr. Brendon will be with you shortly."

Quinncannon hesitated. Then he cocked his head slightly. Both eyebrows went up—one corner of his moustache drew down—his eyes focused on something far away which completely eluded me—and he left the room. It was as though he had divined what Walling was going to say without being told. I felt damned uncomfortable.

The captain poised his pencil above his notebook and avoided my eyes. "I wonder if you would mind, sir, just for the record, answering a few questions?"

I sat down and crossed my legs, and sought to keep my voice casual. "Fire away, Captain."

"Where were you last night, sir?"

The question frankly caught me off guard. "I was at home, in my bed."

"Alone?"

I attempted a smile. "Regrettably, Captain."

He muttered as he wrote: "No corroboration."

"I wasn't aware I would require an alibi." I was determined to keep smiling.

"You don't, sir. Not at all. Just clearing up some loose ends. Do you own a dagger, Mr. Brendon?"

"I don't carry a weapon of any sort."

"What was your relationship with Dr. Burdell?"

"Relationship?" I echoed. What the devil was he getting at? "I knew him—not very well. I did some legal work for him."

"Explain, please, sir." His whole attitude was too damned respectful for my taste.

"Dr. Burdell engaged my firm to handle the divorce of his cousin from her husband. I was assigned the brief."

"The lady—your client—was Mrs. Demis Hubbard?"

"Yes—but obviously, Captain, you already know all this." I fought back my increasing impatience.

"What was your relationship with Mrs. Hubbard?"

I studied him, trying to decide how much he knew and to what degree he was merely fishing. His first question had concerned my whereabouts on the murder night. That bothered me.

"We were client and attorney," I said.

"Nothing more?"

He had already interrogated Demis. I concluded it would be stupid to lie. "Yes, Captain, we were also lovers."

He met my gaze. "I'm sorry, Mr. Brendon. There are certain questions I must ask you. It's my job, you understand." He sounded honestly apologetic too.

"How long did this," he groped for the right word, ". . . arrangement go on, sir? Can you recall?"

"I can recall precisely. It began on the first day I met Mrs. Hubbard and ended in early December this past year."

"Under what circumstances did it end?"

Had Demis told him *that* too?

"I discovered Mrs. Hubbard had not been . . . had not kept faith with me."

"She was seeing another man?"

"Yes."

"Did you learn who this other man was?"

What was the point of forcing him to drag the story from me an inch at a time? "It was Harvey Burdell. And before you ask, Captain, I know because by chance I found them in bed together."

"And this made you angry."

An inane remark! "Yes, and very sad as well. I had duped myself into believing that the lady was in love with me. No man enjoys being made to play the fool. But if you're suggesting that I was angry enough to kill Burdell you are very much mistaken. I shed a few tears and licked my wounds, yes, but those wounds have healed very nicely, thank you." I leaned forward and added earnestly, "Damn it, Walling, if I *had* been tempted to kill him it would have been in the passion of the moment—not two months later!"

"Oh," he said, "I'm certainly not accusing you of a crime of passion. Oh, no, sir. No, not at all."

I allowed myself to relax. "Well, I'm relieved to hear it, Captain."

"No, not at all," he repeated somewhat unnecessarily. He thumbed through his notes. "Do you happen to know, sir, how much of an estate Dr. Burdell left?"

I thought he was unaware of the answer. "I don't know for a fact. Something over two hundred thousand dollars, I believe."

"He died without making a will, didn't he, sir?"

"So I understand."

He gave that considerable thought. At last he said absently, "I suppose that means that his money will go to his nearest relative?"

His expression was an opaque mask. "Since Mrs. Cunningham

appears to be his widow, I imagine she will inherit," I said.

He nodded slowly. "Yes, yes, I imagine so. If her proof of the marriage holds up."

"Well, naturally . . ."

"And if she's acquitted of his murder."

"Mr. Quinncannon and I will do everything in our power to clear her of that charge."

"Will you?" He stressed the word "you" ever so slightly.

"I would remind you that she is not yet even under arrest," I said.

"No, that's true. That's true. Still. . . ." He let his thought drift away. Then, quite suddenly, he said, "Were you aware that Dr. Burdell had a son?"

"A son?" I said warily. "Burdell?"

For the first time Walling sat down. "Yes, Mr. Brendon. The doctor was very young at the time. He married the girl when she became pregnant, but deserted her after the child was born. When she died the boy was placed in an orphanage where he remained until he was ten. Then—" He consulted his notebook. "I'm afraid we haven't been able to trace him past that point—so far, at least. I thought you might be able to help us."

I extracted and began to pack my pipe. "I can't fathom why you should get such a notion," I replied evenly.

"Oh, it's only that Mr. Hoffman's firm apparently handled the boy's affairs at one time. I hoped you might have come across some old files that could give us a clue."

I gave him an easy smile. "Sorry. I've only been with the firm a few months, you must remember."

"Ah, that's the truth, and the young man would have reached his majority before you came aboard. In fact, Mr. Brendon, today he would be— Why, he'd be, as I calculate, just about your own age, sir."

Now he was obviously fishing. I allowed the remark to pass.

"We're anxious to find him, of course, because, as the doctor's son he would be his nearest blood relation and odds on to beat the rest of the family to Burdell's money. Even the widow, if she *is* his widow."

I permitted myself another, broader smile. "What a marvelous motive for murder, Captain."

"The idea did cross my mind, Mr. Brendon. I'd be a liar to deny it." He got to his feet. "Well, well, all is revealed in God's good time as Shakespeare says. Or maybe it's the Bible." He checked his watch. "The inquest will be under way soon. I ought to warn you, it's dead certain Connery's going to order Mrs. Cunningham's arrest. But, then, I know you'll do all you can to defend her, though. . . ."

His pause seemed endless. I waited.

". . . though, it's a fact, her conviction for Burdell's murder *would* close the case."

He nodded to me and left me alone. I remained seated until I had smoked the pipe down to dust, and God forgive me for the thoughts that went through my head.

30

Doctor Mayne Reports

Quinncannon was ascending the stairs to the third floor when I next saw him. I waited for him to reach the landing. For some reason I felt the need to offer an explanation for my interview with Walling. "The captain wanted some information about Mrs. Cunningham's suits against Burdell," I volunteered. "Naturally I told him that was privileged."

Instantly he fixed me in an icy glare. I have never, before or since, seen him so angry. "Toby." The brogue was acerbic. "Don't ever lie to me. Lie to anyone else you please, but don't . . . ever . . . lie . . . to . . . me."

I found myself stammering. "I—I'm sorry. The truth is—"

He cut me off. "Forget what Walling wanted. What I have to know from you, lad—and we'd better get it clear at once—is, can you or can you not provide our client with the best defense of which you are capable?" He raised his hand. "Consider the question carefully, Toby, before you answer."

I *did* think about it. Given all the circumstances surrounding the case, *could* I give it my best effort, or would I hold back at a crucial moment, swallowing the question that ought to be asked, the objection that ought to be made, the strategy that ought to be followed? Walling had said it. Mrs. Cunningham's conviction *would* close the investigation—forever.

A minute passed. Then I met Quinncannon's eyes and drew a deep breath. "Yes, Sir," I said evenly. "Whatever skill I have is at the lady's disposal."

We found Dr. Mayne in the front parlor. "That idiot, Connery, is holding the inquest in the murder room. I suppose you've heard. It's a madhouse up there. We've examined the body. It seems there's not to be an autopsy."

"Why not?" I asked.

"Who knows? Dr. McKnight has been placed in charge. He's the coroner's son-in-law. It appears the whole Connery tribe feeds at the public trough. At all events I'll tell you what I can."

I readied my notebook.

"There were fifteen wounds altogether. They were all made by the same instrument, a dagger between eight and nine inches long and one inch at its widest point. No sign of the weapon yet. The police are scouring the place."

He consulted his notes. "For your convenience I've numbered the wounds. Remember, though, these numbers don't represent the order in which the wounds were inflicted. That may be difficult to tell with certainty. Wound number one is under the angle of the ear and jaw on the left side. The probe shows it extends nearly the whole length through the neck and divides all the great blood vessels of the neck."

"In other words," Quinncannon said, "Burdell was almost decapitated."

Mayne concurred. "Number two is on the left cheek—the malar bone. It went down and inwardly into the face. The third is a cut on the right cheek, not much more than a scratch. The fourth is an abrasion on the left side. Number five is lower down on the right side near the clavicle. It extends directly into the thorax some six or seven inches and runs into the internal portion of the chest.

"Number six is on the right arm, a transverse wound, pretty low down. It looks as if he got it while raising his arm to fend off his attacker. Number seven is on the left arm near the deltoid muscle where the swell is. It went down four or five inches. The eighth wound is on the same arm, lower down. It went in about two inches. All these gashes on the arms, I should guess, are the result of Burdell's defending himself."

Another glance at his notes. "The trunk and abdomen were cut pretty badly. Number nine is on the left side between the fourth and fifth ribs. It penetrated inward almost eight inches. The tenth is two inches lower down and runs upwards into the auricle of the heart. Then there are three wounds close together in the abdomen near the region of the stomach in the abdominal viscera, each of which extends inwards about six inches. I've numbered them eleven, twelve, and thirteen.

"There is another wound, number fourteen, near the margin of the left hip that runs inwardly and then outwardly so that the knife point almost punctured his back from within. And finally, number fifteen. This wound is under the left armpit and extends some seven inches directly inward and down towards the thorax."

"Tell me, Stephen," Quinncannon said, "how many of these wounds would prove fatal?"

"Do you mean fatal by itself?"

The Irishman nodded.

"I would say there are at least five which would have killed him. Numbers one, five, nine, ten, and fifteen. Eleven, twelve, and thirteen might together be fatal. The first was probably the lethal one. It would kill in the shortest time, anywhere from two to five minutes. In Burdell's case it was likely closer to two."

Again Quinncannon nodded. "You both saw the murder room. From its appearance, how long would you say the struggle lasted?"

"Not long," I answered. "Less than a minute."

"Thirty seconds, maybe thirty-five," Mayne said.

"That would be my guess," Quinncannon said. "Now, what are we to make of a murderer who strikes fifteen blows in thirty frenzied seconds and still manages to hit vital targets with fully one-third of his thrusts?" He smiled at Mayne. "Would you say that the assassin had a significant knowledge of the anatomy of the human body?"

"You mean the killer was a doctor?" I exclaimed.

"Well," Mayne said with a sweeping wave of his hand, "if it's a doctor you're looking for, Lon, take your pick. The case is swarming with them."

31

This Most Arrant of Dogberrys

For the first two weeks of February, so long as the inquest continued, Coroner Edward Downes Connery held center stage in the Burdell affair. He eclipsed the victim and Mrs. Cunningham/Burdell, on whom he labored mightily to cast suspicion for the foul deed. He even managed to elbow the district attorney, A. Oakey Hall, out of the light, which wasn't easy because Hall kept elbowing back.

Connery's most spectacular bungling resulted from his uncanny ability to shove his foot into his mouth, but his more costly errors were caused by his appalling ignorance of the law. Quinncannon's strategy was to dignify the proceedings as little as possible by refusing to take part in them, though occasionally he couldn't help himself. Example:

THE CORONER: Did you ever hear Mrs. Cunningham threaten the doctor?

HANNAH CONLAN: Yes. Once she said it was time he was out of the world for he was not fit to live in it.

THE CORONER: Aha! I knew, Hannah, I knew that you carried your tail behind you, by gracious!

MR. QUINNCANNON: Excuse me. Did I hear you say that you knew Mrs. Conlan carried her tail behind her?

THE CORONER: Uh, yes, sir, that is what I said.

MR. QUINNCANNON: Thank you, Mr. Coroner. You understand, I wish my notes to be precise. That seems to me a significant remark. (Laughter.)

The joke was that Connery was forever requiring witnesses to repeat testimony for the benefit of the press. He wanted, he said, their "notes to be precise," particularly when the evidence was detrimental to Mrs. Cunningham's cause. What the coroner meant to convey was that Hannah "carried her tail behind her" as opposed to between her legs—that is, that she had the courage to repeat her employer's threat. But the newspapers found his comment off-color and in poor taste.

Connery's treatment of Daniel Ullman also drew fire from the press. Ullman, who had barely trafficked with his fellow boarders at 31 Bond, was a most respectable man, a leading lawyer, and recent Know-Nothing party candidate for governor in a campaign he'd nearly won. His alibi was airtight and his knowledge of the crime amounted to absolutely nothing but, as he'd been called as a witness anyway, he insisted on reading a lengthy statement into the record, much to the coroner's irritation. Connery prolonged the agony with a constant rattle of petty questions and non sequiturs, all the while feverishly scribbling notes, and then demanded that Ullman inscribe his name to the notes. The witness offered instead his written statement, but this didn't satisfy the coroner who wanted his own interrupting irrelevancies in the record.

Ullman was clearly anxious to escape. He said he would sign. The coroner brightened. "Yes, sir. You may depend upon it as much as if it was *verbatim et literatim.* [Laughter.] If you are hung, Mr. Ullman, I will be the executioner. [Laughter.]"

The Honorable Ullman was gracious to the end, though he bit down hard on his lip. "Well, sir, so pleasant a gentleman would perform an execution in an exceedingly gentle manner—no doubt of it, sir."

The newspapers were not so gracious. They considered Connery rude and insulting. The *Herald,* for example, thought that the coroner's attack on a politician of Ullman's credentials was "the assault of a gnat upon an eagle." And the press wasn't through with Connery yet.

Not that the coroner cut a ridiculous figure on his face. He was, in fact, a rather handsome man of perhaps forty-five with high cheekbones, a straight, only slightly bulbous nose, and a square jaw embraced by a short hedge of black beard. His mouth smiled readily enough, especially at his own jokes, and his lips were wide and full. Too often they were full of his oversized feet. To a witness who, without a jot of proof, accused Emma of having once been a loose woman, Connery asked, "Ever give her the wink yourself?" When one of the doctor's friends quoted Burdell as having spied on Eckel through Emma's keyhole "not dressed as he should have been," the coroner leered, "Dressed in a state of nature, like Timon of Athens?" ("With his nightgown on," explained the patient witness.) A reference to Eckel's canaries brought this bon mot: "Yes, he was a bit of a bird himself!" And when the cook testified that Helen Cunningham had said she watched her mother and Burdell through his keyhole—keyholes having apparently the same fascination for these people as keys —Connery smirked, "Aha! She wanted a peep at the elephant, eh?" (A "peep at the elephant" meant a look at the "great world" outside one's normal experience.)

Whatever Helen saw through the keyhole, however, was hardly outside her normal experience. There had been a time, by my reckoning, when Helen was sleeping with Snodgrass, Eckel was sleeping with Emma, Emma with Burdell, Burdell with Demis, Demis with me, Eckel with Mrs. Prosser—the sexual arithmetic became higher mathematics.

As day followed day in a parade of meaningless witnesses, the reporters went from annoyance at Connery's feeble struggles for cheap laughs to stinging outrage at his clumsy efforts to incriminate Eckel and Mrs. Burdell (as we were now referring to our client). The coroner was catching hell from every side. The *Times* bemoaned his "most extraordinary unfitness for his position." The *Tribune* labeled him "silly, ignorant, incompetent." The *Herald* said he had "the knowledge of a hedge-school-master and the perspicacity of a beadle . . . a bad heart, a loose tongue, a limited intellect and a coarse nature." To the *Sun* he was simply "this most arrant of Dogberrys."

Quinncannon's strategy was working wonderfully. Before the inquest began he told me that Connery would be our staunchest ally. All we needed to do was give him his head and get out of his way. I'll admit to some early doubts when, for the first four days of hearings, the newspapers reported the coroner's inquisition uncritically, and published every vicious rumor and imaginary scandal they could dig up to smear Emma, Eckel, and even poor Snodgrass. In truth the press seemed already to have tried and convicted the butcher and our client. When I informed Quinncannon that I thought it an error to permit Connery's evidence and his innuendoes to go before the public unchallenged, he merely smiled and said, "Have a little faith in the coroner, Toby. His indiscretion is surpassed only by his ineptitude."

The blunder that initially turned the press against Connery actually occurred on the first day of the inquest though it went unreported until the fourth. On that Saturday the coroner had ordered both Eckel and Snodgrass stripped and searched for blood or scratches—any sign they had been engaged in a recent struggle. The searches were carried out by a physician and a deputy sheriff, and nothing incriminating was found. Thus frustrated, Connery had required a strip-search also of Mrs. Cunningham, conducted by the same two gentlemen. True, the doctor was, well, a doctor, but the deputy was only a deputy and the newspapers discovered belatedly that they were infuriated over this gross affront to Emma's privacy.

Stung by these attacks on his insensitivity to a lady's modesty, the coroner fought to regain his dignity, but as the fellow had none, the effort was doomed. Connery produced several letters he had received suggesting that the "image of the murderer will inevitably be retained on the retina of the victim's eye, so that an examination of Dr. Burdell's eye will bring forth certain proofs of the identity of his assassin." This daring experiment the coroner now proposed to assay. The reporters questioned several doctors present and learned that the entire idea was "scientifically impossible and absurd as Mr. Connery, being a physician himself, ought to have known," and we all had another good laugh on the coroner.

The unquashable Connery was back the next morning with yet one more letter that "bore investigation." "SIR: Wishing to assist in the ends of justice, I beg to state that a lady dreamed twice last night that Mrs. Cunningham had left the house early on the morning of the murder, met Mr. Eckel at a bathhouse, and there washed off together some offensive marks on their body. [sic.] This is perhaps all nonsense, but it may lead to some opening."

It was signed "JUSTICE."

Having handed out copies of this momentous document to the press, Connery summoned his first witness, a clairvoyant calling herself Mrs. Seymore, unrelated to the aforementioned "dreaming lady," whose evidence failed to satisfy the coroner, and whom he therefore committed to the Tombs in lieu of $1000 bail. Numerous "witnesses" were already in jail by Connery's courtesy because they could not raise $1000. Most of them were women, including Hannah Conlan, though she'd sworn she'd held nothing back and, "If I knew more I would tell it if I was to go to the gallows for it."

Quinncannon commented to a couple of reporters that the practice of "imprisoning witnesses because they cannot lay their hands on ten hundred-dollar notes, while regrettably within the coroner's powers, seems counterproductive. If there is one soul in this city with information which might solve this mystery, why should he dare come forth and risk the bridewell at the coroner's whim?"

The next morning the papers were off and baying once more at Connery's heels.

The angrier the press became at Connery, the more sympathetic they acted toward Emma, Eckel, and little Snodgrass. All three had been kept incommunicado since the murder—the two men in prison, the woman under house arrest with her daughters—though no charges had been brought against any of them. Snodgrass and Eckel were denied legal counsel and Mrs. Cunningham had been permitted to speak with her attorneys only once, on the day the crime was discovered. Connery, though blatantly exceeding his authority, had failed utterly to find one scrap of evidence against the house's occupants. The newspapers were thirsting for the coroner's blood. Public opinion, in one short week, had swung completely behind Mrs. Cunningham and her fellow suspects. Quinncannon prepared his master stroke.

32

Habeas Corpus

On the afternoon of Friday, February 6, Quinncannon and I became the attorneys of record for John J. Eckel and George Snodgrass as well as Emma Burdell. That same afternoon we applied to Judge John Brady of the New York Common Pleas for writs of habeas corpus requiring the coroner to produce Eckel and Snodgrass before Brady's court on Saturday morning and, at the same time, to issue a return on the writs explaining on what grounds the two men had been imprisoned.

On Saturday morning we obtained a similar writ for Emma, returnable within one hour. During the midday recess two more writs were issued for Augusta and Helen Cunningham so that, by Saturday afternoon, Quinncannon had snatched control of all five of Connery's murder "suspects" from him and assembled them in the courthouse under Brady's protection.

The two men had been committed to the Tombs by the coroner on February 4. The order to the warden on Snodgrass read as follows:

> The Keeper of the City Prison and Bridewell will keep for examination the body of George Snodgrass, until further notice, apart from any other witness.

The order on Eckel was slightly different:

> The Keeper of the City Prison and Bridewell will keep for examination the body of John J. Eckel until further notice.

Snodgrass, you see, had specifically been held as a witness. In Eckel's case it was not apparent whether Connery held him as a witness or a "party" to the crime—that is, as a suspect.

Quinncannon's argument was simple enough. If Eckel was only a witness then the coroner had no authority to confine him once he had posted the $1000 bond, and he must be freed from jail at once—as must Snodgrass who was obviously merely a witness by Connery's own wording of his order. *However,* if Eckel *was* a suspect, then he could not also be a witness at the inquest since a man could not be compelled to testify against himself.

Snodgrass had already twice been questioned by the coroner without saying anything harmful to himself, or Emma or Eckel. He had no value to Connery as a witness and no credibility as a suspect. I argued first for his release and won it easily. Then, following Quinncannon's suggestions, I put it to Judge Brady that Eckel's circumstances were the same as those of Snodgrass. The butcher was also detained as witness—not party—and, as we were prepared to post his bail, he must be turned loose. Connery reacted exactly as Quinncannon had predicted. He stated that Eckel was held as party to the murder. The judge immediately ordered, at my request, that Connery be prohibited from calling the butcher as a witness. Since the coroner had failed, up to then, to question Eckel, that opportunity was now lost to him forever.

During the noon recess someone must have pointed out to Connery that he had twice been badly outmaneuvered. He had lost Snodgrass as a suspect and Eckel as a witness, and he was likely to lose Emma in the same manner. Accordingly, that afternoon, he amended his order detaining her. She was being held under house arrest "as a material witness . . . and on the suspicion of being implicated in the murder, or death by violence, of Dr. Harvey Burdell."

Said the judge, "I do not see how it is possible for me to pass upon the character of this commitment. It seems to be twofold."

The district attorney replied, "It is so. It is what is called a duplicity."

Quinncannon looked up from his papers and smiled. "Duplicity is the term we would use," he said.

Brady shook his head. "I am very much disposed to send it back to the coroner to have it made specific."

"If the court please." Quinncannon got to his feet ever so slowly. "My associate, Mr. Brendon, has already argued (without, I think, refutation by the learned district attorney, Mr. Hall) that under the Second Revised Statutes, fourth edition, section six, page 925, the coroner has no legal power to confine witnesses, and no legal power to detain suspects until *after* an inquest jury has ruled that someone has come to his death by foul means. Despite the fact that the coroner's jury has not yet issued its verdict, we have nevertheless yielded to the point of allowing Mr. Eckel to remain in custody so long as he is protected from giving evidence. But now, Your Honor, the blundering incompetence of Mr. Edward Downes Connery offends this court and strains its patience to the breaking point."

Judge Brady peered down with an offended expression sour with impatience, and nodded.

"The coroner's return on the status of Mrs. Burdell is ludicrous on its face," Quinncannon continued. "His disdain for her constitutional rights is exceeded only by his barbarous ignorance of the law. He wishes to force her to submit, in the guise of interrogation, to his idle speculations in regard to anything that may have occurred to her from her birth up to this hour, without the smallest concern for relevance or substantiation, in the vain hope that some scrap of an answer may escape her which he can snatch up to bolster the bogus charges he is determined to bring against her.

"I could, of course, ask for her immediate, unqualified release, arguing that Mr. Connery's 'duplicity'—as Mr. Hall correctly labels it—is an affront to this court and repugnant alike to the law and to the feelings of all honest men." (I glanced at the press section. The reporters were scribbling their shorthand frantically, recording every word.) "However, I would not have it said that Mrs. Burdell was discharged on a legal technicality, egregious as it is, resulting from the crass stupidity of Coroner Connery. Confident as we are of the final result, we have no wish that our client appear to escape only because of the miserable, the wretched, the contemptible, the disgraceful bungling of this official who has given us yet another written evidence of his blockheadedness, as though it were not already the poorest kept secret in the city."

("Here laughter and applause broke out among the spectators who crowded into every corner of the room," noted one of the papers. "Even Judge Brady was observed suppressing a smile.")

"I therefore ask that the court be adjourned for an hour," resumed Quinncannon, "with directions in the meantime to the coroner that he is no longer to trifle with the court, but that he must make a specific return, and take one ground or the other in reference to Mrs. Burdell."

We had no hope that Emma, any more than Eckel, could escape being charged with Burdell's murder. By forcing Connery to identify them as suspects, however, we could prevent him from requiring them to give injurious, perhaps even self-incriminating, testimony. In his reply to Brady the coroner had no choice but to reassert that Emma was a party. She went back to 31 Bond in police custody and Eckel returned to the Tombs, both now safe from Connery's clutches. It was afterward a simple matter to obtain freedom for the Cunningham daughters who, even the coroner acknowledged, were not under suspicion.

Outside the courthouse the crowd had dispersed and the sun had long ago set when Quinncannon made his last motion. "I ask Your Honor to order that Mrs. Burdell and Mr. Eckel have the right to consult with counsel whenever they please, and that they enjoy that right without the august presence of our great magnate, the coroner, any of his officials, his policemen, or his dignified son John." (Laughter.)

Brady said he supposed no one would contest that "that is a constitutional right that ought not to be interfered with in the slightest degree."

The Irishman turned to the district attorney. "There is no dispute about that, Mr. Hall?"

"Not the least, sir," Hall answered quickly. "I suppose the coroner would have a common-law right to keep witnesses, *quoad* witnesses, apart, but—" He must have seen Quinncannon's eyebrow go up, because he interrupted his half-hearted defense of Connery, and, with an eye on the reporters, "Your Honor, I wish it understood that I was not connected with or responsible for these proceedings. Your Honor knows that I have my sphere of duties and the coroner has his—and that I have not interfered with him in any way whatever."

So desperate was Hall to dissociate himself from Connery that Quinncannon took pity on him. "I never thought of holding you responsible for such outrageous proceedings as have been had before the coroner. I'm certain that you would never have sanctioned such a circus, Mr. Hall."

When the room had cleared I sat alone with the Irishman while we smoked. I remarked we had done a good day's work. "But one thing still bothers me, Lon."

He gave me a tired smile. "Only one?"

"I don't understand the wisdom or the necessity of taking on the defense of Eckel. Never mind Snodgrass—he's of no consequence—but I would have thought we had our hands full with Emma. To be frank, I considered that throwing the crime on Eckel was our best chance of getting Emma off."

"Do you believe Eckel is guilty?"

"Very possibly," I answered. "Whoever killed Burdell was a powerful man. That leaves Snodgrass out, and Eckel was the only other man in the place. If he's innocent then the killer must have come from outside the house and then escaped through a door locked and bolted from inside."

"Perhaps," he offered, "the door was bolted after the murderer escaped."

"An accomplice? But, who?"

He shrugged. "It might have been any or all of them."

"Or," I said stubbornly, "it might have been Eckel."

"Eckel had no motive."

"Yes he did. Mrs. Cunningham—" I stopped short.

"Exactly," he said grimly. "Eckel had nothing *directly, himself* to gain by Burdell's death. If he killed him it was for Emma's sake. The butcher was sleeping with the widow. He disguised himself to look like Burdell and, together with Augusta, they conspired to fake the marriage. After he murdered the dentist, she produced the certificate, planning to claim the estate, and either pay Eckel off or marry him."

"Do you think that's what happened?"

He waved his hand. "Never mind what I think. That will be the theory presented by Hall to the jury. That is one reason why we must represent them both in this case. A second reason is that it is essential that they be tried separately. Another attorney might not agree to sever Eckel's trial from Emma's, or might attempt to prove Eckel's innocence at Emma's expense. But if we can separate their cases, the state will have to try her first, as the principal, precisely because unless she's convicted they can prove no motive for Eckel. Whatever other evidence they may bring against Emma, they'll never convince a jury that she could have overpowered Burdell by herself, and once she's acquitted Eckel won't have to stand trial at all."

I could not help smiling. "You make it all sound so simple, as though a jury had already found her not guilty."

He returned my smile. "Trust me, Toby. Obtaining her acquittal is the least of our problems." By now I was used to his cryptic remarks and I knew better than to question him about them. I refrained from asking him what more serious difficulties he foresaw.

He stood and stretched long arms over his head. "I suggest we search out two tenderloins and a couple of pints, and get some sleep. I've arranged with George Walling to interview several witnesses tomorrow at my rooms and I want you there."

I was preparing to follow him when he turned. "Toby, you told me you had considered casting doubt on Eckel's innocence to save Emma. I assume, at that time, you believed Eckel guilty."

I started to reply but he held up his hand. "As attorneys, lad, we may have to defend the guilty, but we never need to convict the innocent. But, of course, you know that."

Well, I thought, I do now.

33

A Clergyman
and Yet Another Doctor

In his rooms Quinncannon settled into one of the two leather wingback chairs that flanked the fireplace, motioning his guest to take the other. It was his custom to conduct interviews with important witnesses in the warm comfort of his sitting room. The aroma of rich tobaccos and burning piny wood was in marked contrast to the threatening clamminess of the Police Office, and the authorities invariably barked their most innocuous questions while the Irishman put even his sharpest interrogatories in a soothing brogue.

I sat beside the gaming table, removed my notebook, accepted a Scotch. Quinncannon poured an Irish for himself. Our visitor preferred sherry.

He was Reverend Uriah Marvine, the Dutch Reformed minister of Bleeker Street, who had, it was claimed, married Harvey Burdell to Emma Cunningham. He was not a bad-looking man, in his mid-forties, with mild gray eyes and a pointed goatee. Thick, dark hair receded from his forehead and curled round his ears, and there was a substantial paunch beneath his tightly buttoned waistcoat. He said a man and a woman had come to his house on October 28 to be married. They were accompanied by "a young lady of about twenty-one."

He'd seen Emma since and could not identify her at all. He'd also been shown the corpse of Burdell and been taken to the Tombs to see Eckel, and he could not swear to either man as the bridegroom. Burdell "looked a little like him around the mouth," but the dentist's beard was "too full, too high on his face." As for Eckel, he seemed "too small," but then Marvine couldn't even remember if the man he married had a moustache or whether he was going bald.

"When I visited Mr. Eckel in prison he was wearing a wig," the minister volunteered. "The police made him take it off."

"Did you recognize him without the wig?" Quinncannon asked.

"It is my impression that the man I married had more hair than Eckel without the wig, but less hair than Eckel with the wig."

For some inane reason I noted that remark.

"How many times did this man come to see you, Reverend?"

"Three times. On the twenty-seventh he came to arrange for the ceremony. On the twenty-ninth he came for the certificate."

"Are you absolutely certain that *the same man* visited you on all three occasions?"

Marvine looked startled. "Why, yes. That is—I believe it was the same man."

"You have identified the certificate found in Mrs. Burdell's possession as the one you executed?"

"Yes, sir."

"Is your church one which requires the couple being married to sign such a document?"

"No, sir. Some churches do but the Reformed Dutch does not."

"Neither party signed any paper for you?"

"That is correct."

"When you made out the certificate, how did you spell the groom's name?"

"Well," Marvine replied, "at first I thought it was spelled B-E-R-D-E-L-L, but later I happened to be passing the house—31 Bond—with my wife, and I saw the nameplate and realized it was spelled B-*U*-R-D-E-L-L, and I told my wife I must hurry home and change the spelling in my registry book, which I did."

"But you did not alter the certificate?"

"No, for, you see, I no longer had it."

"When the gentleman called for the certificate did he read it?"

"Yes, he did, and pronounced it satisfactory."

"Would you say he read it carefully?"

"He took his time."

"Did he mention that you had misspelled his name?"

Marvine thought about it. "Why, no, he never did." After a moment he added, "He did say one odd thing, but that was after the ceremony."

"Odd?"

"Yes, Mr. Quinncannon. He requested me to keep the wedding a secret."

The Irishman nodded. "Were you asked by the police whether you could identify the young lady who was present during the ceremony?"

"I was, and thought I could not, as I had paid but little attention to her. But when they brought Miss Augusta Cunningham to me I knew her right off."

"You identified her positively?"

"I did, yes, sir."

"No hesitation?"

"None whatever," Marvine said firmly.

We were alone for a few minutes waiting for the next witness. I said, "Well, where does that leave us?"

Quinncannon shrugged. "For one thing it definitely places Emma at Marvine's house being married to someone on October 28th."

"Even though he can't identify her?"

"He can identify Augusta, and he can identify the certificate found in Emma's possession. That's good enough."

"All right," I conceded, "but who was the man with her?"

"Ah, Toby, *that* we don't know . . . yet." He was thumbing through some papers on his lap.

"Lon," I said, "why did you ask Marvine if the man who visited him three times was the same man?"

"Did I?" There was a brief pause. "No particular reason. I just wanted to see how the question might sound to a jury."

Dr. Alvah Blaisdell was the closest thing to a friend and confidant Harvey Burdell had ever had. He was a plump, fleecy-haired, pink-cheeked gentleman of about fifty—an aging cherub whose soft smile and bright blue eyes could easily calm a frightened child or reassure a nervous hypochondriac. I had watched him seated in the dentist's chair at the inquest and pitied his discomfort, so grievously out of his element did he appear in that house of horrors. Even in the pleasant atmosphere of Quinncannon's chamber, with a glass of port clutched in his pudgy hands, Blaisdell seemed as jittery as a white rabbit.

One topic, however, could fire him up. "I *told* Dr. Burdell to get rid of that woman. I told him many, *many* times!"

The dentist had complained of Mrs. Cunningham constantly. "He said she was a cruel and clever woman who would not rest until she had her claws on his house and his money."

"Did he ever mention a marriage to her?"

"Good God, no! He'd have sooner been drawn and quartered!"

Blaisdell had last visited his friend on the day of his death. "He said she had stolen some vital papers from him and would not return them. I again advised him to get rid of her. He said he had taken steps against her—had drawn up a paper which would force her out of the house and made her sign it. He told me he was afraid for his life, Mr. Quinncannon. He dared not leave the house lest they get into his rooms and go through his private papers and learn his secrets. He said that, lately, when he was working at his desk, they would open the door from the hall and peer in at him, but when he turned to see what was wanted they would go away. On that Friday he said there had been trouble the previous Saturday."

"What sort of trouble?" Quinncannon asked, as though he didn't know.

"He had gone out and when he came home that night they had closed the shutters and locked the door against him. He became very angry and berated them for shutting him out of his own house, and they treated him shamefully and cursed him, saying he ought to have his head broke."

"Who did he say cursed him?"

"Mrs. Cunningham and her elder daughter and Eckel—and Snodgrass too I suppose. He informed me they had threatened to take his life and he was terrified they would do so."

"Did you yourself ever hear such threats being made?"

"No," Blaisdell admitted. "I know only what he told me. But he *was* petrified, sir. On the Friday he died he asked me to come and stay with him."

"To spend the night?"

"No, sir, to move in and live with him. He wished me to stay until the first of May. After that date, he said, Mrs. Cunningham would have to vacate and he would be safe."

"What was your response?"

"I told him the idea was impossible. I could not do it. I did agree to return that evening at seven o'clock and remain through the night, but circumstances prevented me."

Quinncannon raised an eyebrow. "What circumstances?"

"Well," the doctor began sheepishly, "there have been a great many garroters about after dark on the streets. There were two cases reported in the papers that morning and I . . . thought it unwise to venture forth in the evening."

"Did you send word to Dr. Burdell not to expect you?"

"No." The answer was barely audible.

The Irishman relaxed in his chair and extracted his pipe and pouch. "Aside from the persons in the house, Doctor, did Harvey Burdell have any enemies?"

"There was difficulty with his brothers from time to time."

"What caused these difficulties?"

"Money, Mr. Quinncannon, always money. Dr. Burdell was one of the most pecuniary men I ever met. To his eye a penny was as large as a dollar is to other men. He could spit on a nickel and give you four cents change."

"Did Burdell make a will?"

Blaisdell chose his words carefully. "He showed me a document which he said was his will. This was at his house on Tuesday, the twenty-seventh of January—a few days before his death."

"How did this conversation arise?"

"I had been after him to make a will for five or six years, sir. Although he then seemed in robust health, he suffered from blood on the heart—apoplexy, you understand—and I had always supposed he would pass away suddenly. Knowing his family —how litigious they were—I thought a will was a wise precaution."

"Did you speak of its contents?" the Irishman asked from a billow of tobacco smoke.

"I admit to some curiosity. I inquired about his brother James, knowing there had been bad feeling and James was in want. He said James was provided for, and also his nephew Matthew with whom he had had some trouble. There was a bequest for his half-sister and even one for his brother William, which astonished me. Dr. Burdell said he had reconciled with William and it was now all right between them."

"And how much did he leave to Mrs. Cunningham?"

"Nothing," Blaisdell answered.

"Not a ha'penny, eh?" Quinncannon did not appear surprised. "Of course, Doctor, you have only Burdell's word that he made such a will."

"I saw it, sir."

"But you did not handle it yourself?"

"No."

"Or read it?"

"No," Blaisdell admitted.

"Aside from the will, did the doctor discuss any other private papers with you?"

"He mentioned a contract he had with Mrs. Cunningham by which she agreed to leave the house on May 1st. He told me she had signed it but was now giving him a great deal of trouble over it. It had something to do with his refusing to marry her."

"He said he had refused to marry her?"

"He did indeed, sir."

Quinncannon nodded. "Did Dr. Burdell ever carry a knife?"

Blaisdell laughed. "He wouldn't have had the courage to use it."

"He was a timid man?"

"I don't believe he would have fought a boy over the age of ten." Blaisdell leaned forward and lowered his voice. "He was, Mr. Quinncannon, a cowardly fellow at heart and the weakest man for his physical size I ever knew."

At the Irishman's signal two constables came to escort Blaisdell out of the room, but one of them remained and handed Quinncannon some writing. "This is a facsimile of a paper found at the murder house last night, sir. It had slipped down behind one of the drawers in Eckel's desk. Captain Walling says to tell you you never saw it and you and me never had this conversation."

He vanished and Quinncannon read the document while his mouth tightened at the corners and one eyebrow arched wickedly. Then he gave it to me. I reproduce it in full:

GENERAL RELEASE

To all whom these presents shall come or may concern, greeting: Know ye, that I, Mrs. *E.A. Cunningham,* for and in consideration of the sum of one dollar, lawful money of the United States of America, to me in hand paid by *Harvey Burdell* of the City and County of New York, have remised, released, and forever discharged, and by these presents do, for myself, my heirs, executors and administrators, remise, release, and forever discharge the said *Harvey Burdell,* his heirs, executors and administrators, of and from all manner of action and actions, cause and causes of actions, suits, debts, dues, sums of money accounts, reckonings, bonds, bills, specialties, covenants, contracts, controversies, agreements, promises, variences, trespasses, damages, judgments, extents, executions, claims and demands whatsoever, in law or in equity, which against him I ever had, now have, or which my heirs, executors, administrators hereafter can, shall, or may have, for, upon, or by reason of any matter, cause, or thing whatsoever, from the beginning of the world to the day of the date of these presents.

I do agree to quit claim and surrender the premises I now occupy, No. 31 Bond street, on the first day of May next, and to pay the rent to said *Burdell* up to that day.

In witness whereof I have hereunto set my hand and seal, the twenty-fourth day of January in the year eighteen hundred and fifty seven. Sealed and delivered in the presence of

E.A. Cunningham (L.S.)

A line was drawn across the page below this in lead pencil and beneath that appeared Burdell's signature and a note from Captain Walling: "Both signatures undoubtedly genuine."

When I looked up Quinncannon was watching me narrowly. I said, "What does it mean?"

"Why don't you tell me, Toby?"

I reread the document. "Obviously this release postdates all other agreements between them. She gave up the suits for defamation and breach of promise, and the right to prosecute for rape. She even binds herself to vacate the house in May after going to so much trouble to avoid it, and all," I shook my head, "all for one dollar."

"Anything else strike you as strange?"

"Well, she signed it only six days before he was killed. And it wasn't found among Burdell's papers, but in John Eckel's desk. That suggests she, or Eckel, removed it from Burdell's safe, possibly after the murder." A new idea hit me. "Lon, Burdell was sure Emma had a key to his safe, and it was found open when the body was discovered. Everyone has assumed the doctor opened it himself because papers and his bankbook were on his desk. But isn't it conceivable the safe was unlocked by someone else, *after* the murder?"

"Mrs. Cunningham?"

"Possibly," I said. "Others of his papers have been found in Eckel's secretary. Suppose they killed Burdell—then took what they wanted from the safe and placed other items on his desk to create the impression he had been surprised by the killer while working there?" I paused. "That theory doesn't help our case, of course, but—" I left my thought unfinished.

"A key to his safe *was* found among her things," the Irishman said.

"Then she could have opened it."

"No, Toby. It was the key to the old lock. Burdell had the safe lock changed in September after he accused her of theft for a second time."

"Still," I argued, "if she'd stolen one key she might have stolen a second." I fixed on his eyes. "Are we defending two guilty clients, Lon?"

"I haven't given that question much consideration," he replied quietly, "and I suggest that you do not dwell on it either."

34

The Shadow Man

Catherine Stansbury, a handsome woman in her forties, had known Burdell for twenty years. She took a chair, declined a glass of wine, and told Quinncannon that the idea she should lease the dentist's house from him had originated with her in conversation in November. "He was very pleased with the notion and spoke of it many times to my husband afterward. I think he was afraid we might change our minds."

"When did you settle on the arrangements?" he inquired.

"On the Friday of his death, although I suppose we had really agreed in principle on January 12th. I came to see him and said my husband would take the house on the first of May if we could be certain that Mrs. Cunningham would be gone. The doctor said she would be. It was with that understanding that I returned on January 30th with my mother to go through the premises and fix on a sum."

She had inspected the apartments without seeing any of the Cunningham menagerie, and then retired to the front parlor with Burdell to discuss specific terms. "He informed me there would be no difficulty with Mrs. Cunningham as he had obtained a release from her in the past week in which she promised to vacate. He said he was keeping it close as she had before stolen papers from his safe and he did not trust her."

"Did he speak of her having duplicate keys?"

Mrs. Stansbury nodded. "He believed she had a key to his safe and other keys that opened the hall doors to his rooms. He was quite convinced of it."

"Did he say anything else about her, madam?"

"Well, he told me she was a scheming woman who would stop at nothing to get his money—that she had deluded him into thinking she was rich. He said she thought he was an old bachelor worth hundreds of thousands, who didn't know his own mind, and she was determined to marry him, but he would sooner be dead."

Quinncannon eyed her. "That was his exact phrase?"

"Yes, sir. He would sooner be dead."

"You came to an understanding on the terms of the lease?"

"Yes, on Friday afternoon. He was to draw up the papers and my husband and I were to return the next morning to sign them."

"Why didn't you come back on Saturday as agreed?"

She waved a gloved hand. "The weather was very boisterous, and my husband thought the matter would wait, as we were not to take possession for three months."

The Irishman sat gnawing on the stem of a dead pipe for a few moments. "On Friday, did Burdell show you the release he said he'd obtained from Mrs. Cunningham?"

"No, sir. But I took it he had it about his person."

"Why did you form that conclusion?"

"Why, he said he kept it close, and when he spoke of it he patted the breast pocket of his coat."

"Do you know whether Mrs. Cunningham was aware of the purpose of your visit?"

"I suspect she was, sir. I would not be surprised if she heard us discussing the house."

He leaned forward. "Was the parlor door open?"

"It was not," Mrs. Stansbury replied, "but when my mother

and I prepared to leave the doctor said, 'When you go into the hall you will find her on the stairs,' and as I opened the door Mrs. Cunningham was on the staircase."

We waited for the last of the witnesses to be escorted up. I said, "What troubles you?"

"The release," he responded, refilling our glasses. "Did you know that Demis Hubbard has told the police Burdell showed it to her on Saturday, January 24th?"

I shook my head.

"That was the evening of the day it was executed. He displayed it at her rooms. He asked her to keep it for him but she claims she did not."

"And you don't believe her?" I ventured.

"Consider," he said, "Emma had just signed it and Burdell obviously did not want to put it in his safe for fear she'd steal it back. If Demis *did* take it from him, then. . . ."

"Then how," I finished, "did it get into Eckel's desk?"

"Exactly, Toby. And who drew it up? Unlike all the other papers exchanged by Emma and the doctor throughout this affair, this document was not drafted by either of them. Only a lawyer could have composed such verbose and convoluted prose."

For some reason I reacted defensively. "I had nothing to do with it."

He observed me over the rim of his glass. "It never entered my mind, lad," he replied mildly.

Our final interview was with Cyrenius Stevens, an elderly gentleman, "retired from business," and a long time acquaintance of Burdell whose wife, Sophronia, was the dentist's patient. He gazed wearily at Quinncannon through bifocals, ran the tip of one index finger under a white, military moustache, and proclaimed that he was willing to do his duty as a citizen, the Lord knew, but the matter was becoming *most* tedious and, "not being

an entirely well man," he would appreciate getting at once to the
point.

Quinncannon gave him a Scotch. "What occurred in early October of last year between yourself and Mrs. Cunningham?"

"I received a message that Harvey Burdell wished to see me at
his home at once. It did not ring true. I could imagine no reason
for such an urgent request. I am sixty-seven, sir, and no longer
leave my house except on rare occasions."

"Did you eventually go to Bond Street?"

"Yes, the next morning, as I thought on reflection there might
be something to it. I was brought to the back parlor and had only
just taken my seat when a lady came in, took a seat near me, and
called me by name. She said she had sent for me, not Dr. Burdell."

"This was Mrs. Cunningham?" I asked.

The old gentleman nodded. "She said my wife was having an
affair with the doctor and had filched money from me and made
use of Burdell to deposit it in some bank for her. I told her I
would think on the matter and see her again, but I did not.
I believed it was all out of whole cloth and considered that she
had great nerve. I thought she wanted to make a tool of me by
working up my feelings against Dr. Burdell. I thought her motive was to ruin Burdell's character and get possession of his
money."

"What made you think so?" the Irishman said.

"Not long before, the doctor had visited my wife and myself
and complained about Mrs. Cunningham. He said a man was
living there who appeared to be a kind of beau to her, and, said
he, 'I have worked hard and got a good deal of money and now
I am actually afraid to stay in my own house.' I remarked to him,
'Why don't you get the people out of your house?' He said he
could not because he had let it till the first of May to Mrs. Cunningham. 'Then,' says I, 'why don't you leave the house? You are
a man of means—I would not stay if I feared for my life.' He said
he was very cautious, and thought he would stay till May and get
the house clear."

"This 'beau,'" I interrupted. "Did the doctor mention his name?"

"John J. Eckel," Stevens answered. "He appeared very frightened of them both."

"Tell us," Quinncannon said, "about the shadow man."

"Yes, well, that is what I call him because he was always careful to stay in the shadows where he could not easily be seen. On the Saturday after my conversation with Mrs. Cunningham a gentleman called and wanted to see me. He said his business was from Mrs. Cunningham. He said she had sent him to ask me to come up and see her. He said he was her counsel. He had got her, he said, out of some pretty serious scrapes. I asked him if he knew what her business was with me. He said he did not know particularly. I asked him if he knew nothing about it. He represented that she was a wonderful, persevering, smart woman, and always accomplished all she undertook. He said she had money, and plenty of men around her who never failed her. He said his name was Van Dolan, that he was a lawyer, and that his office was at number 118 Chambers Street. But there is no Van Dolan in the city directory of lawyers. I became curious and went down to Chambers Street the next day but could not find such a name or any such office."

"Did you discuss any of this with Burdell?"

"I did, a few days later. The doctor said there was nothing between my wife and himself, and I believed him. My wife, Mr. Quinncannon, is thirty-five years younger than I am. I trusted her when we were wed and I trust her now. But an old man may be made the butt of a bad joke, and I am a careful fellow. I did not know but what some scheme or plot might have been laid for me."

The Irishman became pensive. "I realize this man, Van Dolan, remained in shadow, Mr. Stevens, but could you venture a description?"

"He had a beard," Stevens responded. It occurred to me that every man involved in the case, except George Snodgrass, had a beard.

DR. CATLIN

DR. UHL

MR. ECKEL

DR. BURDELL

The Irishman took up an envelope and removed some pieces of paper. I could see they were woodcut portraits of several men that had been drawn for *Frank Leslie's Illustrated Newspaper*. One by one he handed them to the witness with a request to study them carefully and report any similarities with the mysterious "Van Dolan." Stevens adjusted his bifocals and peered at each face intently.

"Not this fellow—his beard is too thick and dark," returning a picture of Harvey Burdell. "Not this one either—entirely too young, and he wears no beard." He was speaking of Snodgrass. "Now, it *might* have been this gentleman." He was studying Eckel's features. "The beard is as I remember it, but the hairline is too high. Of course I have heard it said he wore a wig. As I recall, Mr. Quinncannon, his hair in front curled up into a sort of cock's comb, much like these two men." He was now holding portraits of Doctors Uhl and Catlin. "I might say *this* fellow if he had a moustache and his beard was heavier"—referring to Catlin —"but, on the whole, if you forced me to select one, I should guess that *this* man"—indicating Uhl—"is 'Van Dolan.' " He paused. "It *could* well be this man, however." He was again looking at Catlin.

"Would you swear to that, sir?" I asked, and the old man smiled sadly.

"I would not, young fellow. My eyesight is quite as poor as my memory. Why, sitting in the shadow, as you are now, I'm not certain I could identify *you* ten minutes hence."

When Cyrenius Stevens was gone I observed he would be of very little value to our case as a witness.

Quinncannon collected his clippings from *Leslie's*. "Why do you think so, Toby?"

To me it was obvious. "He can't identify anyone. According to his testimony almost any of these men could have been 'Van Dolan.' "

He smiled with one corner of his mouth. "Exactly," he said.

I was too tired to persue the conversation. I finished my whiskey, stood and yawned, and announced I was ready for an early supper and a long night of sleep, but the Irishman only shook his head.

"Not tonight, lad. I will need you tonight."

I dropped back into the chair with a groan. "Not more witnesses to interrogate?"

"No, Toby." He scratched at his thin moustache and reached for his pipe. "Tonight," he said quietly, "we are going to rob a grave."

35

The Body Snatchers

The journey to Greenwood Cemetery commenced, fittingly enough, at the white door of 31 Bond—"the murder house" it was now universally called in hushed and superstitious tones. The lamp lighter was abroad, scrambling up and down his ladder, flecking the growing darkness with tiny flashes of flame which burned at the end of his wand like St. Elmo's fire and left behind the uncertain glow of the gas lamps. Pools of yellow formed around the posts and shimmered off the soft surface of the falling snow, as yet unmolested by the boots of the silent mob that would again tomorrow gather to gape at the procession of witnesses, police, officials, and reporters streaming unabated through the white door from which I had just emerged.

I watched the lamp lighter retreating toward Broadway, toting his ladder and his little fire-stick, while he seemed to drop in his wake his yellow pools like a trail of breadcrumbs—or droplets of blood. I shivered and drew my greatcoat tighter against the cold, and noticed that, where the pools of yellow light appeared, they were surrounded by a blackness made more impenetrable by the contrast than if the lamps had remained dark. Thus does the lamp lighter, in igniting his flickering wicks, cast shadows deeper, longer, more sable across this gloomy sphere than we should otherwise ever know.

What a topic for a metaphysician to chew upon, thought I, if only one were in the neighborhood. At that moment there was no one in the neighborhood except the rapidly vanishing lamp lighter. My eyes were suddenly diverted from his shrinking figure to a large four-wheeler which trundled past him and approached me at a pace steady but not hurried.

It was a gigantic hearse, drawn by four white horses caparisoned in black, driven by a gaunt shadow of a scarecrow man attired in black with a black stovepipe hat from which a black veil hung half down his back. The coffin he carried was rosewood with brass fastenings, a replica of that in which the remains of Harvey Burdell had been placed. This coffin, however, did not contain a corpse, but rather the tools to be used in excavating a grave. To transport them, Quinncannon had hired the same hearse that had brought Burdell to what—evidently—was not to be his final rest.

"We are going to dig up Mrs. Burdell's husband," the Irishman had told me that afternoon.

The notion was ghoulish enough without the hearse. "Why do we need it when any dray will do?"

"Will do to arouse suspicion, Toby. But nothing is more natural than a hearse in a graveyard. Who expects the body snatcher to arrive in the dead wagon?"

Following the hearse was a coach-and-four. From the box beside the muffled driver Hasty scampered down, dropping onto the new snow with a soft thud, grinning with a boy's anticipation of adventure. "Himself is inside with the two doctors, Toby." He yanked open the coach door. "Whew! What a night!"

I could not make out the features of Quinncannon's two companions until I was seated beside him in the coach. As we swung about and began our progress toward Broadway the Irishman lowered the curtains and lit a lantern. I found myself looking into the familiar but totally unexpected faces of David Uhl and Samuel Catlin. Given the circumstances of the aborted duel, I was astounded to see either of them, particularly Catlin. They appeared unhappy to see me, particularly Catlin. I gathered Quinncannon had given them no more information regarding our purpose than he had provided me.

We rode in sullen silence through the almost deserted streets of the lower city. Only the Irishman smoked and the orange glow of his pipe reminded me of another dark passage we had undertaken, across the North River toward another place of death, the dueling grounds on the cliffs of Weehawken. On that grim occasion I had also stared, almost hypnotically, at the rhythmic incandescence of his pipe, drawing comfort from it as a cold man draws comfort from the fire in his hearth. It is interesting, this finding of solace in another man's pipe. Quinncannon smoked with deliberateness, as he did everything else. We had already stretched the law deliberately. We were about to break the law deliberately. The steady burn of his pipe somehow gave me confidence that he, at least, knew what we were doing and why. God knows I hadn't a clue.

We rolled onto the South Ferry for the crossing to Brooklyn. The ice in the East River had broken up but great chunks of it still floated free and the choppy waters, churned up by gusts of frigid wind, slammed them against the ferry's sides. On arrival at the Brooklyn pier, the boat was tossed about so that we were obliged to leave the coach and assist in securing the vessel and getting the terrified horses ashore.

We wrapped our mufflers over the eyes of the lead animals and half dragged them from the decks while the teamsters cracked whips beside their ears and thundered the foulest of oaths. One horse, to which Hasty was clinging, reared in panic, carrying the boy high over the planking and shaking him like a rag doll. I abandoned my beast and leaped for and caught the lad's legs just as he lost his grip on the harness. We fell—I managed to keep my feet—and, supporting the boy, I spun toward the frightened animal. Uhl had made a grab for its head and stumbled. He lay, stunned, on the deck while the horse again reared, light from the torches flashing off its murderous hooves. I realized in an instant that neither Quinncannon nor I could reach the fallen man in time, and then, to my utter astonishment, Catlin dove forward and covered Uhl's body with his own. By some miracle the surgeon was able to roll to evade the crashing hooves. When the animal reared a third time the Irishman and I managed to drag the two doctors to safety.

At last ashore, I held the lantern while Catlin dressed Uhl's wounds, which were but slight. When he had his patient ambulatory he regarded me with a curl of the lip. "So, Mr. Brendon, perhaps I am not such a coward as you thought me, sir?"

"Perhaps not," I replied.

"Pah!" he exclaimed. "Only a fool would demand squirrel guns at twenty paces."

He had me there.

It was near midnight when we reached the gates of Greenwood Cemetery. The wind was less blustery on the Brooklyn side of the river and the snow had slacked off. The heavy cloud cover had rolled back somewhat and we clattered past the massive stone pillars under the eerie blue half-light of an eerie blue half-moon. With the great hearse leading, we rumbled along a gravel path up an incline identified by a rocky marker as Locust Hill. The carriage wheels screeched in protest against the combined weight of five men and a boy, and the snowflakes turned gradually to a soaking rain, its diagonal streaks visible through the shafts of the side lamps.

The hearse halted near the top of the hill and our carriage, of necessity, also stopped its progress. From the narrow window I could make out the remains of a dwarf wall, not much more than a piled row of loose boulders, which emanated from a gray knoll: bare stone patched haphazardly with grass thatch. Above the plot rose a great, stooped shadow of a tree, a willow by its silhouette, planted many years before to mourn over those who were to be planted thereafter.

I lit one of the lanterns and descended from the coach, followed by Quinncannon and the two surgeons, each carrying his black bag. Hasty, in his excitement, was the first to reach the stone. I lifted my lamp over the marker and stared at it in wonder.

The earth upon which we stood was firm and not mounded. The stone was fixed solidly in the ground and overgrown with weeds and moss. Whoever lay in this plot had not been recently buried.

The moss and wet soil clotted the etching of the name on the marker and I scratched it out with my finger and held the lantern yet higher until the chiseled lettering was legible:

GEORGE CUNNINGHAM
Beloved husband of Emma
Affectionate
Father of Augusta, Helen,
George Jr., William.

1793–1854

"CURSED BE HE WHO MOVES MY BONES"

It was evident from their reactions that both Catlin and Uhl had been as little in Quinncannon's confidence as I concerning which of Emma's former husbands we were going to exhume. The Irishman relit his pipe, shielding it from the rain with the palm of his glove, and regarded each of us in turn with ironic amusement. He said to Hasty, "Fetch the picks and shovels, lad."

Uhl was angry. "What sort of grim joke is this, sir? Dr. Catlin and I understood that we were to further examine the body of Dr. Burdell in hope of finding new evidence favorable to Mrs. Burdell. If we had known your true intent we should not have come."

"That thought crossed my mind, Doctor," Quinncannon replied. "You will recall that I said there was still some mystery over how the lady's husband met his death which I believed you gentlemen could assist in clearing up."

"But," Catlin protested, "there is no mystery over Mr. Cunningham's death. He died of asphyxia brought on by heart failure. I, myself, attended him and signed the death certificate."

"And I assisted in the examination of the body," Uhl said.

Quinncannon nodded. "Precisely why I have asked you two to preside this evening."

Hasty arrived from the hearse, lugging the tools.

"I have reason to expect," the Irishman explained, "that the coroner is going to call witnesses tomorrow whose testimony will suggest that Emma Burdell murdered her first husband."

"That's ridiculous!" Uhl exploded. "I've known her for years. The woman is incapable of such a crime."

Catlin said, "I'm no lawyer, Mr. Quinncannon, but it seems to me such evidence, *if* there were any, is irrelevant and inadmissible."

"In a court of law, before a judge, that would be true. Regrettably, at his inquest, Mr. Connery is free to determine the relevance of testimony, and it is obvious that he is doing his best to incriminate your friend, our client. We must remember that the nonsense spouted at the inquest all finds its way into the newspapers to poison the minds of potential jurors."

"Why, then, you must do something to prevent it, sir," Catlin exclaimed.

Quinncannon shook his head. "Mr. Brendon and I are powerless to keep it out of the record, Doctor. What we can do is request the exhumation of Cunningham's body to prove he died of natural causes; however, before we take that step, we must be certain that evidence will not be found to support a contention of murder. That is our mission tonight and I think we had better get at it."

It did not surprise me that the Irishman had provided a pick or spade for everyone but himself. He relaxed against the neighboring willow while the grisly work progressed. The drivers took no part but sat on the boxes of their vehicles impassively. Every time I swung my pick my eyes fixed on the grim warning chipped into the gravestone: "Cursed Be He Who Moves My Bones." A mound of sodden earth began to rise beside the pit we gouged. At last Uhl's pick struck with a clang against one of the brass hinges, and a moment later I felt my own pick sink with a hollow thud into the rotten rosewood lid of the coffin. The impact was sickening, as though the cruel point had struck the corpse itself. The odor rising from the grave was unimaginably putrid.

Quinncannon stepped forward. "Gently, boys, gently. Do nothing to damage the remains."

A trench was dug around the box and we hoisted it up and frog-marched it to the hearse. With a crowbar the Irishman carefully pried loose the screws until the lid was freed. He ordered Hasty to return to the coach and, after much protestation, the youngster obeyed. Then he turned to me.

"I would advise you to join the boy, Toby."

I said I would not.

I should have.

"Before we open the coffin, sir," Dr. Catlin said, "I wish to tell you what Dr. Uhl and I observed when we first examined Mr. Cunningham. At that time the family was residing in Brooklyn and I was their regular physician. George Cunningham had a bad heart for which I had long treated him. On the morning he died his wife sent her daughter, Augusta, to summon me and, after I had determined he was indeed dead, I caused a message to be taken to Dr. Uhl, who arrived about three hours later."

"Why?"

"Why what, Mr. Quinncannon?"

"Why call another surgeon? And why call Dr. Uhl from Manhattan? Are there no other doctors in Brooklyn?"

"Dr. Uhl is a friend of mine, sir, and he knew Mrs. Cunningham well. I thought it desirable to have a second opinion to corroborate my view of the cause of death."

"Were you afraid the widow would be suspected of murder?"

A cloud crossed Catlin's features. He took his time in replying. "There had been talk that Mr. and Mrs. Cunningham were not legally married. He had abandoned his first wife to live with her. After his first wife died, however, George *did* marry Emma. He acknowledged this to several people including myself and Uhl."

"In fact," Quinncannon said, "he claimed she had gotten him drunk one night and told him the next morning of a wedding he couldn't remember."

"That *was* his version," Uhl conceded, "but he also admitted she had shown him a marriage certificate with his signature.

George never disputed her—they continued to live together as man and wife—and after his death she *did* produce the certificate and settle the matter."

"But Cunningham's relations went to court to challenge the marriage and her right to the estate."

"Unsuccessfully, sir," Uhl reminded the Irishman.

"How large an estate did Cunningham leave?"

"As I recall," Catlin answered, "it was about ten thousand dollars."

I was turning this history over in my mind. The affairs of Emma and Harvey Burdell were starting to assume a pattern—a pattern first established by Emma and George Cunningham. The elements were a common-law marriage that the lady later asserted was legal; a certificate of wedlock suddenly materializing after the husband's death; a squabble between the "widow" and her in-laws over the estate; and suspicions of foul play.

All at once I was vitally interested in whatever findings this second examination of Cunningham's cadaver might disclose. Had Emma gotten away with murder once? Would a jury believe she was trying to do so a second time?

"The appearance of the body when Uhl and I observed it," Catlin was saying, "gave every indication of asphyxia during cardiac failure. The face was congested and pressure-whitened, and there was marked venous and pulmonary congestion. The blood was dark, and there was rupture of the capillaries causing small, punctate hemorrhages in the skin and tissues of the face and throat—all perfectly consistent with death by coronary artery insufficiency aggravated by hypertension. In other words, sir, a heart attack."

Quinncannon appeared unsatisfied. "I'm no more doctor than you are lawyer, Catlin, but are not those symptoms also perfectly consistent with strangulation?" "No, sir—" It was Uhl who responded. "Because strangulation is done either by ligature or manually, and either way there would be telltale bruises on the neck, which we did not find. Moreover, the tiny haemorrhages Dr. Catlin spoke of would have appeared only above the line of stricture, as would the venous congestion. This was not the case. I agreed at the time with my colleague's verdict of Cunningham's death and I find no reason now to change my mind."

"There is an additional argument against strangulation by Mrs. Cunningham," Catlin added. "Three years ago she was attacked with inflammatory rheumatism, which affected both shoulders, but more particularly the right shoulder, the right elbow, and the right hand. The effect upon the joints of her hand was to enlarge them. These joints were not then—are not at present—in a natural condition. The right hand was especially affected, and the joints of both hands were stiffened and weakened. She has not the same power to grasp as before she was afflicted. The strength of her hands was naturally much diminished."

The Irishman listened thoughtfully. "This rheumatic condition persists?"

"Yes, sir. If anything it grows worse."

"Might this prevent her from gripping a dagger with sufficient strength to inflict the wounds found on Burdell?"

"In my opinion it would," Catlin answered, "just as I believe it would have been impossible for her to grasp George Cunningham's throat with fatal results."

Uhl indicated his total agreement.

Quinncannon pondered this new information for a moment. Then he said, "Very good, gentlemen. Let us examine the body."

The lanterns were hung within the hearse above the coffin. Catlin opened his bag and arranged several knives on a black cloth. He pulled up the sleeves of his coat and folded back his shirt cuffs. I admired the cool efficiency with which he prepared for the ghastly operation. I watched him select the ugliest of his blades and test its edge thoughtfully against his thumb.

Uhl and Quinncannon maneuvered the oblong casket so that the full illumination of the lamps fell upon it. Uhl's sleeves and cuffs were also rolled up on his wrists. He nodded to the Irishman and together they raised the lid. The stench that now exhaled from the box into the nearly enclosed wagon was offensive beyond description. I had the sensation that the hearse was a crypt and I was entombed alive within its foul confines with a thing so unspeakably corrupt that the thought that it had once been a man only increased my horror.

The rain could no longer be heard on the canopied roof of the macabre carriage. No wind swayed the heavy draperies that encased us. The lanterns seemed to glow unnaturally rather than to shine. Abruptly I felt a desperation to escape which rapidly became a compulsion. I fled from the hearse and its awful cargo and stumbled and threw myself upon the fallen gravestone. As I lay there I began to vomit.

The others reinterred the corpse and set the marker back in its place. I was of no use at all. I sat in the coach, still choking down the constrictions that rose in my throat. I never did learn the disposition of the hearse. We rode back in the coach, each man engulfed in a black silence. We left Catlin outside his chambers, and, as the ferries were shut down until sunrise, Uhl, Quinncannon, Hasty, and I took rooms in a hotel near the docks. Uhl retired at once and the Irishman carried the exhausted boy to bed while I persuaded the landlord to open his stock of liquor. By the time Quinncannon rejoined me I was on my third bourbon and feeling like a new man. He poured himself a tumbler of Irish. My curiosity got the better of me.

"Well, Lon, was Cunningham murdered or not?"

"I wish it were that simple," he said.

I waited for an explanation.

"The dead man's teeth were broken off," he at last remarked. "The front teeth in the lower jaw."

"What do broken teeth prove?"

"By themselves? Possibly nothing. The circumstance suggests that during asphyxia his lower teeth pressed against the inside of the upper lip or gums with sufficient force to snap them off. That wouldn't happen if his death were natural."

He finished his drink and sat, meditatively, rolling the glass between his palms for so long that at last I prompted, "I gather you found no signs of bruising."

He looked up. "Toby, after two years the flesh is so blackened and decayed"—he must have seen me turning green because he ended simply—"it's too late to hunt for bruises."

He poured another whiskey and left it untouched. "The real problem, lad, is the hyoid bone."

I confessed my ignorance.

"It's a small, U-shaped bone that supports the base of the tongue. You can feel your own by pressing your index fingers together at the point of your chin and moving them straight back against your throat. It's just where the jaw meets the neck, above the Adam's apple."

I found it and nodded.

"Cunningham's hyoid bone was fractured, Toby, and that means murder, any way you view it."

I was confused. "But in the cemetery both Catlin and Uhl recalled that they had found no evidence of strangulation—no bruises from finger or thumb, no mark of a ligature such as a rope or even a length of cloth. Were they *both* lying? Good God, Lon! Do you think that Catlin killed Cunningham and Uhl covered for him? Or—" I did not want to consider this possibility. "Or, did Emma throttle her husband and *both* doctors lie for her?"

He stared moodily into his drink. "Catlin and Uhl claim they failed to notice the fracture because they weren't looking for it. There was no reason to suspect it since there were no other more obvious signs of violence. Still, there should have been a bruise, Toby. At least a small one. If we assume that even one of them is telling the truth, there is only one explanation for George Cunningham's demise. He was not strangled, garrotted, or choked. He was smothered."

The echo of the word escaped me in a breath.

"By the diffuse form of pressure from a soft object, probably a pillow. That would account for all the observations noted by the surgeons during their first examination, and for the broken teeth which eluded them."

"And the bone fracture?" I asked.

"Uhl and Catlin are in agreement on that. During the death

struggle, one of the killer's hands must have lost its grip on the pillow and slipped, striking sharply against the hyoid. It seems that is the way it had to have happened. Except that neither doctor saw a bruise."

Another question I didn't want answered: "Lon, could a woman have done it?"

"Given that Cunningham was an unwell man, bedridden and no youngster, yes, Toby. A woman would have the strength to murder him."

"Emma?"

"Perhaps, but her rheumatic condition argues against it." He added, "Augusta was also in the house."

Augusta? "Well, she's strong enough, but . . . her own father?"

"It's been known to happen, Toby. And let's not forget there was someone else on the premises."

"Someone else?"

"Helen Cunningham," he said and tossed off his whiskey.

36

The Shoestring Witness

Connery had three witnesses in readiness, the first two, as Quinn-cannon had predicted, for the purpose of casting suspicion on Emma for her first husband's death. He called John T. Hildreth to the stand. A fat man, wearing spectacles, past middle age, who managed to be simultaneously prissy and pompous, waddled forward and ascended the dental chair. He turned pale-blue eyes round the crowded parlor and preened.

He gave his name. He was a bookkeeper and resided in Brooklyn. He knew nothing about Dr. Burdell's death but he was a fountain of information on George and Emma Cunningham.

"I first knew Mrs. Cunningham in Brooklyn. Her name was Emma Augusta Hempstead then. That was before she was married, and after, too—that is, if she ever *was* married, but I don't believe she was, though she gave the children Cunningham's name. That was the opinion of a great many people at the time."

"At what time?" the coroner asked.

"At the time her husband was murdered—or rather, the man she claimed was her husband."

Connery was confused. "Which of her husbands are you referring to?"

"Her first husband. At least she *said* he was her husband. She had a paper. She had the reputation of being a prostitute."

Poor Connery's head was swimming. "She had a *paper* saying she was a prostitute?"

"No, sir," Hildreth answered patiently. "She had a paper saying she was married to Cunningham, the distiller."

"Ah! Her first husband was a distiller."

"Yes, a manufacturer of liquid death."

The coroner groped for the joke he knew was there somewhere. "A man-u-fact-ur-er-of-li-quid-death." He flourished his pen. "I will put that down for the benefit of the Temperance Society."

"Put it down. It may do some good."

"When," Connery inquired blandly, "was Mr. Cunningham murdered?"

The question was outrageous, of course, as was the whole line of testimony, but we were helpless to prevent it. It would have been a serious mistake even to dignify Hildreth's "evidence" with a protest.

"Mr. Cunningham was killed in the spring of 1854, sir. It is my understanding that he was pronounced dead of heart failure. But I wish they would disinter his body and examine it, for I believe he was murdered by his wife. I do think so and have always thought so. She was a bad woman, and had no better example from her mother."

"Her mother?" echoed Connery, licking his lips, but a juror observed that telling tales of Mrs. Cunningham's mother was going "a little too far into ancient history."

"I have no doubt," Hildreth persisted, "that her marriage to George Cunningham was a fabrication."

"What evidence have you?" the coroner wanted to know.

"Why, she seduced him from his lawful wife and lived with him in sin until that poor woman's death. All Brooklyn knew it. He was thirty years older than her, but a man of some means when she took him, and what else should attract her to him? Though his fortunes varied he was worth at least ten thousand at his death, and when his relations sought to inherit she suddenly produced a certificate of marriage. The clergyman was dead, and

Cunningham was dead—and his signature illegible—and only her own eldest girl as a witness, yet, nonetheless, the court upheld her, but I knew a lawyer in Jersey City who said he had heard from a fellow in Brooklyn that—"

Connery cut off this hearsay upon hearsay. "Have you," he said, "any proof that Cunningham was murdered?"

"He was sick for more than a year before he died, sir, and it was widely thought that she was slowly poisoning him, for he could seldom keep anything in his stomach, even the most innocuous food, and his bowels were—"

Again the coroner mercifully interrupted. He had gotten from his witness all that he wanted. He waved a transcription of the testimony. "Will you step up here and sign this?"

"Is it my death warrant?" Hildreth asked coyly.

"Yes, sir, your death warrant."

Would that it were, I thought.

Horace Ladd, also of Brooklyn, was the second man on the stand. A short, graying, rather scrawny fellow, he identified himself as a commissions merchant. "Some years ago," he told Connery, "Mr. Cunningham failed in business and applied to me for money to care for his family. I obliged him."

"What did he offer as collateral?"

"He had two life insurance policies, sir. One for ten thousand dollars, and one for half that amount. For much of the last three years of his life he was sick—his final illness occupied nine months—and he owed me one thousand six hundred dollars when he died."

"Who benefited from those insurance policies, Mr. Ladd?"

"Other than a small bequest to his sister, it all went to his wife."

"You got your one thousand six hundred?"

"Yes, sir."

"And Mrs. Cunningham got the rest."

"Well, most of it. I should say about twelve thousand four hundred. I invested it in real estate properties for her—at her request, of course."

"Do you continue to do business with Mrs. Cunningham?"

"I do," Ladd answered. "I collect the rents for her, and from time to time I make new investments on her behalf." He added with pride, "I may say I have done for her rather well."

Ladd, unlike Hildreth, was a dangerous witness. The portrait he painted of Emma was that of a poor wife forced to accept charity and tied to a hopeless invalid—then suddenly transformed into a wealthy woman of property by the "convenient" death of a husband obviously worth more dead than alive.

Connery's last question was as predictable as Ladd's answer:

"Did you ever hear that Mr. Cunningham died under suspicious circumstances?"

"Certainly not!" snapped the commissions merchant. But the coroner had made his point.

It remained, however, not Cunningham's death but Burdell's on which the inquest focused. Connery's next witness was to prove his star, although the coroner very nearly neutralized him at the outset by insisting that the poor fellow was there to testify in a matter of which he was totally ignorant.

John T. Farrell was thirty-two, married, the father of three, a shoemaker, and had a bad back. Those facts are not necessarily given in order of importance. He was a little man, wiry thin, weak-chinned, prematurely bald, with a nose entirely too large and long for his face. He was not the sort of man you wanted at your back in a fight.

"On the night of January 30th," Connery informed him, "on the corner of Bond Street and the Bowery, you witnessed a quarrel between Dr. Burdell and a well-known gambler."

"No," said Mr. Farrell simply.

"No?" The coroner shuffled feverishly through his papers. "You did *not* witness such an altercation?"

"No."

"But, I have a letter here—" Abruptly Connery abandoned his search. "You *did*, sir. I put it to you that I have an anonymous communication here—somewhere—that definitely states that such a quarrel took place."

"It may have, sir," said Farrell, trying his hardest to be accommodating. "I have no knowledge of it."

At this point a plump man of perhaps sixty stepped forward, richly attired, with a perpetually worried aspect. "I believe the coroner may be confused," said retired judge Henry Capron, drawing a universal, unexpected laugh. "I have with me the letter to which Mr. Connery refers," Capron persisted. "It does not refer to a confrontation with a gambler, but it does indicate that Mr. Farrell has vital evidence to offer in this matter now pending. If I may?"

Connery waved his hand and the judge read:

February 8, 1857

Dear sir,

I have today heard that a man by the name of Mr. Farrell, employed in the Appraiser's public store under Mr. Graham, has said that he was in Bond Street at the time Dr. Burdell entered the door; that he saw him enter; heard the cry of murder, and was on the steps when someone came to the door and asked him what he was doing there. This may not be correct but deserves attention. He alleges it as a cause of his not making it known, that he was afraid he would be kept from his family, and inconvenienced by appearing as a witness, as he is a poor man. I am yours, very respectfully,

ONE WHO SEEKS FOR JUSTICE

"Aha, ha!" cried the coroner, at last getting his witnesses straight.

It was Judge Capron, however, who conducted the interrogation. "Have you ever seen Dr. Burdell?"

"If I done, 'twas on the night he got killed."

"Were you on Bond Street that night?"

"Yes, sir."

"At what time?"

"Around ten-thirty. It might have been eleven."

Quinncannon leaned over to me and whispered, "I'm going

upstairs. The police have brought Eckel here from the Tombs. They're holding him in Burdell's bedroom now."

"Lon," I whispered, "what is all this about?"

He merely put a long finger over his mouth and slipped away.

"Can I tell it in my own words?" the witness was asking.

"Yes, tell your story," Capron said.

Farrell was a cobbler who worked at home on consignment. The labor was exacting and required him to sit for long hours in a half-bent posture which, especially in damp weather, could become extremely painful. "I have trouble with my spine, you see," he apologized, "and sometimes I have to get up and walk about for a hour or more until I get straight."

On January 30 his employer had given him a rush job, a pair of ladies' gaiters to be ready the next day, "and they having heels on, which was rather troublesome, I concluded to go out and walk till my back did not ache so much."

He had first visited a friend and then hiked up the Bowery, turning west on Bond, and was within a few houses of number 31 when he noticed that one of his shoelaces was untied and "drawed nearly out," and, "it being sort of sloppy out," he sat down on the front stoop of the murder house, "about the fourth or fifth step," and attempted to fix his lace. The tin tag was off and the string unraveled so that it was difficult to thread it into the hole, and while he struggled he noticed two men approaching him from the Bowery, walking separately. The first man climbed up the steps where Farrell was squatting—the climber on the right side, Farrell "on the left, close to the railing." The man was wearing a shawl—that was the only description the shoemaker could give of him—and he entered the house and shut the door.

If he'd used a key, Farrell wasn't sure.

The second stroller went on by the house. He was still in sight a minute, or a minute and a half, later when the witness heard from inside number 31 a cry of murder. Just one cry. Was he positive the word cried out was "murder"? Mr. Farrell was positive.

About thirty seconds later he heard another sound, "like a

barrel binding. . . . Like a full barrel falling or being overturned. I says to myself, 'There's a muss in this house. They must have been drinking.' "

Another thirty seconds passed, or it might have been a minute. Then the front door of the house opened and a man with a beard, in his shirt-sleeves, peered out at Farrell and said, in a rough voice, "What are you doing there?" The shoemaker said he wasn't doing anything there. He was surprised that he had not heard this man's footsteps approaching the door because he *had* heard the steps of the first man retreat from the same door after entering it. He thought the first man had choked someone inside and then sent this second man to "kick me down the steps."

"I got up," the witness related, "keeping my face to the door. I was still bent over on account of this complaint in my back, and I edged down the steps sideways in the fear the man might assault me." Three or four doors down the street he again sat down and this time managed to repair his shoe.

"When your lace was mended," Capron inquired, "what did you then do?"

Farrell shrugged as though it ought to have been obvious. "I went home."

While the questioning continued, I noticed sheriff's deputies moving through the room, drawing men aside to whispered conferences. Afterward the men thus selected would quietly slip out of the parlor. Every one of them wore a dark, heavy beard. Obviously Connery was preparing to test Farrell's recollection—to see if the bootmaker could pick John Eckel out of a sea of similar faces.

Judge Capron got Farrell to say that the man who entered the house was "at least" five-foot-eight (Burdell's height), while the man who spoke harshly from the door was "about" five-foot-six (Eckel's height). He thought the latter man was forty years old. Eckel was only thirty-five but Capron could not talk the witness out of those five years. Nor would he state positively that the rough-spoken man was balding, as the butcher was in front. ("I could not see the top of his head.") Nor that his beard was definitely black, like Eckel's. ("It might have been reddish, but it were very dark.")

A juror asked what Farrell's drinking habits were, which set Capron off on his favorite subject: teetotalism.

"Were you sober on the night of the murder?"

"As I am now."

"Did you have anything to drink that night?"

"Only some reconstituted spirits."

"Is that whiskey?" the judge asked naively and the parlors exploded with laughter.

"No, sir. It is such as is usually sold in Dutch groceries."

"Well, sir, I do not frequent Dutch groceries," sniffed the judge. "Are you a man who is easily affected by liquor?"

"No, sir!" There was a twinkle in Farrell's eye. "I'm a man who could drink thirty glasses of whiskey and be no more drunk than a fellow who's only had fifteen."

Again the room rocked with laughter.

Upstairs, Connery had arranged his shadow show for viewing in Harvey Burdell's bedroom. His twenty bewhiskered decoys had stripped to their shirt-sleeves but Eckel refused, "on advice of counsel," to remove his coat. The coroner was furious. "It is mine to command and yours to obey," he stormed at the butcher, but our client was adamant and the others put their surtouts on again.

Farrell was brought into the room. I kept my eyes on Eckel. He stood, rocking slightly, near the foot of the bed where the dentist had been laid out. Sweat beaded on his face and palms and rolled down his nose, dropping onto his beard. His hair was matted, his hands trembled, his lips twitched involuntarily. His skin was cadaverously pale. From across the room I could smell his fear.

The tension in the room was almost physically painful. Of all the men packed into that room, only two appeared at all relaxed. Quinncannon lounged against the wall opposite me, absently filling his pipe. Once he caught my eye and gave me a tight smile of resignation. And, to my great surprise, though he gnawed with some anxiety on his lower lip, Edward Downes Connery's features seemed to glow with a triumph that I considered somewhat premature.

Farrell passed by more than ten faces before fixing on Eckel. The suspect gave an almost imperceptible start but managed to retain his composure while the witness, having twice hesitated and turned away, of a sudden impulse put his hand to his head and commenced to stare straight at Eckel as if he were a Barnum exhibit.

The scene that followed might have struck an outsider as comical. All at once Farrell dropped to one knee and peered up at Eckel—frowning, squinting, tilting his head first this way, then that. "This is how I saw him," he explained. "I was down on the steps and he was up at the door." He nearly lost his balance, toad-hopping about while the others cleared a space. I looked at Quinncannon. Quinncannon looked at the ceiling.

At last the shoemaker scrambled to his feet. There was a general intake of breath. We waited.

"Well?" Connery demanded. "Is that the man?"

Farrell hung five. Then, "That *is* the man," he suddenly announced, pointing at Eckel, and again, more firmly, *"That is the man!"*

Eckel went back to the Tombs, a mob dogging his carriage for blocks, uttering (said the *Times*) "a dismal howl of verbal execration." Emma soon followed, Connery having decreed that Farrell's evidence was sufficiently damning against her, though he'd given no evidence against her, to deprive her of the comforts of house arrest.

That afternoon Judge Capron advised John Farrell that he would have a police guard until after the Grand Jury had discharged the case. The shoemaker agreed, but added, "I am a man of family. I wouldn't want to have to go to jail."

"Oh, we merely want to have you when we want you," Capron assured him. "We wouldn't send you to prison."

But they did. Poor Farrell couldn't raise the thousand-dollar bond.

* * *

Farrell's testimony had the unfortunate result of undoing all Quinncannon's efforts to bring the newspapers into sympathy with Eckel and Mrs. Cunningham. When, on Saturday, February 14, the coroner's jury brought in a verdict of murder, naming Emma and Eckel as principals and Snodgrass as either principal or accessory, it did not come as a surprise to the defense. The action of the Grand Jury seemed a foregone conclusion, and the Irishman and I were already preparing for our appearance in court.

What did hurt was the almost universal assumption of our clients' guilt in the press. Even Coroner Connery, whom the reporters had ridiculed so mercilessly, was being given a holiday.

Considering the apparent desperation of our position, I was amazed at the high spirits with which Quinncannon went about preparing our case. For my part I became increasingly despondent, and my depression would have been far deeper had I suspected the vicious little shock the district attorney, A. Oakey Hall, was preparing for me.

37

The Great Police War

Even my younger readers will remember the savage struggle for control of the machines of law enforcement in New York, which racked the city in 1857. The combatants were two separate police forces, the Metropolitans, answerable to the governor and his appointed State Board of Police Commissioners, and the Municipals, under the authority of the mayor, the recorder, and the city judge. These two forces were pitted against each other like rival armies. Skirmishes often broke out between them, and blood was frequently spilled.

Governor King, a Republican, proclaiming his dissatisfaction with the City Police as controlled by Mayor Fernando Wood, a Tammany Democrat, pushed a law through the state senate dissolving the mayor's authority and substituting for the old Municipal Police a Metropolitan Police under King's own commissioners. However, fifteen Municipal captains and almost eight hundred of the one thousand patrolmen refused to take orders from the State Board. These rebels were tried and dismissed for insubordination, but they defied dismissal and continued on duty and in control of the station houses. Subsequently both forces were brought to one thousand men. No love was lost between them. They walked the same beats and collisions were routine. Prisoners arrested by the Metropolitans in the act of committing their crimes were rescued from custody and allowed to escape from justice by armed bands of the Municipals. Writs issued by the courts went largely unserved unless the Metropolitans were accompanied by vigilantes. It was a common practice with the aldermen and city magistrates to proceed to the Police Office immediately upon the arrest of riotous persons and discharge them from custody. This emboldened the dangerous classes, and in early February a battle erupted between hostile gangs of street thugs—the "Dead Rabbits" from the Five Points against the "Atlantic Guard" out of the Battery. These hooligans erected barricades in Bayard Street and fought with clubs, stones, knives, and chains. The Metropolitans were helpless—it took the militia to quell the riot. Six men died, over one hundred were wounded, and it was widely—and accurately—rumored that officers from the Municipal force had abetted the gangsters on both sides.

The crisis was reached on Monday, February 16, when Daniel Conover, whom the governor had appointed street commissioner, was forcibly ejected from his office by Municipal patrolmen and replaced by Charles Devlin, an appointee of Mayor Wood. Conover at once obtained two warrants for Wood's arrest, one for inciting to riot and the other for assault upon his person, and returned to City Hall with fifty of the Metropolitan Police to serve his papers. The mayor shut himself into his office. City Hall was garrisoned by some eight hundred Municipals, prepared to defend their fortress to the death. Though badly outnumbered, the fifty Metropolitans were even more badly commanded. At a signal from Conover they mounted a suicide charge.

At the moment this war commenced I was inside City Hall and unaware of the hostilities seething around me. I had hostilities of my own to deal with—in fact, I was giving serious consideration to bloodying the nose of New York's esteemed district attorney, A. Oakey Hall.

I had arrived at my office that morning to find two Municipal constables waiting in ambush with an "invitation" to call upon lawyer Hall. It was not a warrant, I was assured. They could get a warrant if I chose to be difficult.

The district attorney parted his bushy, gray-tinged hair on the right and wore it short and brushed straight back so that it stood erect on his head. His square jaw was adorned by a whisk broom of a beard, and clipped side whiskers bristled out from pale, hollow cheeks. He wore no moustache, but his eyebrows were unusually thick and S-curved around moody, deep-blue eyes. His nose dropped long and straight from a knob between those eyes on which was perched a pair of steel-rimmed spectacles. He motioned me to a chair in his office and spread some documents on the blotter of his desk. I noticed that he squinted when he read.

"As you know, Toby—" He smiled insincerely. "You won't mind my calling you Toby? The coroner's jury on Saturday found that Harvey Burdell was 'feloniously murdered,' and 'that Emma Augusta Cunningham and John J. Eckel were principals in the commission of said murder, and'—Let me see. Ah!—'that George Vail Snodgrass either joined in the commission of the said murder, or was an accessory . . . that Augusta Cunningham and Helen Cunningham have some knowledge of the facts connected with the said murder which they have concealed . . . and it is the duty of the coroner to hold them for further action of the Grand Jury. In witness thereof, we, the undersigned . . . ,' etc., etc., and so forth."

He looked up at me. "Now, Toby, you see, I must take this case to the Grand Jury, and I need to be positive, when I do, that I am in possession of all the facts. That is why, acting on certain information which reached me last night, I did, this morning, obtain a subpoena to search the files of your former employer, now deceased, Mr. Ogden Hoffman, and to remove one of those files which I now hold aloft in my hand. Its contents, Toby, pertain to you."

I wanted to wipe the superior smirk off his lips with the back of my hand. What in hell did the man mean by commanding my presence and waving the shameful record of my past under my very nose with such ill-concealed glee? And who had been his informant? I thought I knew.

"Damn Leggett! He had no right to communicate with you."

"Don't blame your law clerk, Toby. He defended you valiantly. I wish my employees were as loyal to me."

Hall removed his spectacles and polished the lenses with a bandana, at the same time turning his gaze on a small door that apparently connected with an anteroom. He jingled a tiny bell, the door opened, and a matron escorted Emily Hoffman into the office. I watched her as she became aware of me and averted her eyes from mine. A dozen questions sprang into my mind. Could her father have trusted her with the secret of my origins? To do so would have been outrageously unprofessional. And, if she *did* know the truth, would she have betrayed me to the authorities? That she disliked me I knew, but could the haughty Miss Hoffman hate me that much?

Hall gave her the same sweet, spurious smile with which he had favored me, and told her to be seated. He proceeded to ignore her, addressing himself exclusively to me in a smooth, oily manner.

"You are, I believe, cognizant of the materials in this folder, Toby."

Dull anger stirred in me. "I don't see where those papers are any of your business."

"Don't you?" He put his glasses back on. "I have a murder under investigation, Toby. Any evidence tending to prove a motive for that murder comes within my purview."

At this Miss Hoffman stared at me. Her pretty mouth fell open.

"There is voluminous correspondence here between Ogden Hoffman and a Virginia lawyer named Orion Small who, it seems, was your guardian for the last eleven years of your minority. Prior to that you were a ward of the state of Virginia, having been orphaned in infancy. Your childhood was passed in and out of institutions, chiefly the Brendon Orphans' Asylum in Richmond. When you were ten, Toby, Mr. Small took you in charge and you were sent to a boarding school in Charlottesville, and later to the

University of Virginia. These documents indicate that Small acted entirely on instructions from Hoffman, but Hoffman, in his turn, was merely the agent for another man—a man who paid all your expenses from his own pocket. That man was Mr. Lon Quinncannon."

Hall pushed his spectacles down the bridge of his nose and squinted at me over the steel rims. "Is Lon Quinncannon your father, Toby?"

Would to God that he were, thought I. There had been a few brief minutes on Christmas Day, after Leggett had given me the file, when I thought he was. The idea had stirred in me warm feelings of pride and pleasure. Then, by accident, I had jarred the folder and a slip of yellow paper had fallen to the carpet. I'd retrieved and read it. It was a birth certificate, and A. Oakey Hall now held it between his fingers.

"Mr. Quinncannon is not my father, as you well know."

"This paper," said Hall, waving it about, "is the record of your birth in the charity ward of a Richmond hospital. Your mother was unwed, only sixteen years old. Her name was Mary McCabe, the consumptive daughter of a woman who scraped together a meagre living doing other people's washing and scrubbing their floors. This I learned by telegraph this morning from the Richmond authorities, who also inform me that your grandfather was the town drunk, with numerous arrests for robbery and assault. He seems to have beaten both his wife and daughter rather regularly and with great cruelty—"

He recited this litany of my ancestor's crimes and his abject shame, which was also mine, in an official monotone so cold-blooded and unfeeling that I thought his intent was to abase me, in my own eyes, and in the eyes of the woman he had caused to be brought there to witness. If he sought to humiliate me he had shot wide of his mark. What he had inspired was fury. I was on my feet, my fists clenching and unclenching at my sides. I wanted desperately to knock him down.

"Stop it!" I shouted. "What sick reasoning do you imagine gives you the right to poke at my pain with your filthy finger?"

"Be careful, boy!" he barked back at me. "You are under suspicion of murder. I advise you to behave yourself and answer my questions carefully. Why did Quinncannon assume responsibility for your upbringing and education?"

"Ask him! How the hell should I know?"

"You have not discussed it with him?"

"I have not spoken a word of it."

He slumped back in his chair and watched me intently. "Are you not the least bit curious?"

"I believe to raise the matter with him would be in extremely poor taste. His reasons are his own private business. It is enough for me to know of his kindness and to hope some day to repay it."

I strode to his desk and leaned on it, on the knuckles of my fists, my arms rigid, so that I could look down on him. "Suppose we stop playing games, Mr. Hall. If you're attempting to gain some advantage over Quinncannon by questioning me, you are wasting your time. Your only legitimate interest in my affairs lies in the identity of my father. According to that birth certificate you are holding, my mother gave his name as Harvey Burdell."

I heard Miss Hoffman gasp behind me. It surprised me moderately. I had assumed she knew. I was not yet convinced she had not known.

"Burdell left an estate of nearly two hundred thousand dollars, Toby," Hall said. "Regardless of the outcome of the criminal trial, there's going to be one hell of a fight among the heirs in Surrogate Court. I don't believe for one goddamn second that Mrs. Cunningham really married Burdell, and I don't think you do either, but even if she did, and even if she escapes the noose, she won't get her greedy hands on a dime of his money once you produce that birth certificate."

"I have no intention of asserting any claim to that money!"

"I don't believe you."

"Believe what you like," I snapped. I could have squashed him like a cockroach. "No amount of money could induce me to make public the sorry contents of that folder."

The district attorney shook his head stubbornly. "No man can walk away from two hundred thousand dollars," he affirmed with conviction, meaning, I assumed, that he could not have. "And the money was not your only motive, Toby. You and your father were rivals for your cousin, Mrs. Hubbard, and *you*, handsome devil though you be, couldn't hold on to her, could you, boy? Off you went one dark night, romance in your heart, horny as a hop-toad, and there he was, your *father*, occupying your side of the bed." He shot me a nasty leer. "I've got a witness, boy—a little parlor maid who'll swear to it."

I lunged at him across the desk and seized him by the shirt front. With my free hand I took hold of his cravat and began to twist it tighter and tighter. I honestly believe I would have murdered him. His mocking face swam before me but now the smirk was gone, his tongue protruded from one corner of his gaping mouth, and his spectacles dangled crazily from one of his ears, and then I felt a woman's hands pulling at my own, trying to pry loose my fingers, and a woman's voice crying inarticulate—and I let go of his neckerchief, exhausted with the effort of my rage, and was drawn into her arms, and felt her breathing, felt her bosom heave against my own.

"Oh, Toby!" she cried. "I'm sorry. I'm so sorry. The pain—the terrible pain you must have suffered."

The door flew open and a dozen Municipal Police flooded the room. There were others in the corridor, and there was shouting, and the sounds of men fighting. One of the constables called to me, "The Metros have broken through our lines. The militia is marching on the building. Damn it, man! We've got to defend the mayor's office!" His eyes fell suddenly on the district attorney, sprawled on the floor, his hands at his throat, and the officer, grasping the true circumstances, moved toward me, his club raised, rallying his fellows.

I seized Miss Hoffman's wrist and dragged her to the anteroom. It led into another corridor, also filled with patrolmen, milling about in aimless confusion. I could see the doors that led to the Park but escape was blocked by rival swarms of police

swinging their sticks and bellowing foul oaths. I pulled the girl
toward a staircase and we fled down into the bowels of the building.

We were now in the dungeons of City Hall where criminals
awaiting trial were kept, and I soon realized that, in my desperation to elude the violence of the police riot, I had led us into far
greater peril. The cells, which had confined members of the Dead
Rabbits and Atlantic Guard gangs arrested during the Bayard
Street brawl, had been thrown open by renegade Municipals.
The hoodlums, though free of their fetters, were unable to get
out of the building, their escape prevented, as ours was, by the
police mobs that flooded the upper floors.

Somewhere a cache of liquor confiscated from smugglers had
been broken into, and the ruffians, and their benefactors of the
outlaw constabulary, reeled through the maze of torch-lit passageways in various stages of pugnacious intoxication.

Within moments three of the largest and drunkest set upon us.
One was a Municipal and he carried a pistol. As he lurched at me
I managed to trip up his heels and he spun unsteadily into my fist
as it smashed against his face. He dropped like a rock. I thought
my hand was broken. Then I heard Emily scream my name. I
picked up the gun and turned quickly to find her arms roughly
pinioned by one remaining thug while the other advanced on me.
He was a huge bull of a man with beefy forearms and a lumbering
gait. Shouting threats, he threw a near-empty whiskey bottle at
my head. I dodged it narrowly and heard it shatter against the
stone wall at my back and watched the shards fly past my face like
visible echoes of the explosion of glass. I aimed the gun at his leg
to bring him down and squeezed the trigger. A red hole appeared
in his thigh and gradually widened and began to drip on his boot,
and still he came on. I fired again—this time the red hole was in
the center of his forehead—and he took two more steps and
toppled forward and lay inches from my feet.

I had to step over his bulk to go after the third man, raising the
gun as I did so, but, with a look of suddenly sober terror, he
pushed the girl at me and took to his heels.

I gathered her into my arms and held her as tightly as I could without hurting her, as she had held me in Hall's office, tenderly yet with a strength surprising in a young girl. The dead man, the man I had killed to save her, lay within a yard of us, an eloquent witness to the terrible risks we still faced. We should have been running, hiding, but I could not let her go—I could not let go of the moment. I loved her. It was not infatuation. Not another conquest. I wanted to protect her so that no pain, no danger should ever again threaten her. I wanted, too, to be loved by her —to be held and comforted by her so that no pain could ever touch me.

The two thoughts simultaneously possessed me. We were in ominous peril, and I loved her. I cannot remember such a sense of exhilaration.

"Emily," I whispered hoarsely. "We've got to get away from here. I love you. Our lives are in danger. I'm crazy about you. Isn't this stupendous?"

She lifted her eyes until they met mine. She was laughing and crying at the same time. "Oh, Toby, you are mad! You are wonderful! How could I not have seen it? We're both going to be murdered, I'm afraid. Oh, I do so love you, Toby."

Abruptly there were shouting voices approaching and the sound of many running feet. They seemed to come at us from all directions. Again I took Emily's hand and drew her into the darkest corner of the nearest cell. There was a dirty blanket in a heap on the cot. I had her crouch down and threw it over her. I checked the pistol. Only two bullets remained. I turned to face the cell door, swung it shut, pressed my back to the wall, and waited.

I had hoped, with the door closed, that the hooligans would pass us by, but the footsteps halted right outside. I sucked in my breath and leveled my gun while the heavy door creaked back on rusted hinges, and I could see countless pairs of eyes gleaming in at me from the darkened corridor. I had formed a plan of action. The entrance to the cell was too narrow to admit more than one at a time. I would watch for the first sign of movement, fire the gun point-blank, slam the door, and pray that the gang, not knowing how many shots I had left, would not risk a second attack.

I stood motionless while what must have been a minute dragged by like a year. The door was thrown open. I raised my pistol. Then I heard a light brogue.

"Back to your cages, boys. No loitering."

The mob parted, seeming to melt into the walls. Across the passage, leaning casually on his cane, his pipe in his teeth, stood Quinncannon. I helped Emily to her feet and put my arm around her shoulders to steady her, and perhaps to steady myself as well.

"Come on, children," the Irishman said. "Time to go home."

I led Emily from the cell. "Is it over?" I asked.

He smiled thinly. "The militia has occupied the building. The mayor's in the darbies. The district attorney is a bit disheveled but"—his smile broadened—"the poor nincompoop can't seem to recall who attacked him or why. Well, well, what's this?"

He was observing the two men on the flagstones, one dead, the other still unconscious. He took the gun from me and placed it near the fallen patrolman's hand. "An officer of the law appears to have been waylaid by one of the Bowery thugs. Looks like a clear case of self-defense." He looked back at us. "You two are exhausted. Toby, why don't you see the lady home?"

Emily's hand slipped into mine. I wrapped my fingers around it, surprised at how tiny it was—surprised, too, at the strength in her voice when she said, "Yes, Toby, please get us away from this place."

"One more question," I said to Quinncannon. "How did you get these animals to obey you so meekly?"

He gave me a wry smile. "One man's animals are another man's clients."

"You're going to defend them?"

"That was the first clause in the peace treaty, Toby."

"Not Mayor Wood too?"

He lifted an eyebrow. "No, lad, there are some depths to which even I refuse to sink." He glanced at Emily and put his hand on my shoulder. "Get the hell out of here," he said.

I nodded and she and I went up the staircase and out into the bright afternoon sunshine of the Park.

Book III

DOCTOR BURDELL'S BABY

38

Mr. Quinncannon and
Mr. Brendon Plot Strategy

On the day after the Great Police War Quinncannon and I were to meet at the Astor House for dinner and to lay plans for the upcoming trial. Before keeping that appointment, however, I had two important items on my agenda.

I sent Leggett to the district attorney's office to reclaim the file Ogden Hoffman had kept on me, including the birth certificate, which was my only link with the late, unlamented Dr. Burdell. In my own office, in the presence of my clerk, I burned the file, page by page, in the fireplace, watching each separate paper curl and brown at the edges, slowly scalloping and crumbling into a crinkled black ash. Last to go was the certificate, and when the final ember popgunned into soot I broke into a laugh from which poor Leggett actually recoiled.

"You have just witnessed my baptism," I told the bewildered clerk. "Sweep out the hearth, like a good fellow."

I then knocked on Jeremy Todd's door and invited him to luncheon. Over our second round of ales at the Whistling Pig I brought it out. "I've betrayed your friendship. It would be pointless and hollow to tell you how much I regret it."

He put down his tankard. "What in hell are you babbling about?"

"About Emily Hoffman."

"Oh, damn!" he exclaimed. "That reminds me. The girl is wildly in love with you, Toby, my boy. I've been meaning to mention it, but what with that Cunningham business we never cross paths."

His reaction was hardly what I expected. Completely flustered, I simply went on with the speech I'd prepared. "It happened yesterday, in the midst of that police melee at City Hall, quite by accident. Certainly neither of us could possibly have planned it. I had no idea she would even be there—" I stopped abruptly. Then, "*HOW* did you know she was in love with me?"

He was searching for the waiter. "Good God, Toby. All she ever spoke of was you, and she never had a kind word to say. She might as well have paraded about in a sandwich board proclaiming her affection for you. Ah! Eddie! two more ales for my friend and myself!" He turned back to me with a grin. "As for you, lad, did you know whenever you and she are in the same room, you drool?"

"I do no such thing!" I protested, snatching up my tankard.

"You slobber all over your shirt front, like an infant at feeding time. It's positively disgusting."

I was feeling thoroughly foolish. "I never drooled in my life."

We waited while the waiter delivered the ale. Then Jeremy said, "Of course I will."

"Will what?"

"Why, be your best man. That *is* why you invited me to dine with you?"

This time I returned his grin. "I had rather thought of you for the ring bearer; however, best man, by all means. You should do nicely in a supporting part."

"Speaking of supporting parts," he said, lifting his drink in the gesture of a toast, "my wedding gift to you shall be my old truss."

It wasn't very funny, but with us it never had to be. We broke into spasms of laughter, and for a little while we were again the two giddy schoolboys, inhaling nitrous oxide from a balloon, that we had been that first night in Cedar Street during what now seemed to me another incarnation.

* * *

Quinncannon's table at the Astor House was at the rear of the dining room near the blazing hearth. As usual he sat with his back to the wall, stretched comfortably out in a captain's chair, elbows propped on the chair's arms, pipe between his teeth. A bottle of Irish sat within reach of his long arms. While I shook the fresh snow from my overcoat and spread it across a chair near the fire, a waiter placed a tumbler and a decanter of bourbon beside my seat, and vanished as silently as he had come. A large, single candle burned near me, leaving my companion almost entirely in shadow, save for the orange glow of his pipe. I stamped the snow from my boots and sat down. The Irishman motioned me to take out my notebook.

"Who would you say, Toby, is the most damaging witness Hall has?"

I considered the question. "I would think it was Farrell, the shoemaker. He's the one who saw Burdell enter the house and heard the cry of murder. He fixes the time of death and places Eckel at the scene. It was his evidence that turned the whole inquest against us."

He nodded slowly. "Our first concern, therefore, must be to discredit Farrell."

"You mean to break him down during cross-examination?"

"No, lad. We'll have no need to cross-examine him because he's never going to take the stand."

"How are you going to manage that? We just agreed he was Hall's strongest witness."

He was knocking the ashes out of his pipe. "The key to our whole defense is Coroner Connery and his bungling of the inquest. Recall, Toby, the dramatic calculation with which he produced Farrell and staged the scene in which the cobbler identified Eckel as the man who had come to the door just after the cries were heard."

I remembered it clearly—Farrell peering from face to face among the group of twenty "suspects" assembled by the coroner in the dead man's bed chamber; Farrell finally crouching down at Eckel's feet to squint up at him from the same angle he'd had on the murder night.

"How many reporters were present for that charade?" Quinncannon asked.

"I believe every newspaper in the city was represented."

"And most of them had been ridiculing Connery for days."

I saw his point. "Connery would have been laughed out of office if Farrell had failed to identify Eckel! He *had* to be certain Farrell would point to the right man." All at once it was as transparent as crystal. "Copies of the portrait of Eckel done for *Leslie's Illustrated* had been hawked all over Manhattan. Connery must have showed that picture to Farrell *before* he had him summoned!"

Quinncannon was smiling at me. "Good, Toby, very good. We'll make a lawyer of you yet."

"But, Lon, can we prove it?"

"A police sergeant named Edgar Davis has had a bad attack of conscience," he said, "and will testify that he was present when Connery's son displayed the engraving to Farrell, prior to the taking of the shoemaker's evidence."

I began to laugh out loud, but a disturbing thought caught me up short. "We're not out of the woods yet. We can cast serious doubt on Farrell's identification, but not the rest of his story. Hall can still argue that *some* man must have come to the door, and Eckel, since he lived there, is the logical choice."

"I have a plan to explode the rest of Farrell's story as well."

I asked what it was but he merely replied, "I have put your friend, young Hasty, in charge of the scheme. Consult with him."

This surprised me, but I knew better than to press him for further information. Instead I said, "What other plots are you hatching?"

Quinncannon poured himself another drink and ran his thumbnail thoughtfully along his thin moustache. It was a full minute before he responded.

"You know, Toby, not a day has passed since Burdell's death when I have not received at least five offers from prominent attorneys to donate their services to the defense. The city's four largest newspapers, the *Times, Tribune, Herald,* and *Sun,* have devoted an average of eleven columns a day to reporting the case —not to mention the barrage of letters they print. Other events, which normally would dominate the front pages, such as the Stafford seduction, the Scott/Davis correspondence, the police wars, even the arrest of Mayor Wood, all are stashed between the obituaries and the advertisements for hair restorers and gonorrhea cures. The public sups on horrors, dreams of murders, and gets up the next morning with a renewed appetite for the same dish. Their excitement is inexhaustible."

He paused to light his pipe. I waited for him to continue.

"When a crime becomes this celebrated, a very strange thing happens. The facts become the least important element of the case. The more informed the public is on the details of the murder, the less attention they pay to them. Instead they simply divide the major characters into heroes and villains and prejudge on the basis of rooting interest. And, just at this moment, Toby, public opinion is fixed and decided, and it is against us."

He leaned forward, toying with his glass. "The truth is that this case will be tried in advance in the newspapers and by public opinion rather than in the courtroom by the jury. That being the situation, we must do all in our power to bring the press back into line behind our clients. The press will tell the public what it thinks and the public will then support us."

"How," I inquired, "do you propose to accomplish that?"

"In two strokes, lad. First we take advantage of Governor King's impassioned desire to humiliate the Tammany thugocracy. Within a week Edward Downes Connery is scheduled to be impeached—ordered by King to defend himself against charges of conduct unbecoming a public official during the inquest." Quinncannon smiled slyly. He resembled a fox contemplating a chicken dinner. "When I'm finished with Connery, his treatment of Emma Cunningham will make Bishop Cauchon look fairminded when he burned Joan of Arc."

I returned his smile. We had both suffered the frustration of being effectively silenced through the absurd inquest. The notion of putting Connery on the defensive—and on the stand—was extremely appealing.

"And your second move?"

"The most important cause of public hostility against Emma is the widespread conviction that she induced someone to personate Burdell in the marriage ceremony performed by Marvine. This hostility is intensified by the belief that Eckel was her confederate. The prosecution's whole theory of the crime flows from these two assumptions. If we could prove, or, at least, satisfactorily suggest, that the marriage was to Burdell, and was genuine, then public opinion would leap back to the conclusion that she was innocent of the murder."

He leaned back, observing me over the rim of his glass. "Tomorrow morning we are going before the Surrogate and demand that Emma, as Burdell's widow, be appointed to administrate his estate."

He continued to watch me while my jaw dropped so rapidly that my pipe fell to the table, scattering embers. "But—but—" I was annoyed to find myself stammering. "But—that's *crazy!* For one thing it doesn't even *matter*—it's not *desirable* that she act as administratrix!"

"Absolutely true," he concurred.

"In the second place, you're going to force a battalion of lawyers representing Burdell's relations into the field to band together in proving that the marriage was a fraud. Every piece of evidence disputing the legitimacy of the ceremony will be dredged up again and repeated in the newspapers."

"No, Toby. It's true the next of kin will have to challenge Emma's claim to being Burdell's widow, but that will raise a clear issue of fact, which will have to be tried preliminarily by the Surrogate before he can grant letters of administration to anyone. As we will have the affirmative of the issue, we are entitled to produce our testimony first. All our witnesses must be heard before our opponents can offer rebuttal."

I still didn't like it. "Do we have any witnesses? Do we have any evidence at all?"

He gave me a cryptic smile.

"At least grant me this, Lon. Once we've had our chance to present whatever case we have, the other side will be free to reintroduce all the inquest evidence which convinced the press and public in the first place that the wedding was not genuine."

He slowly shook his head. "In winning murder trials, lad, stamina is half the battle and timing is the other half. We're going to drag out the Surrogate proceedings with requests for adjournments and postponements until just before the trial begins, and then have the case suspended until Emma's fate in criminal court has been decided. You're quite right, Toby. It would never do to give Burdell's relatives their day in court before Emma's been tried for murder. And we certainly don't want the Surrogate to rule on the legitimacy of the wedding prior to her trial. If he decided against us her conviction would be certain."

I thought the risk enormous, but I had unbounded faith in Quinncannon's skills. His point about public hostility toward our clients remained well taken. It crossed my mind that, whether Emma was actually married to Burdell or not, her motive for murder was the same—to get control of his estate. In fact, if she *were* his legal widow, her motive might be strengthened. But this version of the circumstances had not occurred to the public and was not likely to. Quinncannon's strategy was undoubtedly our best hope.

39

Surrogate Court

Proceedings involving our request that Emma be appointed administratrix of the Burdell estate opened on March 3 before Judge Alexander Bradford. Four attorneys appeared for the dentist's kin, while the Irishman and I represented the "widow." The benches reserved for reporters were packed. Journalists had attended from as far away as Boston and Washington City. I doubt an issue of this nature has ever attracted so much attention from the fourth estate. Quinncannon had his audience and he was ready for them.

The crowd had come to listen to testimony, not orations, and my friend kept his opening brief.

"May it please the court:

"It is a source of no small congratulation, both to my client and to myself, that we have at last arrived in a court where we shall be protected in our rights, where the rules of law will be enforced, and where the rules of decency will not be outraged." (A swipe at the coroner, whose back Quinncannon had been battering already for several days during the impeachment hearing.)

"Should I attempt to answer the calumnies with which the community has been inundated in regard to my client, neither this day nor this week would be sufficient for that purpose. I shall therefore endeavor to confine myself strictly to the issue now raised in this court—whether my client at the time of the death of Harvey Burdell was his lawful wife. That she was married to him on the 28th day of October last, I believe will be demonstrated, not only to the satisfaction of Your Honor, but to the satisfaction of the entire community."

Our first witness was Reverend Uriah Marvine. How well Quinncannon and I had prepared him, let the reader judge for himself.

After establishing the clergyman's name, occupation, address, and the fact that he had officiated at a wedding on October 28, Quinncannon led him to the day he had been brought to the inquest.

"I was taken to the house, number 31, by an officer of the Municipal Police and by John Connery, the coroner's son. John Connery told me that rumors were rife that a fraud had been practiced upon me—that Dr. Burdell had been personated. He further informed me that it was well known that the man representing himself as Burdell was Eckel. I was given to understand that Eckel bore a strong resemblance to the doctor and might very readily be mistaken for him."

"Did John Connery say anything else to you?"

"Yes, sir. Just as we were debarking from the carriage he said, 'As you had never seen the parties before, Reverend, no one can blame you for having been duped. But, should you persist in identifying Dr. Burdell as the bridegroom, you will probably become something of a laughingstock.' That, he said, would be a pity for a man of the cloth and a black mark on my church."

Quinncannon's eye was on the reporters. Their pencils raced over their pads. "After your arrival in Bond Street, where were you taken and by whom?"

"I was immediately conducted to the room where the dead man lay—by the coroner himself."

"Was anyone else present?"

"No, sir. There were two patrolmen on watch, but Mr. Edward Connery ordered them to leave and shut the door."

"Please describe what happened next."

"The coroner indicated the corpse and asked me whether that was the man whom I had married on October 28th last. I said I could not give a positive opinion until I had seen Mr. Eckel and had an opportunity to compare them."

"Were you then shown Mr. Eckel?"

"Not at that time."

"Not before you gave your evidence at the inquest?"

"Not until several days after that, sir, when Captain Walling introduced us at the Tombs."

"During the time you and Coroner Connery spent in the dead man's room, what was his demeanor?"

Marvine's face reddened in anger remembered. "He was very officious. With his stentorian voice he wanted me to say 'Yes' or 'No'—'Is that the man on the bed?' He began to lecture me about the solemnity of an oath. I think I replied to him that I ought to know as well as he did what an oath was, and the consequences of a false oath. I—" He looked up at Quinncannon. "Shall I go on?"

"By all means."

"I think Mr. Connery is a very weak-minded man, or a very foolish man—one or the other. He went on at such length about his importance as a public official that I began to suspect he had no great regard for himself. He assumed that loud, strutting, dictatorial way—just as if he was the Lord High Mayor of London —and it did not exactly suit me." He paused, relieved to have gotten *that* off his chest, and then added, almost shyly, "There is one other observation I would make. Throughout our private interview it was Mr. Connery's dearest wish that I should say positively that the dead man, Dr. Burdell, was *not* the man I married to Mrs. Cunningham."

The Irishman let that sink in. I noted the gentlemen of the press scribbling feverishly. "Reverend Marvine," my friend resumed, "while you were in Burdell's rooms, was Mrs. Burdell brought in for your identification?"

"Yes, sir, and at the time I did not recognize her. I thought I saw strong points of resemblance in the dead gentleman, but the lady was not familiar to me at all."

"Have you since been able to recognize the person known as Mrs. Cunningham as the person you married?"

"I have, Mr. Quinncannon. Some few days ago I went to the Tombs at your suggestion. At my first look at the woman, it flashed more upon my mind than ever that this was the woman I had married."

"Was I present when you identified Mrs. Cunningham?"

"No, sir. Only the keeper, Mr. Fosdick, and a matron."

"Are you now satisfied upon that point—that Mrs. Cunningham is the woman you married?"

"I am."

"Perfectly?"

"Perfectly," echoed the witness.

Quinncannon nodded and strolled to the jury box, which was being used to accommodate the overflow of reporters. "On the day you gave evidence at the inquest, Reverend, did you identify Miss Augusta Cunningham as the girl who witnessed the wedding?"

"I did, sir, without hesitation."

"Do you continue in your conviction that Augusta Cunningham was present at the ceremony?"

"On that matter," the minister said firmly, "I have never wavered."

"All right," the Irishman continued. "Please explain again the circumstances under which you gave your evidence before the coroner."

Marvine relaxed in his chair and crossed his legs. He was making, I reflected, an excellent witness—calm, self-possessed, his hands steady, his voice clear.

"I was under the general impression at that time, before I had seen the corpse, that I had married Mr. Eckel to Mrs. Cunningham—I had not then seen Eckel, and the idea was preached into me as soon as I entered the dwelling on Bond Street—before I gave my testimony. I got that impression and supposed the facts were so—but my faith in that thing was mightily shaken when I went up and saw the dead body."

"You were denied the opportunity to see Eckel?"

"The coroner told me it was impossible—that Eckel had not yet been found and the jury could not wait for my evidence."

"When you subsequently met Mr. Eckel at the Tombs, what, if any, opinion did you form as to whether he was the man you had married?"

Quinncannon had moved lightly to one side so Marvine's answer would be delivered directly to the newspapermen.

"I saw nothing in Mr. Eckel resembling the man I had married —not a single thing! In my own mind I knew Mr. Eckel was not the man the moment I visited him."

"Come now, Reverend. Are we to believe there was *no* similarity between Eckel and the man you married? Not in voice, look, size, action, or in any other respect whatever?"

"No, sir!" the witness responded without a second's vacillation. "None whatever!"

The Irishman was positively purring. "Since the inquest, have you taken pains to recall the features of the man you married on October 28th?"

"I have thought a great deal of it—have studied the daguerreotypes of both Dr. Burdell and Mr. Eckel—and the more I have done so the more I am convinced that the man I married was Harvey Burdell."

"State whether you have *any doubt whatever* that the corpse and the man you married were one and the same."

Samuel Tilden, attorney for William Burdell, objected. The Surrogate suggested, "Ask him to state his best belief from comparison."

Quinncannon said, "I will phrase it thus: State whether the corpse of Dr. Burdell—"

"Oh!" Tilden cried as if he'd been shot. "That is the same question, Your Honor. Mr. Quinncannon is asking the witness for an opinion."

"If a clergyman cannot give an opinion under oath," the Irishman smiled, "I don't know who could."

"We don't want opinions," Tilden snapped. "We want *facts!*"

Quinncannon sighed with the air of a patient professor instructing a slow-witted schoolboy. "My learned colleague appears somewhat confused. We are taking, not circumstantial evidence, but direct testimony—specifically whether or not Reverend Marvine recognizes Dr. Burdell as the man who wed Mrs. Cunningham on October 28th. This is not a question of the witness's opinion—it is a question of fact. Is it a *fact* that Reverend Marvine does identify Dr. Burdell as the man he married, or is it a *fact* that he does not so identify him?"

I watched the judge trying to make some sense out of this wonderful doubletalk. He rolled his eyes and screwed up his features and at last he said, "I will allow the question."

Tilden threw up his hands and slumped into his seat. The question was repeated and the witness affirmed he had "no doubt whatsoever" that the bridegroom and Burdell were one and the same.

40

The Cunningham Sisters
Take the Stand

The press treated Uriah Marvine with kindness. Not all the papers were prepared to accept his identification of Burdell uncritically, but they were deeply sympathetic to his confusion at the inquest, given the browbeating he had received from both Edward and John Connery. Their general consensus was that before the Surrogate the clergyman had been a confident, impressive witness. Though we had a distance to go, the tide of popular opinion was starting to turn in our favor.

For reasons of his own Samuel Tilden obtained an adjournment until March 26, at which time Quinncannon got a further adjournment until April 13. With the murder trial scheduled to commence on May 4, it was becoming evident that the Irishman's stalling tactics were working. Judge Bradford had already consented to Quinncannon's request that the Surrogate proceedings be suspended early enough to allow us time to prepare Mrs. Cunningham's defense.

On April 12 Quinncannon went before Judge Henry E. Davies, who was to preside over the trial, and moved to sever Eckel's trial from that of Mrs. Cunningham. District Attorney Hall made no protest, which left me flabbergasted. As the Irishman had explained to me, this meant that the woman must be tried first, since unless she was convicted no motive could be proven against the butcher. It also meant that Hall had to convince a jury that Emma had overcome the powerful Burdell and stabbed him fifteen times after a violent struggle for his life—all this without the aid of a man, or of another woman. I learned much later that Hall's decision was based on the belief that his case against Mrs. Cunningham was by far the stronger, and that by trying the two together he feared he would lose them both.

Quinncannon viewed the severance of the trials as a triumph, and the following morning he was in a jubilant mood. I was to examine our witnesses. Patrolman William Keating, who had ridden with the coroner's son to escort Uriah Marvine to the inquest, confirmed the preacher's account of his conversation with John Connery. A second policeman, Miles O'Leary, testified that, at the coroner's order, he had altered the appearance of Burdell's body before Marvine viewed it.

"In what manner did you alter it?" I asked.

"Well, sir, for example, the doctor always wore his shirt collar down, leaving his full beard visible, but I was told to turn the collar up, which made his beard seem much thinner. Then, too, Dr. Burdell smoothed his hair down at the sides of his head and parted it on the right. I was given a brush and ordered to brush his side hair up into peaks and part it on the left."

"By whom were you given these instructions?"

"By the coroner—well, not directly, sir. 'Twas his son Johnny that told me to do it."

"These changes you effected, Officer O'Leary. Did they change the doctor's appearance markedly?"

"I'll tell you the gospel, sir." The witness grew confidential. "I think his own mother would have had to be introduced to him."

Miss Helen Cunningham, demur and darkly pretty, turned heads when she took the stand. She testified that shortly before October 28 Dr. Burdell had given her mother a ring which Emma had worn ever since.

"Who was present on this occasion?" I inquired.

"My sister, Augusta, was there, and, I believe, my two little brothers."

"What, if anything, do you recall happening on the evening of October 28th, 1856?"

"Dr. Burdell, my mother, and my sister left the house together."

"How do you fix that date so vividly in your memory?"

"From a conversation I had with my mother before she left," replied Miss Helen. "My mother desired me particularly to remember that day, although she gave me no reason. She said that all difficulties between the doctor and herself had been resolved."

I thanked and excused Miss Helen. As with our first two witnesses, there was no cross-examination.

Miss Augusta stepped smartly forward and took a seat in the box. She was our witness, but I had found her to be moody and unpredictable, and I approached her examination with caution.

"Please state what, if anything, occurred on the morning of Sunday, October 26th last?"

"Dr. Burdell," she answered primly, "asked me if I would be willing to witness the marriage between himself and my mother. He told me that he desired to keep the marriage secret until the following June, when he and my mother intended to go to Europe, and said I might travel with them if I wished."

"Was your mother present during this conversation?"

"She was. The doctor asked her if I could be trusted to keep a secret, and she replied that he must ask me. I advised him not to involve me in his plans if he doubted my discretion."

That response, at least, certainly sounded like Augusta.

"Did you ask Dr. Burdell why he wished to keep the wedding secret?"

We had discussed this question. Her answer was to be that he had so often censured matrimony to his friends that he was afraid of their ridicule if his marriage became known.

"He said that he had promised Demis Hubbard."

The attorney's first rule is: Never ask a question unless you know what the answer will be. It was too late now. I stared into Miss Augusta's narrow little eyes and began to take chances.

"What had he promised Demis Hubbard?"

"I can only repeat what he said to me," she replied with the air of one who did not put much stock in Burdell's word.

"What did he tell you?"

"He said he had promised he would never marry anyone while she was single—that she was the only encumbrance he had on his hands at that time, and that she was to be married before June next. Mother then told me I should not ask any more questions about it. I then left the room, leaving the two of them there together."

A dozen ideas raced through my mind. So far as I knew Demis had no plans to marry. If this was a lie, who was lying? Burdell? Augusta? Even, possibly, Demis? If the scene described by my witness *had* taken place, I'd have given a month's rent to have been there.

Whatever the truth was, we had called Augusta to make plausible the secrecy of the alleged wedding. Though I would have loved to drop the whole line of questioning, I had no option but to press on.

"When was the next occasion when the subject was spoken of by Dr. Burdell?"

"I spoke to Mother about it when she came upstairs. She said—"

"Objection!" said Tilden, "to anything not said in the presence of the doctor."

The judge sustained.

This failed to stop Augusta. "I asked mother if *she* wanted to have it kept secret—"

"Miss Cunningham," I interjected quickly. "when did you next hear the doctor say anything on the subject of marriage?"

"I think it was on Tuesday morning in his office that he asked mother her age. She said she was thirty-five."

"State all else that was spoken at that time."

"The doctor had a paper with Mr. Marvine's address on it. He stated that he was going to the bank and would see Mr. Marvine before he returned. I did not see him again until Tuesday evening, about six o'clock. He made the remark, 'I have accomplished it.' Then he passed on upstairs and I went down to tea."

Emma later joined her and her sister for tea. Nothing was said in front of Helen until they were ready to leave. "Mother told Helen she wanted her to remember that night. We then went out. It was between seven and eight."

Marvine met them in his parlor. "He made the remark, 'You see, I am punctual.' " The minister took Augusta's name and age and "Mother said I was her daughter. The doctor introduced Mother to Mr. Marvine."

"What was the next thing?"

"I think he then performed the ceremony."

"What happened next, immediately after the ceremony?"

"Mr. Marvine made a short prayer. The doctor then asked if he would give us a certification. The doctor said it would be better to have one, and Mr. Marvine said he would have it ready in the morning."

The next question was a risk, but we needed corroboration of the clergyman's story: "Was there anything said after the service about keeping the marriage secret?"

"The doctor said that he did not wish Mr. Marvine to publish it."

"Was it the doctor or your mother who said this?"

"The doctor."

The point was important because it had been suggested that the "secrecy" was a falsehood concocted by Emma to explain why Burdell had never mentioned he was married. I pushed the matter hard. "Are you positive it was not your mother?"

She regarded me with vexation. "It was the doctor. I have said several times, Mr. Brendon."

One more time won't hurt, dear heart, I thought.

"Was anything said on the way from Mr. Marvine's to your home that you recall?"

"I made the remark to the doctor that if I should ever tell it, what would he say? He said he would kill me."

Every head in the press section bobbed up. No matter how often a lawyer rehearses his witnesses, there is always the danger of an unanticipated ad-lib. Of course that wasn't the answer I expected, and I couldn't let the topic rest there. "Was it your impression that he meant that for a joke?"

She looked at me with perfect seriousness. "Mr. Brendon, I don't know whether he said it in jest or in earnest."

Before I could get in any more trouble I said, "No further questions."

41

Mrs. Schwartzwaelder
Hears a Murder

On the evening of Saturday, March 29, Mrs. Katrina Schwartzwaelder heard screams of terror that froze her blood. She lived with her husband, Colonel Franz Schwartzwaelder, on the second floor of number 29 Bond Street, immediately next door to number 31, and their rooms abutted those which Harvey Burdell had occupied, except that the Schwartzwaelders used their front room for a parlor and slept in the back room, whereas the dentist had his bed in his front room. It had not escaped Mrs. Schwartzwaelder's notice that, on the night of January 30, she and her spouse had been sleeping only a few feet away (though separated by the walls of the dwellings) from the murder room where the most grisly, violent, horrible crime in the city's history was being committed. Fortunately, as she often told the neighbors, the noise of the death struggle—though it must have been "simply dreadful!"—had not wakened her or the Colonel.

The neighbors nodded knowingly. The Colonel was retired—no one was quite sure from what army—and he spent his evenings at a saloon on the Bowery. Mrs. Schwartzwaelder was also suspected of taking a nip or five after sundown. No doubt, said the neighbors, someone could have shot off a cannon in Burdell's rooms without disturbing the Schwartzwaelder slumbers.

Nevertheless, at near eight-thirty the night of March 29, in her parlor, waiting for her husband's return and "taking a sip of gin to keep out the chill," Katrina Schwartzwaelder heard loud noises, "angry voices and the crashing of furniture," coming through the wall. The sounds grew louder when she went into her bedroom, and then she heard "such a piercing shriek of 'murder' that I thought someone was being slaughtered like a hog!"

She ran to a window in her front room, threw it up, and cried for the police at the top of her lungs.

I paid the hackman and stepped down from the cab outside 31 Bond at just 7:30 P.M. I was to attend an "experiment" Quinncannon had arranged in preparation for the trial. A dray was already at the curb and a coffin was being unloaded by two strapping young men under the direction of, of all people, Zachariah Lamentations Hasty. While being lowered, the box swayed and the boy yelled in alarm, "Careful, you fellows. We don't want him to tumble out in the street and get all mussed up!" He was taking his authority with the utmost seriousness.

"Who have you got in there?" I asked.

"Oh, that's Teddy. That's what I call him. He sort of looks like a Teddy. Doc Carnochan says he died of apoplexy—threw a fit when his bosses over at the horse barn wouldn't promote him."

"What did he do at the horse barn?"

"He worked with a shovel," the boy said.

"Is Dr. Carnochan here?" I asked.

"Uh-huh. He came over from the New York Medical College about a half hour ago with two students of his. If I was asked I'd say he looks more like an undertaker than a surgery professor, and them two students look like cadavers he forgot to bury." He winked broadly. "Anyway, they're up in Burdell's office with the other doctors—Dr. Mayne, and a few more I didn't recognize. The house is crawling with police, too. Captain Walling's here from the Metros and Captain Dilks from the Municipals, and about fifteen detectives in plain clothes. You better go on up."

I nodded and started for the street door, but Hasty called me back, handing me a satchel. "Do me a favor and carry this with you, Toby."

It occurred to me that this was the way we'd met, except that our roles were now reversed. "What's in it?" I asked.

"Teddy's clothes."

I didn't inquire why Teddy wasn't wearing his clothes. If it didn't bother Teddy, it was no concern of mine.

When I reached the "murder room" Teddy was already unpacked and sitting on the floor in the corner of the room where the dentist had been found. His back was against the closet door, his arms dangled at his sides, his legs were straight out in a "V" angle, and he was buck naked.

I had to enter through the front room and the tiny laboratory. About twelve men were crowded into the office including Walling, Dilks, and Mayne. Dr. John Carnochan introduced himself to me as Professor of Surgery. He was well above six feet, stooped and scrawny, with no facial hair and a pate almost totally bald. His students appeared no healthier. All three wore laboratory coats of a dingy gray which hung from their shoulders like winding cloths. The two students carried daggers the dimensions of the missing murder weapon. The three of them paced before the corpse in ever-smaller semicircles like a trio of bloodthirsty crows.

Carnochan began to lecture in a squeeking, pedagogic tone. "I have never known a case where so many wounds were inflicted in vital parts. I should say that the blows were struck by a person or persons who had anatomical knowledge.

"My opinion is that the first blow was received by Dr. Burdell while he was sitting at his desk, and that it was effected by a person leaning forward behind him. The natural inference is that the victim, so struck, jumped up, panic-stricken, and made towards the door, and that the assailing party tried to intercept him and prevent him from getting out. A single assailant of less strength than the doctor could not have inflicted those wounds without showing marks of the struggle. Supposing that single assailant were a woman, the probability of marks being left upon her person would be greater than on the person of a man. Females show bruises much more easily than males. The tissues are more delicate, and a lady's arm even when moderately pressed will show marks there next day.

"Now, gentlemen, if you will watch closely, I will conduct some experiments to see the amount of force necessary to inflict certain wounds."

At this Dr. Carnochan gave a signal and his students began poking their daggers into Teddy in the approximate places where the killer had struck Burdell. The purpose of this, I gathered, was to prove that very little force was needed to pierce the body while it was naked. As the dentist had not been naked when he was murdered, the significance of all this somehow escaped me, but I supposed Quinncannon thought this bit of business would impress a trial jury.

After they'd had their fill of puncturing Teddy, Carnochan and his assistants removed his clothes from the satchel and dressed the poor fellow completely in the same woolen fabric—though not the same suit—which Burdell had worn on the night of his death. Once more they prepared to stab the cadaver and did so relentlessly. Naturally the force needed to penetrate the skin was much greater this time—the daggers even recoiling from the woolen substance—and at last the professor announced grandly that he had just proven "beyond a shadow of a doubt" that it was easier to stab a naked man than one attired in a woolen suit.

This seemed rather obvious but it was well, I suppose, to have it confirmed scientifically. Carnochan informed me he was now ready to testify to this effect, and that this would prove that a lone woman wasn't strong enough to have knifed Burdell.

Teddy was then packed away like a ventriloquist's dummy in his box and the professor prepared for a second experiment. The assembled members of the police were directed to go where the house's inmates had claimed to have been while the murder was in progress. Three of the bulkiest patrolmen, for example, were packed cheek-to-jowl in the third floor bed that Emma had supposedly shared with her daughters. They looked, if possible, more uncomfortable than embarrassed.

Another constable occupied Eckel's room, yet another Ullman's, and still others were cast as Snodgrass and Hannah the cook. Four or five more officers were stationed on the front stoop, it now being gauged that the foggy light was as poor as on the night Farrell claimed to have recognized Eckel.

(Up from the basement, where he had been hidden, to the front hall, escorted by Hasty, came a tall black man. He was forty-five years old—with thick black hair, a thin moustache, and only a tightly clipped beard. He wore one shirt-sleeve rolled up while the other hung loosely at his wrist. He had on a gray slouch hat and a brown vest.)

From the window of Burdell s front room Dr. Carnochan waved his handkerchief and at once a man began walking down Bond Street, climbed the stoop of number 31 (past the five squatters positioned there), and fumbled through his keys before letting himself in. Dr. Mayne—for it was he playing the role of the victim—ascended to the second floor and opened the office. He threw off his coat and rubber boots, ignited the fire, removed ledgers from his safe, and sat down to open them at the desk. Meanwhile, Captain Walling, portraying the killer, concealed himself in the small laboratory.

Abruptly Carnochan dropped his handkerchief. Walling rushed forward with a growl, holding a pencil aloft as if it were a dagger. He seized Mayne's neckerchief and thrust the pencil downward while Mayne struggled to stand and twist away from his attacker, emitting a most horrific screech. He staggered to the hall door, Walling in grim pursuit, and tried to turn the lock, but there was no opportunity—Walling was upon him—and this time Mayne screamed the words "Help! Murder!" as shrilly as he could while Walling fell upon him.

At number 29 Mrs. Katrina Schwartzwaelder dropped her gin bottle with a crash and glued her ear to her bedroom wall. Land sakes! she thought. Those lunatics next door were at it again.

The policemen in the rooms of Eckel and Ullman said later that they had heard nothing during the staged "murder"—in fact the constable in Eckel's bed had been found asleep. But, then, so had Eckel claimed to be.

The trio crammed into Emma's bed were so entangled in bedclothes and otherwise convoluted like a Chinese bent-nail puzzle that they heard nothing but themselves cursing each other.

Walling finished inflicting all fifteen "wounds" before escaping through the bedroom (Mayne's fallen form blocking the office-to-hall door just as Burdell's had). Walling groped down the stairs without gaslight, reaching the cellar door. Meanwhile, about a minute after the scream of murder, the front door opened and a man appeared briefly silhouetted against the inside hall light. He looked in turn at each of the five officers sitting on the stoop, ordered them away in a gruff voice, and returned inside.

At the same moment Mrs. Schwartzwaelder raised her front window and commenced a hysterical, banshee shriek, announcing to all in the city that there was again murder in Bond Street.

The next morning I said to Quinncannon, "Just *what* did we accomplish?"

"A great deal," he responded over steaming coffee. "We have a reputable professor of surgery prepared to swear that no woman, and certainly not Emma, would have the strength to stab a dead man through heavy wool, much less a powerful man fighting for his life. And we've just about blown their witness, Farrell, out of the case. Three of the beadles posted on the stoop last night identified Captain Walling as the man who came to the door in his shirt-sleeves, two others said it was Mayne, and one picked *you*, Toby. Not one of them even realized it was a black man." He smiled. "Between that and the proof that Farrell was shown pictures of Eckel in advance of his identification, I seriously doubt Hall will dare to summon the cobbler to the stand."

"It's true that none of the police in the various bedrooms acknowledged hearing the screams or the sounds of the struggle," I said. "I suppose that means the household might have slept through it."

He nodded. "Remember, lad, all we have to do is raise reasonable doubt in the jury's minds. I think we have more than enough ammunition to do that."

I had been giving our position at the trial deep consideration. "You *did* once tell me, Lon, that winning an acquittal was the least of our problems. The prosecution has no weapon, no trustworthy direct evidence. I'll admit I was not at first in favor of opening up the issue of Emma's marriage in Surrogate Court, but your tactics worked wonderfully. The press again tends to a belief that the wedding took place. Hall cannot, I think, call Reverend Marvine after his testimony in Surrogate, and without strong evidence that the marriage was a fraud, Hall really has no motive."

I finished my coffee and reached for my pipe. I was feeling better about our chances to win this case than I had from the outset. "Of course, Hall *can* call Hannah Conlan to show bad blood between the dentist and Emma—that business about the seduction and the foetus. And there are police witnesses to his charges of safecracking—and naturally he has Demis and Uhl and Catlin and Alvah Blaisdell."

Quinncannon laughed out loud. "I don't think so, Toby. Uhl assisted at the autopsy so he'll have to be called, but you won't see Blaisdell in the box, nor—especially—your old paramour Mrs. Hubbard. And, if Catlin testifies, it will be for the defense, to establish Emma's arthritic condition." He gave me a smile. "Nor will the state want evidence from Snodgrass or any of the Cunningham children, particularly Augusta."

"Do you think that Cyrenius Stevens and his wife will also be left off the witness list?"

"What can they say," he responded, "except to describe the mysterious Mr. Van Dolan, the 'shadow man' whom the old gentleman can't even identify?"

I was recalling what I had read of many of Quinncannon's earlier cases—trials that had ended dramatically when the Irishman had suddenly saved his client by forcing a confession from the real killer in front of a stunned courtroom. I now realized how eagerly I anticipated that climactic triumph—how much, perhaps because of our unique relationship, I wished to participate in and savor such a moment.

"Lon, you've told me that you've given little consideration to who the killer really is."

"Have I?" he said absently.

I watched him closely. "Lon, do you know who murdered Harvey Burdell?"

He did not avoid my eyes, but neither did he answer me. He'd been packing his pipe and he took his time in lighting it. After what seemed an interminable wait he said, "Are you certain you want to know?"

"As certain as I am of anything," I said earnestly.

Still he exhaled tobacco smoke without responding.

"I look forward," I added, "to proving the solution in court."

"Oh," he replied languidly, "we would not be able to prove it in court, Toby."

That took me by surprise. "Even so," I persisted, "you owe it to me, Lon. I know we're not—equals. But we *are* partners and, I hope, friends. If you know who killed him you must tell me. I have the right to know!"

He put down his pipe and let the smoke drift away until I could see him clearly. He was smiling, without humor, but with warmth. "Yes," he said slowly, "you do have that right. I should have realized that myself. If you will return to my rooms this afternoon at one, Toby, I will tell you as much as I know."

42

Startling Revelations

I went back to Quinncannon's chambers precisely at one o'clock, in a fever of both anticipation and foreboding. Though the day was bright the sitting room was dark, for my host had drawn his drapes and only a single gas lamp burned above the mantel. The Irishman greeted me from his chair. He was, as usual, smoking his pipe, and the effect of its measured glow and the flickering of the gas flame served alternately to throw his features into light and cast them back into the shadows. At such times he seemed to me a man of almost impenetrable mystery, a Merlin, a Druid priest.

He motioned me to take a chair at the gaming table. I found a bottle there and took a whiskey to steady my nerves. "The drapes are drawn," he explained, "for the comfort of our guest."

"We are to have a guest?"

"Shortly, Toby, shortly."

With that I heard footfalls on the stairs. They ascended slowly, as if with great reluctance, and lightly so that I concluded we were to entertain a woman. At length there was a tap at the door. A figure entered enveloped in a dark cape, a woman's cape, the hood worn over her head, concealing her features.

Quinncannon stood. "Please take this chair," he said, indicating the wingback opposite his own. "There is a glass of sherry on the table beside you."

She seated herself on the chair's edge and folded gloved hands in her lap.

"Before we begin," he said, "I want you to understand that you may speak before us with perfect freedom and without fear. Our oaths as attorneys commit us to silence. Nothing discussed during this interview may ever be repeated to your detriment or that of any person we represent. Is this entirely clear to you?"

I thought she nodded. She reached up with both hands and drew back the hood that had covered her face. Our guest was Augusta Cunningham.

"I have not come here of my own will, Mr. Quinncannon. I wish that understood from the beginning. I am submitting to your interrogation because you are my mother's best and only hope of escaping the gallows, and because, whatever else I may feel, I trust you."

Her voice was low and filled with a sadness of which I would not have thought her capable. I removed my notebook and she turned to me with frightened eyes.

"Put it away, Toby," Quinncannon said. "There is to be no record of this meeting."

I returned it to my pocket and she relaxed, slightly.

"You feel very deeply for your mother, don't you, Miss Cunningham?" the Irishman said.

"I love my mother," she replied simply.

"There is nothing you would not do if it were in her interests?"

"I think," she said, "you already know that, sir."

"On October 28th you accompanied your mother to witness her marriage to a gentleman?"

"I did."

"Was that marriage legal?"

"It is given to me to understand that it was not."

"Why was it not?"

"Because the name of the bridegroom provided to the clergyman and recorded on the certificate was not the name of the man who participated in the ceremony."

"You conspired with your mother and another man to obtain a fraudulent certificate of marriage between herself and Dr. Burdell?"

"Yes, sir," she answered without emotion.

"You did so at your mother's request?"

"Yes, sir."

"Was Dr. Burdell, at any time, aware of this?"

"He was not, Mr. Quinncannon."

"And when you testified at the inquest that you had witnessed a wedding between your mother and the doctor you were committing perjury?"

"I was, for my mother's sake."

Had I, however ignorantly, suborned perjury? "Then," I interrupted, "you also lied deliberately before the Surrogate?"

"That is true," she responded.

I looked wildly at Quinncannon. He caught my look. "I ask this question for Mr. Brendon's peace of mind, Miss Cunningham. Were either of us aware at any time while you were before the coroner or the Surrogate that you were perjuring yourself?"

She looked at him, then into my eyes. "No, sir, you were not. I lied to you also. My mother thought it best. Despite your reputation, Mr. Quinncannon, she feared you would drop her case."

I allowed a sigh of relief to escape me.

The Irishman said, "Do you know your mother's purpose in fabricating this marriage?"

Augusta shook her head. "She did not confide so far in me."

"But you can guess," I said, probably more harshly than was necessary.

"My mother wished to wed the doctor, Mr. Brendon. She wished that above all things, and I believe he would have married her last summer except for Mrs. Hubbard. Mrs. Hubbard seemed to assert a great power over him—he could refuse her nothing and she made a great many demands. He could become violently jealous over her. She used—" She turned to me and, it seemed, smiled with a hint of malice. "She used you, I'm afraid, to make him jealous. Whenever they quarreled she would mention your name."

I returned her smile in kind. "I am well aware of that, Miss Cunningham."

Other things were also becoming clear to me. Emma had tried to fight Demis for Burdell and lost every battle. She slept with her rival but this did not prevent Demis from slipping away to the dentist's bed. She evicted Demis and succeeded only in martyring her in Burdell's eyes and driving him to late night rendezvous in Brooklyn. Worse yet, Demis became a source of constant estrangement between him and Emma. She had then tried to use the lawsuits to force his hand and that, too, had gone awry. It struck me, not for the first time, that for a woman who was perpetually scheming and plotting Emma Cunningham was an incredibly inept blunderer.

Her next ploy was the fake marriage. But why go to the trouble? She could never claim to be the doctor's wife so long as—

A very ugly thought came suddenly into my mind.

Quinncannon said, "How much of this does your sister know, Miss Cunningham?"

"Oh, we have told Helen nothing. She could never have kept the secret. Mother has been very cunning about it. She bought a ring. On the Sunday before we saw Reverend Marvine she asked the doctor to put it on her finger as she found it tight and ill-fitting, and he did so. She made sure Helen and the boys saw him. On Tuesday evening, as we went out the door, Mother went back to Helen and told her never to forget the night but, of course, she did not give her reasons. Helen believes Mother and the doctor were married. That is why she made such a wonderful witness, you see. But we could *never* have told her the truth. She is such a *child!*"

There was a question I had been waiting for the Irishman to ask, but as he showed no inclination to do so, I put it. "Miss Cunningham, who was the man who impersonated Burdell?"

"Why," she replied, "I should have thought you had guessed it, Mr. Brendon."

"I have, miss," I said grimly. "I merely wish you to corroborate it."

"Then," she said, "of course it was Mr. Eckel."

My worst fears were being confirmed. Well, not yet my *worst* fear.

"I gather," I said, "Mr. Eckel disguised himself in some manner."

"He wore a wig on his forehead and false whiskers to make his beard appear fuller, and he wore boots to make himself taller. Mother borrowed some of the doctor's clothes." She could not keep out of her voice her pride in the cleverness of the charade.

Quinncannon knocked the ashes out of his pipe. "Miss Cunningham, on January 24th your mother signed a document for Dr. Burdell in which she released him from all her claims upon him and promised to vacate the house, number 31, at the termination of her lease. Do you know why she did this?"

"It was to quiet the doctor, so that he would not again call in the police. It was Helen's idea really, but Mother went along even after the doctor had it drafted by a lawyer. She thought—"

I finished the sentence for her. "Your mother thought she could always steal it back from him as she had other papers." I was angry and she knew it.

"Mother took nothing from him that was not rightfully hers," she snapped defensively.

"Was it also your mother's right to pilfer his keys, to prowl through his safe, to spy on him from his door, to abuse him in front of the boarders in his own house and encourage others to do the same, to spread lies about him among the husbands of his patients?"

Even while my anger increased a part of me wondered why. Was it because he had been my father? The idea was ridiculous. I owed him nothing, not even my anger. Dead and alive I loathed the man.

Or was it because I was growing more and more certain that the woman I was defending had murdered him?

"My mother," Augusta said coldly, "never spread lies to other women's husbands."

"Have you ever heard of Sophronia and Cyrenius Stevens?"

"Mother never spoke about—"

"She did, miss. On two occasions. I suppose you have no idea who Mr. Van Dolan was either."

"Van Dolan?" She seemed bewildered. "No, sir, I take my oath—"

"And we know what value to place on your oath, Miss Cunningham!"

Abruptly Quinncannon's soft brogue drifted out of a billow of smoke surrounding his head. "Miss Cunningham, tell us what occurred on the night Dr. Burdell was murdered."

She threw him a look of alarm. "Must I?"

"Yes, miss," he replied quietly, "you must."

For the first time she leaned back in the chair. She took her time. "May I," she at last inquired shyly, "have another sherry please?"

He poured it for her. I noticed her eyes never left him. She gulped at the wine.

"The doctor went out at his usual time," she began. "Helen was going away to school the next morning so we all helped her pack—putting labels in her clothes, chores like that. George played his banjo and we sang—a little. Later on George went down to the kitchen for cider. We were all in bed by eleven. After that I heard nothing."

"Did you and Helen and your mother sleep together in the same bed?" His tone told her he knew the answer.

After some hesitation she said, "No, sir."

"Recall, Toby," he said, "the morning after the murder the police found Helen's clothing tangled with Snodgrass's on his bed. The girl spent her last night at home with her young man, didn't she, Augusta?"

"Yes, sir."

"As landlady, your mother had a passkey which opened all the interior doors?"

"Yes."

"Including Burdell's?"

"Yes."

"Did she also have a key to his safe, Augusta?"

"No, sir," she answered quickly. "She *had* one—the police found it—but that opened the old lock. The doctor had the lock changed."

"All right," Quinncannon said. "Now I'm going to ask you another question, Augusta, and you must tell us the truth. After the others had gone to bed and you and your mother were left alone, did your mother go out of the room?"

The girl sat for a long time, quiescent, her gloved hands clasped tightly. Then she said, barely audibly, "Mother went downstairs."

Of course she had. She went down to await Burdell's return and murder him. I shook my head slowly. How could I ever have doubted Emma's guilt? All along, every fact we knew had suggested it—insisted on it.

But she could not have killed Burdell without help. There were no bloodstains on her clothes and no marks of a struggle on her body. She did not possess the physical strength, even without the rheumatic condition in her hands to which her doctors were ready to swear. There had to have been an accomplice—a man.

"Miss Cunningham," I inquired, "did Mr. Eckel go downstairs with your mother?"

"I don't know," was her response.

"When your mother left the room that night, did she go out through Mr. Eckel's room?" I asked, remembering that the two bedrooms connected.

"No, Mr. Brendon, she went into the hall."

So, I thought, she'd already arranged to meet Eckel on the second floor. Her passkey admitted them to Burdell's rooms and there they waited for their victim's return—Emma in the bedroom, Eckel in the tiny laboratory, grasping the dagger.

While she waited Emma must have thought of Burdell in Demis' arms, for she could not have doubted that's where he was. That's where he'd been the previous week when, in her anger, she had locked his own street door against him. Well, tonight she had a more interesting surprise in store for him. He was romancing his cousin for the last time.

The sound of his key in the street door. His footsteps trudging slowly up the stairs, along the hall, stopping outside his office door. The clank of more keys, the lock turning, the door clicking shut and doubtless locked again. The sudden illumination of the gas lamp, the unoiled screech of the safe door, the scraping of the desk chair across the wooden floor. I could close my eyes and see Emma's face at that moment. Her eyes burned brightly with hate and triumph. Her complexion was flush with thrilled excitement. Her mouth was set in a grim, rigid line. She held her breath. Then the laboratory door was flung back and her accomplice sprang.

When Quinncannon returned from escorting our guest out I had taken the chair she'd occupied and poured another whiskey. I had brought the bottle with me. He sat down facing me and picked up his pipe.

"Our client is a cold-blooded murderess," I said in as even a tone as I could manage. "You should have told me, Lon."

He was studying my face. "Yes, Toby, I should have told you."

"How long have you known?"

"For some time," he said. "There were several signposts beginning with the room keys. Because the body was wedged against the office door the killer had to escape through the bedroom, yet that door was locked and Burdell's key was in his pocket. The only other known key was the passkey in Emma's possession. Still, there *might* have been a third key. I stopped searching for it when you told me Burdell had inquired of you, through Blaisdell, as to Emma's disposition of the lawsuits in *January*. He would not have been concerned over the breech of promise charge if he'd married her in October. She had gone to great lengths to obtain a false marriage certificate which would have been useless to her while the dentist was around to deny it. What sealed the matter was the general release she signed on January 24th, just six days before he died. Emma would never have signed that document if she had not been certain Burdell would not be alive to enforce it. Of course, by the time I realized the truth I had long been her attorney of record and was ethically committed to defend her."

"*Ethically?*" I echoed in disbelief. I took a drink and sat in a black silence.

"Toby," he said, "the only alternative would have been to violate a client's trust. We are attorneys, not judges, not jurymen. As professionals we give our best efforts to the defense of our clients."

"Guilty or innocent?"

"Guilty or innocent. I grant you it might be a better world if life were like a romantic novel—if the Providence so dear to our Christian neighbors *did* always intervene at the last moment to punish the wicked and reward the virtuous. And I'll confess to you also that I prefer the world as I believe it to be, with all its many imperfections, shaped and reshaped by the men who live in it."

"Emma Cunningham," I said with heavy sarcasm, "is not a nice woman."

"Nice people seldom commit murder," he replied. "Nice people are also seldom murdered. By what measure of arrogance are we to presume to make moral judgments?"

My head was spinning. I began to realize that it was not Emma's guilt that most disturbed me. The whole situation seemed a bitterly ironic joke on me, the nature of which I had not yet fully grasped.

"You can withdraw from the case now, Toby," he said. "It's not too late."

"It *is* too late," I shot back. "The trial hasn't opened and she's as good as aquitted. We—*you* have done your job too well. The prosecution is tied in knots, disarmed and helpless. Lon," I cried suddenly, "*why* didn't you tell me the truth?"

He smiled sadly. "I thought to protect you, I suppose, lad. I wanted to spare you the very recriminations you're now feeling. I was wrong. You had a right to know. Your protection is none of my business."

"Why did you arrange for Hoffman to bring me into his firm?"

He raised an eyebrow. "I imagine, Toby, I was curious to see how you'd turned out."

"I was somewhat rough around the edges."

The sadness vanished briefly from his smile. "You were that, lad."

"Why did you take me out of the orphanage in the first place?" Now that we were at last into the subject I had to know the answers.

"Hoffman told me your story, Toby. I could not understand what Burdell—what your father had done. In all my life, lad, my one great regret—" He cut himself off abruptly. He took a sip of his whiskey. "To me," he said at last, "a son is the most precious gift a man can receive. To have received that gift, and then to cast it away, unvalued, was beyond my comprehension. I could not give you a father, Toby, but I could do something to redeem— to rectify—the cruelty you had suffered at his hands. That's the best explanation I can give you."

It was all spoken simply, almost without emotion, yet it came to me that he had never opened his heart even thus far before. It was hard for him and I made it harder.

"You're not my father, Lon." It escaped from me before I could call it back.

"Do you think I don't know that, Toby?"

That was all he said. I cannot describe his tone. I couldn't answer him. I remember thinking that he *did* believe I was his son. That I had *had* to tell him. I wanted him to be my father and he was not and there it was.

I rose and went to the door. With my hand on the knob I paused. "The trial begins tomorrow," I said.

"I'll see you there, Toby," he replied in his easy brogue.

I went out and closed the door behind me.

43

The Prosecution Opens

There were many who felt that District Attorney Hall's opening address was the high point of his conduct of the Cunningham case, which may be a way of expressing how abysmally he handled the rest of it. In all fairness A. Oakey Hall did not eventually rise to be mayor under the Boss Tweed Ring or chief bagman for the Tammany mob on his forensic skills.

Someone in his office had figured out that it would be difficult to prosecute a woman before an all-male jury. In attempting to blunt any natural juridical sympathy Hall took two interesting positions: though women were inherently twice as vicious as men, they were also twice as stupid.

The killing of Burdell, he proclaimed, "was the deed of a woman—a deed to a great extent unartificial—a deed planned and contemplated from a different standpoint from which men of the world contemplate crime, perpetrated to a great extent with that ignorance of human nature which, compared with men of the world, women at all times in history have possessed and at all times in our own history claim."

As for Burdell: "This hunted, haunted man is dead, and she who was his deadly enemy in life lives—and *there she sits!* GEN-TLEMEN—a veiled picture of sorrow, as the world would say— she challenges you today as jurors by her looks, demanding the

sympathy which belongs to a woman, but not to a murderess! Day
by day as you sit here in the discharge of a solemn public duty,
eloquence and ingenuity will attempt to force upon your minds:
'Remember, gentlemen, you are trying a woman.' We appreciate
fully the difficulties which the prosecution labors under from the
outset, but in the discharge of our duty we shall mince no words
before you, gentlemen. CRIME HAS NO SEX!' "

Hall faced the jury squarely. "Oh! It is no wonder that all these
holy associations that cluster around the name of woman should
force themselves into the jury box when a case of this kind comes
before the public eye. When we remember the mother of our
prayers; when we remember the sister of our household adoration; when we remember the wife of our life until death; when we
remember the children who are to be the future women of the
world, that sit upon our knee, and we feel as we look upon young
girlhood and growing maidenhood, we say, can it ever be that this
being, upon whom God Almighty has put his own seal of purity,
should ever live to be the perpetrator of crime, the midnight
assassin, to cherish hate and revenge and jealousy?"

Quinncannon appeared to be asleep. A few of the jurors were
nodding off.

The prosecutor began to explore history, mythology, even the
Bible and the immortal Bard. ". . . we read of Messalina who,
having murdered her husband, the servant of Imperial Rome,
drove her chariot over the dead body of her father; and Fulvia,
when the head of Cicero was brought to her, she spat upon it,
drew from her bosom, which had nourished children, a bodkin,
and drove it through the tongue until it quivered; and the drama-
tist speaks of Agnes, Queen of Hungary, who bathed her feet in
the blood of sixty-three knights, and said, 'It seems as if I were
wading in May dew. . . .' "

I have no wish to try the reader's patience. Enough to say that
Hall got round to Salome and Lady Macbeth, and concluded with
a rather interesting proposition, theologically speaking, that Lu-
cifer was one-half female, and that half the worse, *if* the two

halves could be separated (which, he acknowledged, was an entirely separate debate).

When he finally reached the state's theory of the crime, however, Hall's presentation contained nothing new or original. In truth Hall had abandoned most of his most damaging evidence. To establish the quarrelsome history of Emma and Burdell he relied heavily on the cook and a small number of the dentist's friends. He called the police before whom Burdell had charged Emma with theft and the undersheriff who had served the warrants on Burdell. Physicians who had examined the body, including Mayne, were summoned—and that was just about the state's whole case.

No Alvah Blaisdell to speak of the alleged will—now missing and an excellent motive for murder—or to tell the jury of Burdell's fears for his life on the very evening he died.

No Demis Hubbard to establish the existence of the *ménage a trois* at Bond Street which infuriated Emma and which might easily have been made to strengthen the "woman scorned" motive the district attorney was at pains to stress.

No Catherine Stansbury to testify that the doctor was murdered on the eve of his signing away the much coveted house from under Emma—and, naturally, no Uriah Marvine. After the minister's evidence at Surrogate, Hall had now decided that "whether she be called Emma Augusta Cunningham, or Emma Augusta Burdell; whether she be the mistress or the wife; whether she had the simulated or the real marriage, SHE!—woman though she is—is GUILTY OF THIS HEINOUS CRIME!"

John J. Eckel was in the courtroom in irons but Hall wasn't going to put him on the stand: "There was an effort to cover up the base act in one's own house, and the effort may—we are not saying it was—but this effort may have been abetted by a man; and yet the prosecution are not bound to bring before you the man who saw the deed done, for he might lie, and he might be the enemy himself."

This portion of the address was outrageous. Hall asserted, without proof, that Eckel had helped Emma to clean up after the killing, or might actually have killed Burdell himself, though he had chosen not to try Eckel either as accessory or as principal. While I was choking back my astonishment at this unprofessional, incompetent stupidity, Mr. Hall outdid himself.

"The prosecution will bring before you such circumstances as convinced twelve men, as they swore yesterday, that that crime was done by somebody inside the house. Away with justice forever, if circumstances like these do not call, trumpet-tongued, upon the defense to reverse the rule of law; let the innocent prove that he is not guilty if he can!"

I shook my head grimly. "Did he just say what I thought he said? That because the Grand Jury indicted, that is *proof* of Emma's guilt, and the responsibility for proving her innocent lies with *us?*"

"That's the thrust of his meaning," Quinncannon answered.

I began to rise in my chair and felt a restraining hand on my shoulder.

"Lon," I half-whispered, "that can't pass unchallenged."

"Leave him alone," Quinncannon replied. "Hall's only demonstrating how bankrupt his case is."

44

A Ride in a Hansom

On the evening of the day the prosecution rested I took Emily to
supper and the Park Theater. I don't recall the play except that
it was a comedy. It was a night when I felt very much the need
to laugh.

We had not seen each other since before Quinncannon's and
my interview with Augusta Cunningham, but she had been constantly in my thoughts. I never fell asleep without picturing her
delicate features. Her deeply jade-green eyes, so lustrous and so
penetrating—times they seemed to probe my soul to its core but
with a gentle, perceptive compassion such that, though I half-
sensed she understood me better than I would ever understand
myself, the notion gave me only reassurance, never alarm. In
another girl the same power to comprehend my private feelings
would have disturbed me. I was beginning to realize that my
other relationships had been not simply superficial and self-serv-
ing, but oddly competitive. With Emily I could be myself without
yet knowing who I really was. When we talked I never weighed
in advance what I was about to say. I never concerned myself with
what impression I might make on her. And when she talked, I
listened and never planned, while she was speaking, what I would
say next. That she was beautiful was important to me, but not,
as it had always been before, crucial. I loved the soft throaty

quality of her voice, the gentleness of her touch. I admired her quiet strength and the sharpness of her mind. With her I always relaxed. It was strange because our acquaintance had begun so inauspiciously and yet we were so comfortable together.

The four days since we had last been together had been among the four longest of my life. A gap had opened between Quinncannon and myself for which I felt responsible and which I had no idea how to close. There was also the matter of defending a client who I knew for a certainty was guilty of the most hideous of crimes, nor was it Emma's guilt alone that ate at me. Her acquittal was a foregone conclusion and when she went free so did John Eckel, another of our clients, who, I was morally convinced, had slaughtered Burdell as he had once butchered beef, and who would walk away without even suffering the ordeal of a trial.

I could not hide my depression from Emily and when we had left the theater and hailed a hansom she said, "Toby, let's not go right home. It's such a beautiful evening. Why don't you ask the cabman to drive around for a while?"

I did so and she took my hand and drew me toward her. I let my head rest against her shoulder. We rode for a few minutes in silence and then I began to speak and it all came pouring out of me.

When I had finished she took me in her arms and held me with the same tender strength she had shown in Hall's office on the day of the police war. I embraced her and felt the rhythm of her heart against mine, and for a while we communicated all that was necessary without a word being spoken.

Then she said softly, "Toby, you've defended guilty people before."

"Not for a crime like this."

"Is it because Dr. Burdell was your father?"

"I've thought about that." I had found that I could look at his corpse in my mind's eye with the same emotionless detachment I had felt viewing it on the morning of his murder. In a real sense I had destroyed Harvey Burdell when I threw my birth certificate into the fire. For me the man had no existence.

"No, my dear Emily," I answered. "That has nothing to do with it. I feel—" I tried to find the phrase. "I feel as if I were an accessory after the fact."

"Oh, Toby," she cried, "you can't blame yourself. Not for any of this. You didn't kill him."

"I could have. God! there were times when I could have. Don't you understand? I could have killed my father, but Emma Cunningham beat me to it, so I'm doing the next best thing. I'm defending my father's murderer."

And there it was. At last I had said it, admitted it—to Emily and to myself. This was the bitter irony I had sensed in Quinncannon's rooms without being able to articulate it. I was standing beside the man who was more to me than a father—the man whose son I had devoutly wished I was—and together we were defending the woman who had killed my father—a man who had disowned and deserted me before I was born, and whom I had hated enough to murder him.

I began to laugh. "Good God, Emily! The situation is comical. Patricide by proxy! Damn it! There's something about it that's downright Greek."

Her soft voice caressed me. "There's a system, darling, and if you're a lawyer you're a part of that system. I learned that much watching Papa work all those years. Someone prosecutes, someone defends, and someone judges. I know Papa defended guilty people. Many times they were acquitted, because he was a good lawyer. He wasn't proud of it—it was part of the job. He never boasted about it, but he liked to boast that, while he was district attorney, he never knowingly prosecuted an innocent man."

I listened to what she was saying. It made sense, I thought, but— "It's Quinncannon I don't understand," I almost exploded. "All that talent and skill, that brilliance! And he wastes it—perverts it—on that scheming, brutal woman!"

"Do you feel he's betrayed you?" she asked quietly.

"No!" I said too loudly. But I did feel exactly that.

"I remember a conversation Mr. Quinncannon had once with Papa. It was after Papa had won a case and then discovered that the man he had represented was guilty. Mr. Quinncannon said being a criminal lawyer was like being the groom in a Turkish marriage. You can't see the bride until after the wedding and when she lifts her veil it's too late.''

She touched my hair gently. "I know how much you admire and respect him, Toby. When I was growing up he was Papa's best friend. I admire him too, and love him. He is like an uncle to me. But he isn't a god. Don't expect that of him. I think he wants very much your respect and admiration. It's not fair of you to demand perfection as the price for that admiration.''

She continued to stroke my hair. I began to feel the tension draining out of me. "You mustn't feel guilty, Toby. Guilt is such a destructive and futile emotion—worse than jealousy, I think—worse even than hate because it's really hatred of one's self. You are making the best of unsought circumstances—practicing your profession with a man you respect. There is nothing shameful in that.''

I lay back against her shoulder and lost myself in the gentle swaying of the hansom and the clopping of the horse's hooves. At last I looked up at her and said, as lightly as I could, "How can you be so young and beautiful, and know so much?''

"I don't know so very much,'' she smiled. "I know you, darling, I think, because I love you.''

I gathered her in my arms and kissed her. I won't swear to it, but I believe that kiss lasted for three city blocks. Then she rested her head on my shoulder and I asked her to be my wife.

45

Doctor Burdell's Baby

The Cunningham trial ended on May 9. The jury took thirty-five minutes to bring in a verdict of not guilty. I could not imagine what had delayed them.

Emma went back to number 31 Bond Street to the house which held so many warm memories for her. Georgie Snodgrass was immediately released from the Tombs. Eckel had to remain a while longer behind bars but the district attorney began proceedings to drop all charges against him.

The Surrogate Court prepared to resume deliberations over whether Emma was Burdell's legal wife, an issue hardly settled by her acquittal. Neither Quinncannon nor I attended. The Irishman turned her representation over to an old colleague of his, former judge Gilbert Dean. I assume he told Dean the complete truth of the case. I never inquired. All I wanted was to leave the ugly memory of Emma Cunningham and John J. Eckel far behind me. But Emma and I were not finished with each other yet.

On the morning following the verdict I received a message to go to Quinncannon's office. Dr. David Uhl was also present, clutching his top hat in his lap and trembling uncomfortably with nervous excitement.

"Tell Mr. Brendon what you have told me, Doctor," the Irishman ordered.

"Yes," Uhl stammered, "well, last evening, Mr. Brendon, after she had returned to Bond Street, Mrs. Cunningham summoned me. She—she informed me that she was *enceinte.*"

"She's pregnant?"

"She says she has been carrying Dr. Burdell's child for six months."

I threw Quinncannon a tired grimace. "Oh, Lon. For God's sake."

He held up his hand. "Hear the doctor out, Toby."

"Shortly after Mrs. Cunningham was confined in the Tombs," Uhl continued, "she sent me a note requesting my professional attendance. She described her symptoms and I immediately suspected their cause, but I said nothing until our sixth or seventh consultation when I asked her if she were in a family way. She responded that she had not told that to anybody and would not answer my question at that time.

"Frankly, gentlemen, I was concerned for her health and I urged her to be examined by other physicians, but she simply would not hear of it. When I continued to press the matter she became extremely agitated and at last she dismissed me, saying that from then on Dr. Catlin would attend her. But last night she again sent for me."

"And this time she confessed everything," I said drily.

"Yes, sir. She said she feared a miscarriage, which must not happen as she wished to produce an heir to the Burdell estate. 'I shall never forgive myself,' she said, 'if I lose our child, and I know Harvey is watching us from heaven and would never forgive me.' "

I shot a glance at Quinncannon. Quinncannon studied the ceiling.

"Mrs. Cunningham has arranged for her widowed sister to come and stay with her," Uhl went on, "and a friend of hers, a Mrs. Wilt, has a sister living with her who is a nurse, and who will attend her when the infant is born."

"My, my," I said. "She seems to have thought of everything."

A sudden curiosity led me to ask, "Do her daughters know of this?"

"I don't believe Helen has been told. Augusta is aware of it but it seems to have upset her. She called me aside last night and admitted she wished she had not learned of it—that ever since her nervous system has been deranged. I prescribed a tonic."

I could almost sympathize with Augusta. Her conscience, such as it was, was already weighed down with too many of her mother's dark secrets.

"Mrs. Cunningham, against my advice, still refuses to submit to examination by any doctor save for Catlin or myself; however, as long as she shows no signs of aborting the child and has her sister with her, I suppose there is no great danger." The physician peered uncertainly at each of us in turn. "I hope I have done right in confiding in you gentlemen. Mrs. Cunningham does not know I am here, and I'm certain she would not approve, but I thought, as you are her attorneys, you should be informed. I mean, this *will* affect her hearing before the Surrogate, won't it?"

"We no longer repre—" I began but Quinncannon cut me off.

"You have done exactly the right thing, Doctor," he replied in his most soothing brogue. "Now I must ask two more favors of you."

"Anything, sir."

"I think it unwise that you mention Mrs. Cunningham's pregnancy to anyone else just at present. And we would appreciate it if you would keep Mr. Brendon and myself fully abreast of any new developments in the matter as they arise."

Uhl nodded vigorously. "Consider it done, sir," he said.

When the physician had gone I took a pencil from the desk and flung it into the air so that it ricocheted off the ceiling behind me. Quinncannon relaxed in his chair, gnawing on the stem of a cold pipe, and then he threw back his head and laughed—a deep, rich laugh that rolled out of him in waves—an infectious laugh that I soon caught from him and for a while we roared with hilarity like two lunatics in an asylum. At last we were forced to stop from sheer exhaustion. I slumped back in my chair while he fell forward on his desk, resting his chin on his crossed arms, and the laughter still periodically burst out of us in sporadic hoots and gasps.

When I finally regained some measure of self-control I said, "What do we do? Expose her?"

"Good God! No, Toby. Give the lady her head. This is classic —absolutely priceless. I wouldn't miss it for the world." He drew in a deep breath and paused a moment to be sure he had stopped laughing. "What we do, Toby, is nothing. We sit tight and await Dr. Uhl's report. I won't even attempt to guess what our ex-client will do next."

He looked at me with a funny smile on his face and suddenly we were again helpless with laughter.

A week later Uhl was back, pensively solemn and, if possible, even more nervous than during his first visit. "I am in a state of shock, Mr. Quinncannon—upon my word, I am prostrate with astonishment. I never for a second would have suspected it." He leaned across the Irishman's desk and lowered his voice to a whisper, turning his head from time to time as though spies were lurking everywhere.

"Last evening, gentlemen, Mrs. Cunningham offered me one thousand dollars to attend her during her pregnancy. Naturally I told her the fee was exorbitant out of all reason. She insisted on the amount, explaining that she would have plenty of money at her command once her baby inherited Burdell's estate. But when I again remonstrated with her she told me very plainly that—"

Uhl flushed with confused embarrassment. Quinncannon finished his thought. "She told you that the baby was to be delivered at the back door."

"Exactly!" the doctor exclaimed. "She was quite candid about it. She admitted she was not in a family way, and that we would have to get hold of a child in some way or other. She suggested one might be purchased from one of the charity hospitals."

Quinncannon was trying hard not to smile. "And how did you respond, Doctor?"

"I did not give her any satisfaction. I said I must sleep on her proposition, but, of course, I shall refuse. Really, I want nothing more to do with her. I did promise to keep you informed, Mr. Quinncannon, and so I have come here this morning. I—I thought too that perhaps you might advise me."

"You haven't spoken to anyone else?"

"No one, as we agreed. I considered that possibly I should see the district attorney."

"By no means," Quinncannon said. "The authorities must be contacted at the appropriate time, Doctor, but as yet we have only your unsupported word. I'm afraid you'll have to pretend to fall in with Mrs. Cunningham for the present. If you abandon her it will only put her on her guard, and unfortunately there are many physicians in New York who would be all too willing to assist her plot for the thousand dollar reward."

Uhl sighed and looked unhappy. He said, "What would you have me do?"

"First you might discover what is Dr. Catlin's role in this scheme."

"I asked her that. She replied that there was no need to be concerned about him. She said he could be trusted in the matter, for she had him so completely in her power that he did not dare disclose anything connected with it. She told me Catlin had adhered to her interests during all her troubles with her first husband, and she could rely upon him."

I watched Quinncannon take that in and turn it over slowly in his mind. "I see," he said. "All right, Doctor, what would you say is the best time for Emma to produce the little heir? Keep in mind that she cannot risk a question of bastardy or her grasp on the estate could be lost."

Uhl did some mental calculations. "I should say the earliest possible date would be July 28th if we are speaking of the ordinary gestation period. Perhaps the first week in August?"

"The first week in August by all means," the Irishman echoed with a smile. I was enjoying myself watching him enjoy himself. All the tension I had felt between us during the trial had disappeared.

"I want you," he explained to Uhl, "to return and tell Mrs. Cunningham that you have located a 'California widow' who is due to birth a child at the appropriate time and is willing to give the infant up secretly for adoption."

A California widow, it may be remembered, was a wife left behind while her husband panned for gold a continent away. Such women often became pregnant with other men's children whom they had to dispose of when their husbands sent for them to come west. The phenomenon was regrettably common after the great strike at Sutter's Mill. As a result the traffic in illegal babies was brisk and virtually immune to official interference.

"We will need a place for the baby to be born," Quinncannon said.

"Why not the hospital?"

"Well, it will actually be born in the hospital, Toby, but Emma and whomever she sends as her agent to pick up the child must think it was delivered in a more secluded spot for their own safety."

"What do you say to Elm Street?" I suggested. "It's only a short walk from Bond and it's always filled with vacant apartments."

My friend nodded. "That sounds satisfactory. Very well, Doctor, you may go back to your patient. Inform her of the arrangements you have made to obtain little Harvey and keep us posted."

June passed and then July. Uhl's visits became weekly reports. It was his opinion that Helen Cunningham honestly believed her mother was carrying a child. Augusta knew the truth but she and Emma never spoke of the business; in fact it was Uhl's impression that Augusta and her mother seldom spoke at all.

Emma's friend Mrs. Wilt, and her sister, Jane Bell, the nurse, had pretty well become fixtures around the place. They busied themselves bleaching and mending old baby clothes once worn by Emma's older children. The little mother-to-be had had herself moved from her bed to Burdell's old quarters where she spent much of her days pillow-propped where the dentist had once been laid out for viewing. There she received such female well-wishers as chose to call and sewed booties for the expected arrival. She was often heard humming little lullabies half to herself.

To promote the illusion cloth wadding was gradually added to the front of Emma's dresses. She developed odd appetites and cravings, and kept more and more to her bed for fear, as she said, of miscarriage. There were times, Uhl acknowledged, when if he had not known the truth he'd have sworn she really was, as he insisted on phrasing it, "in a family way."

It was Ann Barnes, Emma's widowed sister, who held the household together. There were, of course, no longer any servants. Poor Ann, though nearly ten years Emma's senior, and somewhat crippled in that one leg was shorter than the other, was nevertheless kept hopping. Emma kept a bell on her bed table the ringing of which called Ann from any remote corner of the house. Ann Barnes was in on the secret, Uhl reported. He thought Mrs. Wilt was also but could not be certain.

Quinncannon advised Uhl to avoid Dr. Catlin but one afternoon, to poor Uhl's chagrin and annoyance, they walked right into each other on Broadway. "He insisted upon conversing with me on the subject, right there on the street. I told him I supposed we understood each other—there was no necessity for any conferences. He said no; we must arrange things together. I did not say much. During the conversation he said he had devised this plan while he was in the Tombs visiting Mrs. Cunningham. It was a mere matter of justice to her, for she had been a very much abused woman. They discussed it in her cell, and made up their minds that they must have another doctor, that they could not get on without one. He said they thought immediately of me, although they would have had no difficulty getting hold of any physician, for Mrs. Cunningham was a brilliant and much admired woman who never lacked for men around her to support her. I told him I was in a hurry, and if he wished to see me he must call at my office. I then got into a stage and went uptown. Truly, gentlemen, the entire exchange was most unpleasant. I thought I should never break away from the man."

Quinncannon said something sympathetic and the doctor went away. "He won't hold up much longer," I observed. "His nerves are beginning to crack."

"He won't have to," my friend replied.

It was July 26.

46

The Blessed Event

Quinncannon had a friend in Timothy Daly, the warden of Belle-vue, through whom it was arranged to "borrow" a baby for the last act of the masque. That much managed, the Irishman at last confided in George Walling. They agreed that District Attorney Hall must be let in on the plot, but not until the last possible minute. That would be Monday, August 3, the day selected for Burdell's heir to be delivered. The infant in the case, therefore, must be born on Saturday the first or Sunday the second.

My first assignment was to locate a suitable apartment on Elm Street. With Hasty tagging along I spent the better part of Satur-day hunting without luck. At last we found two rooms that would do on the third floor of a house set back a bit farther from the curb than its neighbors and somewhat hidden by an oak tree. The landlord was a German named William Vieser, who ran a lager-beir potshop and lived just above it. He was positive we were up to no good at all. Though his sign indicated rooms were rented by the week, Vieser demanded a month in advance and I paid it. Instead of placating him it only made the fellow more suspicious. We had a further problem. Our chambers were devoid of furnish-ings. For all we knew Emma's agent would insist on inspecting the premises and unfurnished rooms would destroy the illusion. I was left with only one option.

"Herr Vieser," I said, "we must rent your furniture."

The German eyed me as if I was crazy.

"It is only for three nights. Then you may have it all back as good as new." I watched the gleam of greed shining in his beady little eyes and added, "How much?"

"Vun hundret dollars," he said without blinking.

I did the blinking for both of us. "Ten dollars," I said firmly. "Not a penny more!"

"Vun hundret dollars," said Herr Vieser.

"You're a hard man, Hen Vieser, but I'll make it twenty dollars."

"Vun hundret dollars," he replied stolidly.

"Damn it, Hasty," I said under my breath. "I'm not getting anywhere."

"Sure you are," the youth answered. "You're slowly getting up to a hundred dollars."

When I had given the German swindler his one hundred dollars I suggested he might assist in carrying the furniture up to the third floor. He took time out from counting his money to eye us up and down.

"You look strong. Boy look strong."

For an hour and a half Hasty and I hauled Vieser's furniture up a narrow staircase to our rented apartment: a sofa-bedstead, rocking chair, rugs, tables, lamps, five straight-back chairs, a full-length mirror that weighed a ton.

"Toby," gasped an exhausted Hasty, "what do we need with a *mirror?*"

"For 'vun hundret dollars," I replied through gritted teeth, "we're not going to leave that Saxon sharper with a stick!"

Elizabeth Ann Anderson, twenty-seven, had been deserted by her drunken brute of a husband when she was three months pregnant. She supported herself by sewing—making aprons and sun bonnets which she peddled at the Washington Market. It was a meager existence, barely enough for her own needs much less those of a child. On Saturday, August 1, being conscious of the symptoms of confinement, she attempted to reach Bellevue, riding the Third Avenue car to Twenty-seventh Street and walking toward the hospital. The pains of labor seized her before she had traveled a block and she sank down on a stoop. The Irish maid who heard her groaning would not take her in as her mistress was away but she sent the neighbor's boy to Bellevue. The doctor arrived after Elizabeth Ann, having managed to crawl into a small outhouse, gave birth to a pretty, blue-eyed little girl. Mother and daughter were at once rushed to the lying-in ward in Bellevue's charity wing.

MONDAY, AUGUST 3, 2:18 P.M.

The Elm Street chambers had taken on the appearance of a command post in wartime. Present and awaiting Quinncannon's orders were, besides myself and Hasty, Captain Walling, Captain Dilks, and Dr. Stephen Mayne, whom the Irishman had recruited into the plot to take charge of the baby in transit from the hospital. We were prepared, we thought, for any contingency.

I realize as I write that many, perhaps most, of my readers will hesitate to credit my account of the events of that interesting afternoon and evening. I can only give my assurance as a gentleman that every word is true.

Uhl had been dispatched to inform Emma that the heir's birth was imminent and she should prepare her agent to take delivery that night after dark at number 190 Elm. Hasty was perched on the window seat on sentry duty. Suddenly he shouted, "Cab approaching! Cab stopping! Dr. Uhl stepping down!" He turned to face us. "Boy! gents, the doc's in a panic!"

We heard Uhl taking the stairs two at a clip—then a frenzied knock and the door swung in and slammed against the wall. The physician glared at us frantically.

"She's done it! I knew it! That mad woman has upset all our plans! It's doomed, I tell you—doomed!"

Dr. Mayne pounced on him, shoving camphor under his nose.

Quinncannon took hold of his shoulders and pushed him as gently as circumstances would allow into the rocking chair. I poured a stiff dose of whiskey down his throat. The Irishman still gripped his shoulders.

"Easy, now, Doctor—easy, easy. We don't want to get upset, do we? We know how bad that is for our system, don't we?"

Gradually Uhl calmed down. There was still a wildness in his eyes. "She's sending someone over here to scout the place," he at last sputtered.

"When?" Quinncannon asked.

"NOW! RIGHT NOW, man! They may be minutes behind me." He gave a choking sound. "Don't you understand? They may want to look at the rooms. They may want to see the mother. *We don't have a mother!*"

"Well," my friend said, "we're going to have to get a mother." His eyes roamed around the parlor until they fixed on Captain Dilks.

"Ooooh, no!" the policeman exclaimed.

"There's nothing to it," Quinncannon assured him, producing a frilly nightcap. "All you have to do is put this on and get into the bed and, should Emma's spy insist on gaining entrance, you just moan a little."

The burly officer shrank back from the nightcap. "I got orders to cooperate with you, sir, but I'm drawing the line right here. Why can't the boy do it? Or this young fellow?" He was referring to me.

"Unless I don't know the lady at all," the Irishman answered, "Mrs. Cunningham is coming here herself. She would recognize the boy or Mr. Brendon and then the cat would be out of the bag. You're the only man present that Emma's never seen. I'm afraid you're it, Captain." He pulled the nightcap down over poor Dilks' ears. The cap had seen better days—the lace border was torn and hung down over one eye, giving the officer the appearance of a sissified cyclops.

"Just climb into bed," Quinncannon said, leading Dilks into the bedroom, "and pull the blankets up to your chin, and if you get a signal, give us a few moans. Try to sound like a woman in labor. Now, Dilks, let me hear a moan or two.''

Dilks looked as unhappy as I've ever seen a man but he offered a few half-hearted moans.

Quinncannon shook his head. "No, no, you sound like a wounded hog. Louder, Dilks, louder. Put some soul into it, and pitch it higher, shriller. You're a woman, remember, in terrible pain.''

The policeman gave out a series of shrieks, followed by the most pitiful groans, while Hasty, who was again posted as lookout, cried out, "Enemy sighted!" He added to Quinncannon, "It's old Emma, herself, just like you figured.''

The Irishman took charge. "George," he said to Walling, "get in the bedroom closet. Stephen," to Dr. Mayne, "you and Uhl let her in if she knocks. Remember you're caring for our little mother. Hasty, into the window seat and stay put. Toby, stand by the bedroom door. If Emma comes upstairs signal Dilks to start moaning." He was preparing to step into the closet in the parlor.

"If she comes up," I asked, "where do I go?"

"Under the bed, lad, as fast as you can move.''

Downstairs we could hear the street door opening. "She's inside the house," Mayne said from the window. Quinncannon lay one finger aside his moustache, winked at me broadly, and disappeared into the closet. Emma began ascending the stairs. When she reached the second floor she halted, evidently trying to decide whether to venture the rest of the climb. Then we could hear her footsteps once again. She was coming up.

I gave Dilks the sign. "Aargh! Oooooo! Argh ooooh! Yiiiiii!" The captain was giving the performance of his life. I heard Emma on the landing just outside and dove under the bed.

The bedsprings were beyond repair. They screeched with nearly as much agony as the policeman in the bed. To get in the mood for his role Dilks was writhing and twisting above me. There was barely space for me to squeeze in out of sight. The springs were grazing my back and the top of my head. "Ooooooh!" Dilks bellowed. "Ugh! Argh!"

Listening at the hall door, Emma could not have failed to hear Dilks' act. Apparently she assumed that it would be unwise to disturb the inmates of the apartment because soon her steps could be heard descending the stairs. At last Mayne came to the bedroom doorway. "She's gone," he announced and I wriggled out from beneath the bed. Dilks was so anxious to escape that he almost stepped on my hand.

In the parlor Quinncannon was rocking slowly in the chair, barely suppressing a grin. The rest of us stood in various states of shivering fidgets. I thought he really ought to be ashamed of himself.

Dr. Mayne went by carriage to Bellevue to borrow Elizabeth Ann Anderson's daughter, the infant who was about to rise from indigent obscurity to become the most famous baby in New York, if not the nation. Other police captains began to arrive, and Quinncannon and Walling spread a map of lower Manhattan on a large round table in the parlor. Plainclothesmen were deployed throughout the area like troops before a battle. Watching the Irishman I could think of nothing else but Wellington and his generals preparing for Waterloo.

Captain Dilks had shed his nightcap and vowed to murder the first man who did not keep his secret. Another "mother" was needed. Uhl had a friend, an apothecary on Spring Street named William Gilchrest, who had a talent for amateur theatrics. Hasty was dispatched to fetch him, and when Gilchrest arrived he whimpered and moaned so satisfactorily that he was engaged on the spot. I can still see him standing before the full-length mirror Hasty and I had struggled to carry upstairs and admiring himself in the tattered lace nightcap.

About seven o'clock Mayne returned with the baby and a young Irish nurse from the hospital. Her name was Mary Regan, a no-nonsense, down-to-earth lass with flaming hair and a turned-up nose who seemed surprised by nothing that was happening around her. She went right to work in the bedroom fussing over her tiny charge.

Dr. Mayne had remembered to bring a basket to transport the child but he'd forgotten something else. "You're the expert in these things, Stephen," Quinncannon told him, "but shouldn't there be a placenta?"

Off went Mayne again in his carriage, back to Bellevue. By now the doctor's nerves were a bit jangled and Hasty went along to keep him company. I gathered later that en route Mayne explained to the boy what a placenta was.

Sundown was to be at eight-thirty. An hour earlier the police captains left the apartment to begin stationing their men. Walling was the last to go. He took from Uhl some lunar caustic and dabbed it on the baby, a little behind the left ear and some under each arm. The stuff was harmless and, at that time, invisible, but the following day it would turn black, clearly identifying the infant. Walling wasn't about to let Emma claim they'd switched babies on her.

At seven-forty-five Uhl returned to Bond Street. He was back at eight-thirty with another tale of the amazing Emma: "I was shown upstairs to the second story. The room was very dark indeed. I walked into the front room where Mrs. Cunningham is pretending to have labor pains. She informed me Dr. Catlin had been summoned. She said she would call the lady who was to go for the child, but she would not tell her name. I don't know why because I recognized her sister, Mrs. Barnes, at once. Mrs. Cunningham asked her if she was ready to go. She said yes, and asked where the black dress was. Then Mrs. Cunningham said that the lady would come half an hour after me, and I should wait in the front door of this house for her. The lady is to hold in her hand a white handkerchief by which I can recognize her."

Quinncannon laughed. "What a gift for intrigue that woman has! A little white handkerchief. What a wonderful touch. I could almost regret this charade is nearing its close. I'm going to miss her."

There was something in his tone when he uttered that last sentence that made me study him. For a second I thought I had read his mind, but the insight, whatever it was, was instantly gone.

From the street there was a thunder of hooves and the scream of brakes, and then young feet scrambling nimbly up the stairs. The door burst open and Hasty stood there holding aloft a roll of silk oilcloth. "I've got it—I've got it!" he shouted in triumph. He looked uncertainly at Quinncannon. "What do I do with it?"

"Take it into the bedroom and give it to the nurse."

The youngster bolted into the bedroom. Inside "Mother" Gilchrest was already under the covers, practicing his groans. Dr. Mayne appeared in the hall gasping. "I'm getting too old for this sort of thing," he panted to no one in particular.

I felt an urgent tug at my sleeve. Hasty was standing beside me, his eyes sparkling with excitement. At that moment I realized how great a thrill it was for him to be a part of all this elaborate nonsense. I smiled and sent him back to the window to keep a weather eye out for our visitor.

Quinncannon advised Dr. Mayne to go into the street and wait in the shadows with one of the patrolmen. Uhl went down to await the mystery woman with the white handkerchief. That left only Hasty, the Irishman, and myself in the parlor. In the bedroom Gilchrest keened softly, Mary Regan hummed a lullaby, and the baby slept like—well, like a baby. Outside the sun had been down for forty minutes. We waited.

At length Hasty said, "Here she comes, gents."

Quinncannon remained in the rocking chair but I went to the window and peered out over the boy's shoulder.

The woman who hurried down Elm Street was unquestionably Emma. She wore a black dress and long black cape that swept along the sidewalk. On her head was a black, coal-scuttle bonnet with a black veil to conceal her features. Her gloves were also black, but as she neared the house I could see that in her right hand she clutched a white handkerchief. She disappeared from my view under the window. A moment later we heard her on the stairs following Uhl's heavier tread.

Hasty jumped into the window seat. I went into the bedroom and hid myself behind the door. It was now so dark that I saw no need to crawl under the bed. Quinncannon had stepped into the parlor closet. Gilchrest was groaning away. Having moved to the parlor rocking chair, Nurse Regan cradled the baby in her arms and crooned to it softly. The door from the landing opened.

The only light in the apartment burned dimly on the center table of the sitting room. By its glow, through the crack between the bedroom door and the frame, I could just see the silhouette of the lady in black. She crossed to the bedroom and stopped inches away from me. I held my breath while she glanced in at the figure on the bed. Gilchrest kept up his bleating. After a long minute, evidently satisfied, she turned back without entering the chamber.

"I must now ask you, madam," Uhl said, "are you the person who has come for this child?"

Her response was to shake her handkerchief at him.

He went to the nurse, took the baby, placed it in the basket, and handed it to the veiled figure. Without a word having ever been spoken she accepted the basket, slipping her arm through the handle, and went out, closing the door behind her.

Gilchrest was sent home with thanks. Uhl, according to the plan, returned to Bond Street. Hasty engaged a cab to take Mary Regan back to Bellevue. I watched Quinncannon press a green-back into her hand and then helped him light two or three lamps. "Should we be leaving?" I asked.

"No rush," he replied, dropping into the rocker. "I have a carriage waiting, we know where she's going, and the police have her in sight every step of the way."

He massaged his temples with the tips of his fingers. I had seen him like this before. He seemed to be gathering his energies for some final ordeal the nature of which I could not guess. The plot had gone off without a hitch and, I observed to him, we had Emma in the trap.

He looked up at me. "For what crime, Toby?"

"Lon, she's going to pass that baby off as Burdell's heir to get hold of his money."

He shook his head. "She can't be arrested for what she's planning to do until she does it. It's not illegal to pretend to have a baby. It's not illegal to falsify the name of the father of the baby you pretend to have. Not until she actually goes to court and swears that child on Burdell will she be guilty of anything."

"Good God!" I cried. All along I had believed we were going to put Emma in jail where she belonged. Not for murder—it was too late for that. But for *some* crime. "If she can't be charged with anything, then why in the name of God have we gone to all this damn trouble?"

He stood and put his hands on my shoulders. His eyes burned straight into mine. "Toby," he said evenly, "if you've ever trusted me, trust me in this. I will not— Damn it! I will *not* risk your life."

He turned away toward the door. I said, "Lon! Don't shut me out. Whatever you're going to do, please, don't shut me out of it."

He looked back at me and a smile gradually creased his face. He withdrew a gun from his pocket. "You do know how to use this."

I nodded quickly.

"Then take it, little brother," he said in that quiet brogue, "and tonight keep your back to mine."

47

The Last Act

It was nearing eleven o'clock when our carriage rolled into Bond Street. We halted several houses down from number 31 and joined George Walling and two other officers. Dr. Mayne was with them and so was A. Oakey Hall. The district attorney and I exchanged glares.

"Who is in the house?" Quinncannon asked.

"So far as I can tell, besides Mrs. Cunningham and the baby, there's her sister, Mrs. Barnes, her two daughters, and the doctors, Catlin and Uhl." Walling was counting them off on his fingers. "The little boys have been sent away. A few minutes ago one of my men intercepted a Mrs. Wilt who says she was on her way to fetch her sister who's a nurse. We detained her."

"What about John Eckel?"

Walling indicated a police wagon parked some distance away. "I got him out of the Tombs like you requested, Mr. Quinncannon, though I'm damned if I know how he figures in this business. He's been locked up the whole time."

"Let's get straight on what we're going to do," the Irishman said to Walling. To this point he'd addressed only the captain, ignoring Hall. The district attorney had grown increasingly irritated.

"Look here, Quinncannon, I'm the senior official here. We'll handle this my way."

"Shut up, Hall," my friend said. Just like that the prosecutor fell silent.

"A recent law," Quinncannon said, "allows the police to enter a building without a warrant if they suspect a felony has been committed there. We're going to get into Emma's house using that law, George."

"Yes, sir, I remember the plan. I'm to knock on the door and flash my badge. Once we're in we go upstairs to Burdell's old rooms. Then you and—" He looked at me quizzically.

"Mr. Brendon will go with me," Quinncannon said.

"Yes, sir. Well, you and Mr. Brendon will go into the bedroom, leaving the door ajar, and Mr. Hall and I will stay back, out of sight, in the office. We'll keep Eckel with us, in the darbies of course, under the charge of Officer Welsh. We're not to enter the bedroom until the appropriate moment." He frowned. "But how will we know the appropriate moment?"

"Don't worry, George." The Irishman patted his shoulder. "You'll know."

Welsh escorted Eckel from the police wagon and the butcher was ordered to keep his mouth closed or have it gagged. Then the six of us crossed Bond Street and Walling rang the bell.

A frightened Helen Cunningham admitted us and informed us her mother was confined and could not be disturbed. "The doctors are with her now. We've sent for a nurse."

Without warning Quinncannon seized her by the wrists. "Helen! On the night of the murder you slept in the attic with George Snodgrass, didn't you?"

Stunned by the sudden accusation, the girl stammered out the truth.

Just as quickly he released her and spoke in a reassuring tone. "That's a good girl. No need to be afraid, child." He put Helen in Welsh's charge and another officer was sent in to guard Eckel. We commenced the climb to the second floor.

I puzzled over Quinncannon's purpose. We already knew how the girl had passed the fatal evening. True, our information came from a privileged source, but what was the point in raising it now? Emma no longer needed an alibi.

The dental office was dark except for a candle flickering bravely on the center table. Emma had taken time out from her labor for a bit of supper, for there was the remnant of a meal of cheese, bread, and jam. The door leading to the front room through the laboratory was closed. Quinncannon knocked.

Ann Barnes began talking before she had the door fully open. "I'm glad you're back, Helen, dear. Who was it downstairs?" She stopped abruptly when she saw us. Quinncannon stepped inside and I followed him.

Emma lay on the bed with the baby beside her in the crook of her arm. Uhl stood nearby chafing her hand in his. Augusta lurked, rather guiltily it seemed to me, in the shadows at the head of the bed. She was wringing her hands in great agitation. For the first time I noticed how large and strong they were.

Catlin was soaking some sheets in a bucket of blood and putting them into a washtub half-filled with water. He looked up at us with surprise but not a hint of alarm. I noted the placenta on a bloody towel on one of the chairs. A single gas lamp burned low near one of the draped windows.

Emma smiled when she recognized us. "Good evening, gentlemen. I don't know what has brought you here but your arrival is most opportune. As you can see, I have just given birth to the child of my late husband. You might inform your friend, Judge Dean, who is representing me before the Surrogate. I feel certain this joyous news will influence the court to decide the pending matter in my favor."

It made me sick to watch her. She was so cocksure of herself, so smugly triumphant.

Quinncannon took off his hat and gave her a slight bow. "I have come to congratulate you, Emma. At last it appears you have what you so desperately wanted, control of Harvey Burdell's estate. You stand acquitted of his murder—"

"For which I have you to thank, sir," she interrupted graciously. "Your reputation, may I say, is well deserved."

He bowed again at the compliment. "There seems little doubt the Surrogate will declare you the doctor's legal widow."

"Again thanks to you, Mr. Quinncannon, and the remarkable memory for faces possessed by Reverend Marvine."

"Remarkable is the word, madam. Reverend Marvine remembers clearly whatever was last suggested to him."

He took a few steps toward the bed and looked down at the baby. "Who would you say the child most resembles, madam? You or the doctor?"

"Why, she's the very image of Dr. Burdell."

"Hmmm. Perhaps," he replied, "just a bit around the eyes." All at once his voice took on an edge. "I must say, Emma, that after a few false starts, you managed the affair brilliantly. I've defended guilty clients before, but none, I think, were quite so clever."

Suddenly she was on her guard. "I really don't take your meaning, sir. Besides, there is such a thing, I have heard, as double jeopardy."

"Exactly. You may discuss the matter now with as much freedom as you wish, though the district attorney himself might be eavesdropping in the next room."

I saw that he was preparing to amuse himself at Hall's expense. But surely that was not our only purpose in being there.

The Irishman found the most comfortable chair and stretched out his long legs, resting one boot atop the other. He removed his pipe. "Let me see if I can accurately reconstruct the murder of Dr. Burdell."

"I have told you, sir," she said warily. "I cannot be prosecuted again for that crime."

He smiled at her. "As you have acknowledged your debt to me on that score, I would ask you, madam, to indulge me in this. Now, we know that about eleven o'clock you and your daughter, Augusta, were left alone in your rooms. You went downstairs and let yourself into the doctor's suite with your passkey. Then you waited in the bedroom—this room—for Burdell's return. Your accomplice waited in the laboratory."

"Oh," she said, "did I have an accomplice?"

"You did, madam, and your accomplice had a dagger. When Burdell came home your accomplice attacked him as he sat at his desk and stabbed him to death, inflicting fifteen wounds during a brief, violent struggle. There are several reasons for believing in an accomplice, all of which we brought out at your trial. You are physically too frail to have overpowered the victim, and your hands are further afflicted by a rheumatic condition of long standing, as both these gentlemen"—indicating Uhl and Catlin —"testified. There were no bloodstains on any of your garments, which by itself would not be conclusive, but you were forced to submit to the infamous body search and no marks of violence were found as there would have been on the killer."

"It seems to me, Mr. Quinncannon, that all you are proving is that I did *not* kill my husband."

"In December," my friend went on, "Burdell changed the lock of his safe. You had stolen a key to the old lock, which was found in your possession, but he had the only key to the new one. There were two important papers in that safe. Had the doctor not opened it before his death, you could have taken the key from his body. Either way you removed those documents: the will he had recently made disinheriting you, and the release you signed promising, among other things, to leave this house in May. You destroyed the will but kept the other.

"Burdell's body lay six inches from the door connecting his office with the corridor, making escape through that door impossible. His key was on the inside, in the keyhole. Upon entering he had locked the door behind him, against you, as he habitually did. Your accomplice removed the key and carried it out through the front room into the hall. You followed, leaving Burdell's bedroom key in his pocket and using your passkey to lock the hall door. That was your first mistake, madam, for it proved the murderer could not have left the apartment through either door

DR. BURDELL'S OFFICE

without a passkey, and you had the only one. Then, almost immediately, you made your second mistake."

"And what, pray, was that?" She appeared amused, entering into the spirit of the game.

"You had your accomplice insert Burdell's office key outside his door. Your idea was to make it appear that the killer must have entered originally by means of that key, but of course the doctor would never have left himself so vulnerable to an intruder, and in any case you had left the imaginary intruder with no way to get out."

"Please continue, sir. I find this fascinating. Tell me, who was my mysterious accomplice? Mr. Eckel, I suppose."

"No, Emma," he replied, "though, if the worst happened, you were prepared to make it look as though Eckel, acting alone, was guilty. You first involved him by paying him to pose as Burdell during your bogus wedding."

"There you are in error, sir," she snapped. "The doctor and

I *were* married. Reverend Marvine identified my husband in court."

"You forget, madam. I am the man who created the illusion of your wedding before the Surrogate. Marvine has no idea whom he married. He first refused to identify Burdell because the coroner's son told him it was Eckel. Then he identified Burdell because Mr. Brendon and I told him it was Burdell. Initially he could not recognize you at all. Now he swears you were the bride. His evidence, like that of most eyewitnesses, is worthless. However, the point is not worth arguing since, if you were the dentist's legal wife, your motive to murder is actually strengthened.

"At all events allow me to assume, for the sake of the argument, that Eckel was thus far involved in your plot. Recall, madam, that shortly before he was killed Burdell sent Alvah Blaisdell to Mr. Brendon to inquire into your disposition of the suit for breach of promise, something which would not have concerned him if he were your husband. When he learned you could still activate that suit he was furious and insisted on your executing a release. On the day of his death he arranged to lease the house to another party when your agreement terminated, and he asked Blaisdell to live with him because he feared you would take his life. I submit, Emma darlin', that these are not the actions of a married man."

All bemusement was gone from her eyes. She propped herself up in the bed and scowled at him. Quinncannon puffed contentedly on his pipe and went quietly on with his narrative.

"Eckel knew of the false marriage but he was ignorant of your plans for murder. You planted some of the papers you had stolen from Burdell in Eckel's secretary, including the promise to befriend you, the statement that he had never made a will, and the release, which was no longer enforceable—this to further implicate the butcher. You knew his employer had summoned him early on Saturday—you had received and delivered the message to him at seven-thirty Friday night. You believed his early departure would cast suspicion on him. You even suggested as much to me. And of course you established him in a room which communicated with your own and shared his bed from time to time, not particularly discreetly. Your notion was that if the police suspected the killer was someone inside the house, it would appear that Eckel had murdered the doctor on his own hook in hopes of becoming your next husband and sharing the inheritance. The scheme was not well thought out. For all your guile, madam, your schemes never are. But you viewed it only as an ultimate contingency."

He gave her a thin smile. "However, your accomplice was not John Eckel."

She waited. "All right, Mr. Quinncannon, you have my attention. Whom do you suspect?"

"It had to be someone totally loyal to you, madam. Someone who loves you deeply. Someone who would do anything you asked—lie for you, conceal your crimes, even murder. And it had to be someone possessed of enough strength to overcome Burdell—someone with powerful hands. All along everyone has assumed that your accomplice was a man—"

"NO!" Augusta Cunningham screamed. She broke into a fit of tears. "It is all true. I knew that mother would murder the doctor. I lied under oath about everything—the wedding, our sleeping arrangements, everything—" She was almost hysterical. "But I did not kill him, Mr. Quinncannon. Oh, God! You must believe me. I DID NOT KILL DR. BURDELL!"

"Augusta!" Her mother barked an order. "Be still!"

"Who did kill him, Augusta?" Quinncannon asked sharply. "Who really held the dagger?"

"I don't know," the girl wailed through her sobs. "I don't know! I thought it was Mr. Eckel. Oh, I know I've lied to you before, Mr. Quinncannon, but I swear to God I'm telling the truth now. I don't know who killed him!"

Catlin went to her and put his arm around her shoulder, seeking to calm her. She shook violently with weeping.

Uhl said, "Really, Quinncannon, is all this necessary?"

The Irishman said to Emma, "There was considerable evidence that the murderer came from outside the household, both in what was found and in what was not. What was not found was the murder weapon, though the police tore the house apart. Nor was any bloodied clothing discovered though even the ashes in the hearths were sifted for unburned swatches and buttons. These things were carried away from the house by the assassin. He dropped the first blood spot on the sill of the murder room when he put Burdell's key in the door, and from there on he left a trail of his victim's blood down two staircases and along two corridors until he escaped through the front basement door, leaving a sanguine smear where he'd felt unsuccessfully for the knob.

"You, madam, admitted him by prearrangement at eleven. He brought the dagger with him. Together you waited in Burdell's rooms and, when the doctor returned, he dispatched him as I have described. You were afraid a light might be observed so he had to grope his way through the dark, unfamiliar passageways with you behind him, madam, to direct him, and when he was fled you made another foolish mistake. You bolted the door behind him. You had hoped the police would believe that an enemy of Burdell's, or perhaps a disgruntled relative—he had plenty of both—had come in and killed him. But there was no sign of forced entry. Of course the killer might have come back with his victim or the doctor might have let him in, but he could hardly have locked the house behind him, and the first-floor windows and all the doors were locked from inside."

Quinncannon looked around the darkened room with a half-smile until his gaze fell upon one of the circle. "It must have been a gruesome experience for you, Catlin," he remarked in his easy brogue. " 'Who would have thought the old man had so much blood in him?' "

Dr. Catlin's eyes narrowed. "You can't prove a thing," he said.

"You realize," the Irishman said, "it all points to you. Four doctors testified for the defense that the murderer must have had anatomical knowledge. Consider that Burdell was struggling for his life in a wild, flailing panic that could not have consumed longer than thirty seconds, and yet, of the fifteen wounds you inflicted, no less than five would have proved fatal. Allowing for some gashes delivered while defending yourself, that is a remarkable circumstance. Obviously you knew exactly the points on Burdell's body which were most vulnerable. I have a feeling that, properly presented, those facts would make a strong and damning impression on a jury."

"It isn't proof," Catlin shot back.

"Then there's your fierce loyalty to Mrs. Cunningham over the years. At the moment I can't prove that you posed as Van Dolan, Emma's imaginary lawyer, in a conversation with Cyrenius Stevens, but I suspect in the hands of the right attorney the Colonel's memory might improve to the point where he could identify you as that shadowy figure. I find it intriguing that the unabashed admiration 'Van Dolan' expressed for this lady sounds suspiciously like the sentiments you imparted to Dr. Uhl a few days ago on Broadway. You may recall the conversation, Catlin, as the same one in which you admitted, in fact bragged, that the scheme of the bogus Burdell baby was your idea. You know, Doctor, when a jury learns that a defendant has plotted with a confederate to commit one crime, they're much more likely to believe him capable of plotting a second crime with the same confederate, especially when both crimes are inspired by the same motive."

Catlin glowered at him. "It is my word against Uhl's. So far as the world knows this is Harvey Burdell's baby."

Quinncannon shook his head. "I'm afraid you're mistaken, Doctor. The authorities have been aware of this ploy since its inception. This business won't do your chances with the Surrogate much good, Emma."

"You traitor!" the lady shouted at Uhl.

"She offered Uhl a thousand dollars, Catlin," my friend said. "I shudder to think how much she offered you—or did she promise to marry you and did you believe her . . . again."

Something in his tone alerted me. I watched him. It was coming.

"Frankly," Quinncannon said, "I would despair of ever bringing either one of you to justice if I couldn't prove you murdered George Cunningham."

"No, Mother!" Augusta broke free of Catlin and knelt at her mother's side. "Don't let him do this! You didn't kill Father. I know you didn't."

"Be still, child," Emma hissed. "For my sake be still!"

"I won't be still!" the girl cried. "I won't be still any more." She was on her feet, her fists clenched at her sides, facing the Irishman, tears again rolling down her cheeks. "Father was ill. He was dreadfully ill for such a long time. That last morning he was so bad. We feared for his life. I remember Mother took up a pillow and went into his room, just to put under his head to make him more comfortable. I didn't go in. I couldn't bear to see Father suffer so. Mother was with him only a few minutes. When she came out she was ghastly white. 'Augusta,' she said, 'you must go at once for Dr. Catlin. I'm afraid your father is dead.' She said he'd had a seizure. I was so frightened. I ran for Dr. Catlin.

"He came with me at once. Helen was upstairs. Mother told me to say nothing—that she would tell Helen. She and the doctor went into Father's room and I watched from the door, and I saw—" She fought for control. "I saw Father *move!* He wasn't dead, don't you see? Then Mother came out and closed the door and said we must let the doctor alone to help Father, but . . . but, after five or six minutes Dr. Catlin came out and told us that Father was dead." Her shoulders were now heaving with sobs. "Don't you understand? Mother couldn't have killed him. She was with me when he died."

With his head Quinncannon motioned Uhl to care for the girl. Then he gave his attention to Emma. "Your husband had insurance policies totaling fifteen thousand dollars. His illness was a heavy financial drain on you and his chances of recovery were nil but he might have lingered on for years. You took that pillow, Emma, and pressed it over his face in an effort to smother him. You kept it there until you thought he was dead. But those rheumatic hands betrayed you, and old George had more stamina than you credited him with."

"That's not true." She was trying to sound defiant but there was terror in her voice. "My husband died of a heart attack."

"No, darlin', because if he had his teeth would not have been broken. His lower teeth pressed against the inside of his mouth while he fought for breath and they snapped off. Those teeth and your daughter's story will prove you attempted his murder."

"But he wasn't dead. You heard Augusta. He was still alive when I left him to comfort her."

"Emma, Emma." Quinncannon sighed. "You bungled that murder the way you've bungled everything else. All Catlin was supposed to do was cover your crime and sign the death certificate. Instead you left him to finish George off."

He turned to Catlin. "And you, Doctor, were just as careless. It never occurred to you to look in the old man's mouth and notice those broken teeth. But it was the fractured hyoid bone— that was your fatal blunder. You see, Catlin, the bone was broken but there wasn't any bruise. Had there been, Uhl would have seen it. That bothered me. What you must have done was press your thumbs against the middle of your victim's throat just above the adam's apple. A slow, steady pressure would close the carotid arteries that carry blood to the brain, but the pressure would be sufficiently slight that the skin would not be bruised. The hyoid is delicate, however, and in the process it snapped. The whole operation would take about five minutes, the length of time Augusta says you were alone with her father. Afterward the snag in your plan worried you, and you sent for Uhl to corroborate heart failure and co-sign the death certificate. It was a risk but not a great one. Uhl was your friend and Emma's. It never occurred to him to look for evidence of murder."

Quinncannon drew on his pipe and asked with the air of a man who really wanted to know: "What *did* she promise you, Doctor? My guess is she said, after a decent interval, she would marry you. But she met Harvey Burdell, who was worth, not fifteen thousand, but more than thirteen times that. What did she tell you? It would be easy. She would marry Burdell and then the two of you would murder him and she would inherit and, after a seemly mourning period, she would marry you. You're in love with her, Catlin, aren't you? You have been for years. And look at her now. Turn your head, Catlin, and look at her."

Emma's eyes gleamed like a cat's in the shadowy darkness. There was a strange twisted smile on her face.

"Right this minute she's plotting to betray you, Doctor," Quinncannon said. "Look at her, man! She's getting ready to swear the whole dirty, brutal business on *you.*"

A harsh, bestial growl that I had difficulty recognizing as human rumbled deep in Catlin's throat and rose in pitch into a scream of agony. Suddenly there was a gun in his hand. I had not seen him reach for it. He fired at Quinncannon wildly. I yanked out the pistol the Irishman had given me. Catlin held his weapon in both hands to steady it. The Irishman started to get out of his chair. Catlin fired at him again, point-blank. His bullet tore through Quinncannon's arm. The impact drove him back into the chair. I aimed at the doctor and squeezed the trigger. My shot caught Catlin in the shoulder and spun him a half turn. Before he could recover I lunged at him. We crashed to the floor. I was on top of him. In the corner of my eye I saw his gun skidding across the floor. I slammed my fist against Catlin's face and he stopped struggling.

At my back I heard the door from the office slam open and the sound of scuffling feet. Then a breathless Walling said, "Mr. Quinncannon, do we come in now?"

There was a brief pause before I heard the tired brogue.

"Now, George."

Epilogue

Poor Samuel Catlin had, as Quinncannon suspected, been in love with Emma for years. That passion had motivated all his actions including, I now saw, his intense anger at me on the night he challenged me to a duel. His adoration did not, however, prevent Emma from turning on him like a cornered cobra, just as the Irishman had predicted.

Judge Dean defended her at her trial. He claimed that Catlin, desperately infatuated with the lady and covetous of her husband's insurance, had planned George Cunningham's murder alone. He had tried to smother the old man with a pillow and, that failing, he'd used his thumbs to cut off the supply of blood to his victim's brain. The jury bought part of this fable but they couldn't quite believe that Emma had not dropped a hint or two to the doctor that George should be put out of his misery. She got five years, of which she served two. She then headed west to California where, the story goes, she married a sourdough who'd struck it rich in '49 and soon after became an immensely wealthy widow.

Samuel Catlin was convicted of murder and hanged.

The "Bogus Burdell Baby," who'd been arrested in the general confusion and released the next morning for lack of evidence, was for a time paid twenty-five dollars weekly by P. T. Barnum to gurgle at the gullible in his museum.

Emily Hoffman and I were married in the autumn of 1857. Jeremy was my best man. Quinncannon gave the bride away.

It was Emily's idea to adopt Hasty. Under her tutelage he has actually become a scholar and a gentleman. His ambition is to go into law, and Jeremy and I have left room for his name on the new shingle that hangs outside the Reede Street office proclaiming The Firm of Hoffman, Todd, and Brendon.

About a year after the Cunningham/Burdell trial I met Quinncannon's ship at South Street when he returned from Dublin and took him to the Astor House for drinks.

"You won't believe the metamorphosis in Hasty," I said. "He still scratches his ear with his fork but now he knows the proper fork to use."

The Irishman smiled at me. "Marriage evidently agrees with you, my friend."

"More than you know," I answered. "I'm going to be a father."

His smile widened at my obvious pleasure. "Everything that goes around. . . ." He raised his glass and we drank a silent toast.

"Of course we want you to be the godfather."

One eyebrow went up. "A bolt of lightning would demolish the font."

"Well, at all events," I said, "you shall be a grandfather of sorts."

He shook his head. "No, Toby, you once told me I was not your father, and you were right. We both know that fatherhood can be merely a biological accident. You and I are much closer than that. You and I are friends." He observed me over the rim of his glass. "And you know what a friend does for his friend." He reached for the menu. "A friend picks up the dinner cheque."

"Greater love," I muttered, "hath no man than this."

Quinncannon said, "The lobster looks good."

Acknowledgments

You ought to be ironical the minute you get out of bed.
You ought to wake up with your mouth full of pity.
—Ernest Hemingway

This being Quinncannon's third adventure, it occurs to me that
he and I owe a debt as yet unpaid to three of the most brilliant
legal minds of the last century: Hugh Maxwell, Jeremiah Mason,
and Henry Clinton.

My special thanks go to my agent, Fred Hill, for reasons that
are nobody's business.

I am grateful to Patterson Smith who lives surrounded by the
records of human iniquity and crime through which he permits
me to prowl; and to Randy Kelly who once again advised me on
medical matters.

And Abby, sounding board, cheerleader, advisor, friend—to
whom this volume is affectionately dedicated.

Troy Hills, New Jersey   RP